Y0-BUP-152

BRIDGING BOTH WORLDS

The Communication Consultant in Corporate America

Edited by

Rebecca L. Ray

HD
30.3
.B75
1993
West

UNIVERSITY
PRESS OF
AMERICA

Lanham • New York • London

Copyright © 1993 by
University Press of America® Inc.
4720 Boston Way
Lanham, Maryland 20706

3 Henrietta Street
London WC2E 8LU England

All rights reserved
Printed in the United States of America
British Cataloging in Publication Information Available

Library of Congress Cataloging-in-Publication Data

Bridging both worlds : the communication consultant in
corporate America / edited by Rebecca L. Ray.
Includes bibliographical references.
1. Communication in organizations—United States.
2. Business consultants—United States. I. Ray, Rebecca L.
HD30.3.B75   1993
658.4'6—dc20   93–28996 CIP

ISBN 0–8191–9278–3 (cloth : alk. paper)
ISBN 0–8191–9279–1 (pbk. : alk. paper)

The paper used in this publication meets the minimum requirements of
American National Standard for Information Sciences—Permanence
of Paper for Printed Library Materials, ANSI Z39.48–1984.

PREFACE

It is probably the last thing you thought you'd do in your career: corporate training. There were probably no references to it, much less courses offered in it while you were a graduate student. But here you are, years of university teaching and a list of publications to your credit and you are intrigued by the prospect of a new challenge. At professional conferences, colleagues speak of their experiences in the corporate world: their clients are household names, the places they travel to are exciting, and the money they talk about is tempting. Or perhaps you are a graduate student now and your professors speak of their consulting practices and it all sounds so interesting. But you have questions: Where do I start? What does the actual training look like? How do I present a professional image? How do I compete? How do I take what I know and translate it into a training session? Can I run my own business? Could I really be successful?

When I began my consulting practice seven years ago, I knew very little about the business world. I had chosen academia; that was the world in which I was most comfortable. So when I began to use my teaching skills in this new setting, I really knew nothing of research in the area of corporate training or how this was supposed to be done. I did what I thought was right, what made sense, and what worked. I have learned a great deal about business, made some mistakes, and known the clarity of vision that is possible only with hindsight.

For many of us who have ventured out, it has been a process of trial and error, of success and failure. Many academicians do not believe that what they know and what they can help others to know is of value to corporations; indeed as the face of America's workforce changes and becomes more global in its outlook, strong communication skills will become even more critical in America and the world marketplace. The transition from the academic world to the corporate one can be a difficult one to make. There are a variety of new challenges, new mindsets, and ways in which we must be retooled. The transition forces us to see ourselves, as well as the corporate world, in a new light.

Bridging Both Worlds: The Communication Consultant in Corporate America was envisioned to be a very practical guide for those whose academic training in the field of speech communication did not encompass involvement in the corporate sector. As the editor of this text, I sought out members of our profession who had attained recognition in particular aspects of our discipline and who also maintained an active consulting practice. I asked each to speak to the experiences they have had as a consultant, highlight consulting opportunities and challenges in their area of specialization, and suggest ways in which training and consulting might be conducted. I gave each contributor free rein in the format and content of the response, letting readers see the varied approaches and viewpoints. I hope that readers will find the chapters informative and thought-provoking.

Bridging Both Worlds

No single book could hope to capture all that is known about the field of communication. Certainly, that is not the purpose of this book. Rather, it asks the reader to consider taking communication competency and applying it to new settings with new challenges. Designed to provide an overview of communication consulting, from starting the consulting practice to the types of communication training being done by active consultants, this text is not an exhaustive look, but rather the groundwork to begin thinking in more concrete terms about consulting. Each of us has tried to distill a select few pearls of wisdom for those of you who may be considering training as a career option or in conjuction with university teaching.

I would especially like to thank the contributors for their substantive help in providing a more comprehensive overview of consulting opportunities in the field of communications than I alone could and I am honored to be included in such company.

Rebecca L. Ray

CONTENTS

INTRODUCTION:

THE ACADEMIC AS CORPORATE CONSULTANT

Rebecca L. Ray

Training in Corporate America

Corporate training in America has experienced tremendous growth. In 1992, corporate America spent roughly $210 billion on training equipment, materials, and services, according to the American Society for Training and Development (ASTD, 1992), the largest professional organization for trainers and human resource professionals. That figure can only increase throughout the 1990s, as training needs become more varied and intense. Witness the sudden explosion of training programs in the areas of sexual harassment, diversity, and disability which were the direct result of media attention and such legislation as the 1990 Americans with Disabilities Act. There are predictions that up to 75% of today's workers will need to be trained or retrained by the year 2000 (Grazian, 1992).

There is great concern about the skills of American workers and their competitiveness in a global marketplace. Federally mandated training may become the law of the land. Candidate Bill Clinton pledged 1.5% of corporate payrolls would be devoted to training when he became president. While that pledge has yet to become a reality, Anthony Carnevale, chief economist for ASTD and president of the Institute for Workplace Learning, estimates that a 1.5% percent of payroll increase in the training dollars spent would add another $21 billion to the current annual sum of $30-45 billion paid to independent trainers and training firms as well as create 2.6 million jobs within five years (Carnevale, 1992). While the concept of mandated training raises questions about the implementation and quality of training programs, the training tax does send the message that the government is concerned enough to put some teeth into the soundbite of most politicians, that, of course, "training is important."

In an era of economic recession, corporate "right-sizing," and budget slashing, the conventional wisdom is that training would be among the first items to be cut, right after limousine service, holiday bonuses, condos and other flashy corporate perks. For the independent consultant providing training to corporate clients, the surprising news is that external consultants are doing better than one would expect. Kimmerling (1991) identifies three factors for training providers riding out the recession: the breadth of the client base; the quality of the planning, and offering training which is tied closely to business strategy. Suzanne Hodvey, director of corporate communications for the Los Angeles-based Times-Mirror Company, which recently acquired three training firms, Zenger-Miller, Learning International, and Kaset International, cites three reasons for the need, and increasing profitability, of training: corporate downsizing, the weakness of the educational system, and rapid technological change (Kimmerling, 1991). These trends contribute to the corporate educational system which trains roughly 46 million workers each year, more than 3.8 times the number enrolled in higher education (English, 1992).

Given the economic and demographic changes, training, especially communication training, will look different. Corporations are gearing up for the changes, looking to maintain competitiveness (Pope, 1992). Stephen Cohen, president and CEO of the Learning Design Group, predicts that there will be 15.6 million new workers by the year 2000 and 23.8 million more jobs. Ten million of these jobs will require complex cognitive and interpersonal skills (Cohen, 1991).

The educational system may continue to produce graduates without the skills corporations want. Add to this a work force which is more culturally diverse, and the result is that more training will be needed in the areas of basic skills, writing, diversity, teamwork, listening, empowerment, personal integrity, sales, and interpersonal communication. With a more challenging labor pool, managers will need training in the areas of coaching and mentoring, conflict management, sexual harassment, stress management, interviewing strategies, and time management. Middle and upper management will need training in sales, presentation skills, media training, leadership, and ethics as competition becomes even more cut-throat. As competition becomes more global, training in cross-cultural communication will become critical.

The delivery of training will be different. More training will done on or close to site in order to reduce the average two-thirds of the training budget now spent on travel. Training will be delivered by employees who become "certified" to act as trainers for others, keeping the learning process active. The training methods will differ as well. Learning styles, individual backgrounds, and cultural diversity will account for training variations: more ways to teach the same thing to many. Teleconferencing and satellite transmission will be more common. Simulators and virtual-reality training will enter the workplace and join computer-assisted instruction and interactive videodiscs, using hypertext, hypermedia, and CD-ROM (Reid, 1992; Cohen, 1991). Sears, Nissan, Union Pacific, Allstate Insurance, Hewlett-Packard, Goodyear, and Bethlehem Steel are among the many who now use multimedia in training employees. Hughes Aircraft, Aetna Life & Casualty, USWest, Ben & Jerry's and countless others use multimedia in presentations to the public as well as to potential clients.

Training dollars and proposed programs will be heavily scrutinized. Management will be looking to justify these expenditures and trainers, especially individual practitioners, will be expected to demonstrate a return on investment (ROI). Consultants will be expected to track employee performance, making needs assessments done prior to training that much more critical as they will now be used to determine whether employees actually mastered the skills which were initially identified. Clearly linking learning objectives with business objectives helps keep training focused as well as easier to quantify. Managers will look for demonstrable proof that training accomplished goals and was cost effective. Consultants will need to construct evaluation instruments and develop ROI formulas which document not only improved employee behaviors but significant cost effectiveness as well (Davidove & Schroeder, 1992). Post-training assessment, in the form of evaluation instruments and follow-up program evaluation surveys and interviews will be pro forma in an effort to substantiate training benefit claims.

Outside consultants will still be in demand. A survey conducted by the ASTD revealed that the activity of consultants had remained constant for the last three years with many indicating increased activity (ASTD, 1992). As full-time training staffs are streamlined, outside consultants, many with advanced degrees, publications, and sterling reputations, will be available at much less cost than in-house trainers and with the ability to achieve the same results.

Major corporations and/or industries will set up "universities" where university professors will be "on-call" to present a variety of training programs for executives. These training programs will have a core curriculum, similar to that of universities, where university professors are "on staff" as trainers to deliver workshops and seminars as needed at the corporate center. Ford Motor Company has established the Leadership Education and Development Program in partnership with the University of Michigan. Merrill Lynch offers an annual "University Week" at its training center in Princeton where industry leaders and innovators speak and university professors conduct workshops and seminars. General Electric currently has two hundred professors "on staff" at its Crotonville, New York "campus."

More formal, traditional associations will continue to exist between business and academia, such as Cornell University's School of Hotel Administration's forum for industry, the Center for Hospitality Research, to augment its regularly sponsored programs at the J. Willard Marriott Executive Education Center on campus (Ray, 1992).

The decision to set up their own "universities" is driven by the cost of training. Corporations, who currently spend $15-42,000 per executive for a five week training program, are deciding that these university-affiliated programs are too expensive, too time consuming, and too theoretical. This will cause major universities who currently offer high-end executive development/training programs to reevaluate the way in which training is conducted. No matter what the format, these partnerships mean that corporate America will have much greater influence on what is being taught to the young people who will soon join the ranks of the corporate world. Corporate executives will be called upon to teach and serve as mentors to young people.

Some companies believe in training to such an extent that they make a commitment to train every member of the organization every year and actually increase the training staff and budget, believing that training could produce the difference between staying alive and striding ahead. This is where consultants can really have an impact for once they have proved themselves, they will then be "on call" for a variety of training needs.

Many have heralded the effectiveness and competitiveness of small businesses and independent professionals (Tuller, 1992; Peters, 1992). Through corporate downsizing, economics, or personal choice, there are an estimated 1.3 million people who identify themselves as consultants (Nussbaum, Cuneo, Carlson, & McWilliams, 1993). By the year 2000, half of the businesses or consulting practices in America will be owned by women, a trend driven, perhaps, by the "glass ceiling" factor.

What do front-line training specialists think of the future of training in general and of communication training in particular? Brown & Rancer (1993) cite the emphasis that senior executives place on communication skills, specifically speaking and listening. Some companies are making an all-out effort to train in a few key areas, primarily diversity, sexual harassment, teams, and mentoring and sponsoring. Another trend is the move to make internal, individual business units behave more like outside consulting units: recognizing their contribution to the corporation while being responsible for the bottom-line. They also cite a trend toward the inclusion of "high-tech" presentation tools like multimedia in general training sessions and in presentation skills training. This highly expensive shift is necessary to remain competitive.

Top-notch corporations will continue to bring in outside consultants for training as long as they can get quality programs and expert advise, even if they have to pay higher rates. They are not going to send their employees to inexpensive, commercially-available training sessions because the perception is that if you only spend "X," you are only going to get "X" amount of training. Additionally, ego becomes a factor and the employees whose companies are well-respected are going to feel that they are worth a great deal more than a general session with lesser players. They do not respect what can be had cheaply.

Some foresee major changes for the consulting sector. Tuller (1992) believes that state and federal licensing is on the horizon as well as a surge in the number of universities which will train individuals specifically for careers in consulting as well as an increase in the number of degree and certification programs in consulting.

Of all the trends and innovative projects on the table, one thing is clear. There has been, and will continue to be, a significant increase in the emphasis on communication skills in the overall training programs in most of corporate America. This communication training is delivered both alone and in conjunction with technical training, often in an experiential format. Lower level employees often receive communication training that reflects a communication skill with a direct implication for the performance of their job. The more senior the executive, the more often communication skills are taught alone. For example, upper management is the more likely recipient of training in the areas of managing diversity, conflict management, negotiation, or individualized presentation skills coaching. However, no matter what the organization, the employee experiences, or the economic times, communication skills will continue to be an important part of training in corporate America.

The Corporate Consultant

When an individual is retained by management to analyze, advise, offer solutions, or serve in a variety of capacities where the individual's knowledge, skills, and experience are brought to bear, he or she serves as a consultant. The projects may be long or short term but they are, or should be, clearly defined, mutually agreeable, business arrangements. For our purposes, the term "consultant" will be taken to mean one who has been retained by management to perform either as a consultant, in the sense of being an agent for change, or a trainer, who delivers the program designed to have a direct impact upon the knowledge, skills, or attitudes of the participants.

The consultant has always worn a variety of hats: the trainer who delivers the training and provides learning experiences; the provider who designs, maintains, and delivers training programs; the consultant who analyzes and advises; and the innovator who serves as an agent for change (Steinberg, 1992). Lippitt and Lippitt (1978) identify the multiple roles of the consultant, ranging from objective observer to joint problem solver to trainer/educator to advocate. As outside consultants take on more of the traditionally in-house functions of the training department, we will be called on to do more than simply deliver a stand-alone workshop on some aspect of communication. It will be left to us, as outside consultants, to learn how to design and deliver communication training programs which reflect the changing demographics in the workplace as well as new theories about how people learn and work. We will be expected to help corporations value diversity, eliminate discrimination, comply with EEOC and ADA guidelines when interviewing and managing, increase sales, project a powerful image in the media, and a host of other challenges.

Carnevale (1992) in his book, *America and the New Economy*, posits that people who understand how learning takes place and who build experiences and structures to make that learning happen, are the agents of learning, the critical technology. A major portion of learning process will be experiential and self-reinforcing with formal and informal learning networks built on "shared expectations, complex behaviors, and patterns of interaction" (p. S10).

As consultants, the training experiences we provide will underscore such trends in the workplace as quality, teamwork, and empowerment. Those informal working structures will radically alter the way in which we present information and design experiential opportunities to demonstrate competence. Rather than present information in a lecture format, we will serve as facilitators, allowing others to learn by building on past training, what Carnevale calls cumulative learning, and from each other.

The Academic as Consultant

As academicians who choose to consult, we must make every effort to understand the tremendous changes taking place in the corporate sector, present ourselves as ethical professionals, strive to master developments both in our own field of communication and in business, and understand that we provide a service which must be sold to customers who demand a great deal. We will be expected to know about things we may not have experienced, use language from a business world we have not visited, and compete with people for consulting work who have been specifically trained to do what we are now going to attempt for the first time. But take heart. It is possible to compete and win. Your experiences in the business sector will make you more valuable to your students who are eager to glimpse the world they will soon enter. You will know exactly what communication skills are important to teach because you train executives who know they desperately need it. Your knowledge comes from the workplace of today, not the textbook of yesterday. Consulting will allow you to document effectiveness in a new setting, providing information for further research. Consulting may even bolster your self-confidence for now you know that you can "swim with sharks" and still emerge from the waters with limbs intact.

Those of us who consult do not see the mutual exclusivity of the "successful" consultant and the "outstanding" academic, though many will argue the point (Phillips, 1992; Jarboe, 1992). In most cutting-edge institutions, your business acumen and the work you do for corporate clients will be viewed as a positive contribution to the university as it reflects well on the university and underscores that what you teach in a classroom can be adapted and of worth to corporate America. Only in rare cases will professional jealousy mean that you have to defend your contribution to the department or university or your involvement in the nationally recognized area of applied communication. A full-time teaching position necessitates the fulfillment of teaching and departmental duties and your consulting practice will need be adapted to that schedule. However, even with the most ethical of practices on your part, you may find that there is no support whatsoever from department chairs or other academicians who cannot fathom the choice you have made, much less successfully consult themselves. If that happens, you will need to decide whether or not it is worth your time to educate you colleagues or if you will simply persevere and bask in recognition from your professional associations and your corporate clients as well as the respect from your students who recognize that you can give them what others cannot.

A Consultant's Skillset

Before considering consulting in a corporate setting, you should take inventory of the skills you posses. Certainly, a mastery of the field of communication is critical. Just as important are superior presentation skills adapted to a training setting. An understanding of the adult learner, current learning theories, flexible teaching and facilitating styles, and the ability to design and measure training effectiveness in terms of behavioral objectives will become more important as training dollars are scrutinized. Your interpersonal communication skills should be finely tuned, as well as your powers of negotiation, diplomacy, observation, and self-control.

In terms of actually running a business, you will need to become "bottom-line" oriented. Know what you have to offer, know what your competition offers, and know what the market will bear. Become computer literate and have access to electronic mail (email) and links with both business and academia. Hunter and Allen (1992) offer a roadmap to adapting to email for the newly initiated. Since many of your trainees use this form of communication, as well as on-line information services, you'll want to discuss the implications of electronic communication. Rice et al.(1992) discuss communicator style and organizational level in the evaluation of email usage. Learn to juggle numerous clients and still be attentive to detail. Learn to wear a variety of hats: chief financial officer, researcher, writer, desktop publisher, purchasing agent, press agent, audiovisual specialist, and travel agent.

All consultants must determine what personality styles, methods, and ways of organizing work best for them. There are, however, some skills that are critical. Block (1981) breaks the skills necessary for success into three broad categories: technical skills specific to the discipline, interpersonal skills, and such consulting skills as contracting, diagnosis, feedback, and decision-making. Rudolph & Johnson (1985) cite emotional maturity, assertiveness, tough-mindedness, social sensitivity, conscientiousness, self-discipline, initiative, analytical capacity, the ability to plan and organize, critical thinking skills, and self-confidence (p. 15).

Changing Audiences (and hats)

Training adults and teaching college students are, in many ways, quite different. As you move from academia, you will need to rethink the way in which you deliver information, utilize time, motivate, give feedback, and present yourself. You may be challenged by adult trainees who believe that you have nothing valuable to offer simply because you do not bring business experience to the table. You may be challenged by trainees who dislike the concept of training in general or you in particular. You cannot rely on the grade held as a stick over the college student. Adult learners, especially at the middle and upper management levels have been known to become hostile or simply get up and leave if you aren't, in their opinion, dynamic, informative, and worth the time out of their hectic schedule. Your Ph.D. and your impressive client list may get you in the door, but you are on your own from there.

Arnold & McClure (1989) identify several of the principles of adult learning: people learn best by doing, often have prior experience, have different motivations, and struggle with preoccupations during training. Additionally, trainees expect that you will distill the research and jargon into "bottom-line" benefits for them in their work, and, sometimes, personal lives. We must offer a variety of training styles to reach the majority of our trainees.

You will need to look, speak, and act as though being in a business setting is second nature. You will need to acquire business suits and personal effects which stand up to close scrutiny. Your personal grooming must be impeccable. We all know that nonverbal cues communicate your rung on the ladder and nothing is more noticeably academic than tweeds, polyester, neoprene-soled shoes, and worn briefcases. You will not be given the opportunity to deliver long-winded monologues, displaying your ability to drop names and quote current research. You will be expected to draw examples from business and show how anything you claim is important relates to business success. You will be expected to show respect to all trainees, even the ones who challenge and confront you. Management will expect you to conduct your consulting practice in accordance with standard business practices: power lunches, business letters which confirm your agreements, invoices which look professional, telephone practices which underscore your professionalism, and business etiquette. Baldridge (1985) offers an exhaustive treatment of business etiquette; the market is flooded with books to help avoid faux pas when conducting business across cultures.

Having said all that...

Assuming that you are still interested in becoming a communication consultant in corporate America, please read on. Part One: The Consulting Practice will allow you to hear what your potential clients are looking for, how to start your practice, and how ethical considerations will shape your relationships with clients. Part Two: Communication Skills Training examines how your colleagues have offered training in their areas of specialization, the challenges they have faced, and suggestions for the delivery of training. Even the longest journey begins with the first step.

References

American Society for Training and Development. 1992. Who's Who in Training and Development Alexandria: American Society for Training and Development.

Arnold, W. E. & L. McClure. 1989. Communication training & development. New York: Harper & Row.

Baldridge, L. 1985. Complete guide to executive manners. New York: Rawson Associates.

Block, P. 1981. Flawless consulting. San Diego: Pfeiffer.

Brown, R. E. & A. Rancer. 1993. Senior corporate executive perceptions about communication skills: A research note. The Speech Communication Annual 7: 25 - 32.

Carnevale, A. P. 1992. Learning: The critical technology. Training & Development (February): S1.

Carnevale, A. P. 1992. What training means in an election year. Training & Development (October): 45.

Cohen, S. L. 1991. The challenge of training in the nineties. Training & Development (July): 31.

Grazian, F., ed. 1992. Keep your eye on training. communication briefings, (XII): 6.

Davidove, E. & P. Schroeder. 1992. Demonstrating ROI of training. Training & Development (August): 70.

English, J. K. 1992. Defining the continuing education professional. Journal of Continuing Higher Education 40: 30-37.

Harris, T. E. 1992. Applied Organizational Communication. Hillsdale, NJ: Lawrence Erlbaum Associates.

Hunter, J. & M. Allen. 1992. Adaptation to electronic mail. Journal of Applied Communication Research 20 (August): 254-274.

Jarboe, S. 1992. They do it for the money(?): A response to G.M. Phillips. Journal of Applied Communication Research 20 (May): 225-233.

Kimmerling, G. F. 1991. Are we in a bull market for training? Training & Development (August): 27.

Lippitt, G. & R. Lippitt. 1978. The consulting process in action. LaJolla, CA: University Press.

Loden, M. & J. B. Rosener. 1991. Workforce America! Homewood,IL: Business One Irwin.

Newman, T. 1993. How do we know training makes a difference? Training & Development (April): 80.

Nussbaum, B., A. Cuneo, B. Carlson, & G. McWilliams. 1993. Corporate refugees. Business Week, 12 April, 58.

Peters, T. 1992. Liberation Management. New York: Knopf.

Phillips, G. M. 1992. They do it for the money. Journal of Applied Communication Research 20 (May): 219-224.

Pope, B. 1992. Workforce management: how today's companies are meeting business and employee needs. Homewood, IL: Business One Irwin.

Ray, R. L. 1992. Spotlight on higher education/industry collaboration; Cornell University's Center for Hospitality Research. ASTD: Continuing Professional Education Network Newsletter 1 (Fall): 2.

Reid, R. L., ed. 1992. High-tech training. Technical Trainer/Skills Trainer (Fall): 6.

Rice, R. E., S. Chang, & J. Torobin. 1992. Communicator style, media use, organizational level, and use of evaluation of electronic messaging. Management Communication Quarterly 6 (August):3-33.

Rudolph, E. E. & B. R. Johnson. 1985. Communication consulting: Another teaching option. Annandale, VA: The Speech Communication Association.

Sternberg, C. 1992. In practice: The changing role of trainers. Training & Development (March): 14.

Tuller, L. W. 1992. Cutting edge consultants. Englewood Cliffs, NJ: Prentice Hall.

Part One: The Consulting Practice

THE BUSINESS OF RUNNING A BUSINESS

Rebecca L. Ray

Business details do not have to become the bane of your existence. It is possible to set up your home office and operate your consulting practice with a minimum of hassles and time-consuming paperwork. Not intended to substitute for legal or financial advice from experts, what follows are thoughts on how you might consider setting up your consulting practice.

Before Making the Leap, Ask Hard Questions

Nothing is so clear as hindsight. Before you leap, take a hard look and ask these questions about your self as a person. Can you make a frank assessment of your strengths and weaknesses? Are you comfortable taking risks? Do you thrive on challenges? Are you willing to reinvent the way you share information? Can you package yourself to fit into another world, with different ways of operating? Are you able to totally commit to new ventures? Most of the consultants with whom you would compete have a Ph.D. in hand and years of experience. How do your credentials compare? Are you willing to upgrade your skills?

How much time and effort are you willing to put into launching a consulting practice? There is no end to the number of small details that go into client service, training materials, participant materials, travel logistics, research, and office detail. Long hours, out-of-town travel, and anxiety are the norm. Can you handle the feelings of isolation that come from working on your own?

Here's another question. Do you have the temperament to be a consultant? You need great listening and facilitation skills, a level of diplomacy that gets you through tight spots, flexibility, and the ability to turn on a dime. You need to be a great salesperson - selling yourself is probably the hardest task of all and the most potentially damaging to your psyche. You need to like living on the edge, attempting the impossible, and juggling a great many things at once. You also need to become a political animal - know who key players are, how to protect yourself, and how to get important players to "buy into" your training.

With a new business failure rate of almost 80%, there are factors to consider which have nothing to do with your expertise or your hard work: inexperience, undercapitalization, high overhead, and low cash flow (Freeman, 1993). Can you afford to become a consultant? There are may hidden start-up costs and you still need to meet your current obligations. I would suggest that you continue to teach or maintain some steady source of income as companies notoriously stretch their payments cycles to 90 days or more. Do you think that you can beat the odds?

If you can honestly answer yes to these questions, read on.

Find Your Niche

As with any new venture, the first step is to determine what, if anything, you have to offer that doesn't already exist in the marketplace in great numbers. You have to ask hard questions - "What do I really know that others will pay to know?" and "How would I be different from others who offer similar services?" This is key - you need to find a niche and stick to it. You cannot offer all communication training services to all people without a loss of credibility not to mention that offering a wide range of services will take away from available preparation time. It's a great deal like having six or more preparations in a semester. With all of the consultants and major firms out there offering training in the areas of presentation skills, negotiation, interpersonal communication, listening, conflict resolution, and sales training, how will you fit into the framework? I knew the areas of communication in which I felt especially comfortable - presentation skills, media training, interviewing, and vocal coaching - and I decided to zero in on those.

I sat down and looked at the promotional literature of companies like Communispond, Executive Techniques, Motivational Systems, Decker Communications and a host of others and ar lyzed their programs in those areas. Their two or three day open sessions cover the basics of presentation skills training but do little more than introduce the concepts, ask people to give a brief speech of introduction and/or a speech on an innocuous topic, and send them home. As an educator, I knew that real learning only happens when reinforced over time and when a trainee has an opportunity to use these new skills in a practical setting.

I decided to offer something I didn't see out there already - individualized presentation skills training sessions at a price most companies charge for group sessions. Conducted over ten to twelve weeks and on-site so that there is a minimum of disruption during the work day for trainees, this seemed to be a distinct difference. Not only do trainees get private, practical experience giving business presentations for which they can prepare and rehearse, the training and followup sessions allow them to reflect on their progress between sessions. I also knew that I could offer this extensive training schedule of individual training sessions for the same price that the big companies charge for groups of 15-20 people for two days. When viewed in that light, my services are a bargain.

Most successful consultants find out what they are good at, fine-tune it, and stick with it.

Ask Experts

Talk to everyone you think has good advice or has traveled this route before you. Network at professional conferences, attend applied communication interest group panels and meetings, and introduce yourself to people whose practice is off and running. Seek out other consultants in a variety of fields and ask if they will be willing to sit down with you over lunch and talk about their experiences. Seek out small business development centers at local universities as well as representatives of the Service Core of Retired Executives (SCORE). They can be especially helpful in writing business plans, which you will need when applying for operating capital (Freeman, 1993).

Read voraciously about general market trends, industries, and the business climate in your area. Know what business publications your clients are reading and read them. Not to know major developments and trends or blockbuster bestsellers is like taking out an advertisement that you don't have a sense of the business world in which your clients operate.

Many universities now offer courses for the prospective communication consultant: New York University, Cornell University, Bloomsburg University, and the University of Akron, to name only a few. In addition, most colleges and universities offer general courses which relate to running your own business or serving as a consultant. There is no end to the number of books, audiotapes, and seminars on the market which may be helpful in plotting a general course.

Get the Word Out

One of the best ways to get started is to start very slowly while you still have your "day job." If your friends in business get you in the door, consider offering a seminar or series of training sessions. This is a little tricky because you are offering services without having been told of a need and there could be resistance to your presence and your training. But you should take the chance because it will be good training for you in a fairly safe setting and you'll be able to use the name of the company in your own brochures and materials. Offer to speak to business groups about some aspect of communication which is covered by your training. Offer to teach a course in a continuing or adult education program. The pay is usually low but that's not the point: you are building your resume and reaching potential clients and their networks.

Send out brochures to a target audience but know that the return on these expensive mailings can be minimal. Advertising can help but until you can afford the higher rates of the publications which reach your target audience (the kind that can afford your fees), pass. Nothing looks more amateurish than advertising in the local "free" newsletter. It takes a pretty keen business sense to know where to place the ads and you might want to hold off on this for awhile. A listing in the yellow pages under communication or speech training can also be rather expensive (Milano, 1992).

Join professional organizations, especially the Speech Communication Association and the American Society for Training and Development (ASTD). ASTD publishes Training and Development and Human Resource Development Quarterly, both a wealth of information as well as a marketplace for the kind of materials and suppliers you will need. ASTD offers Info-Line, which offers research and training tips, and TRAINET, the on-line computer database of training events and courseware. Other professional organizations include the International Association of Business Communicators, International Communication Association, the American Business Communication Association, and the National Speakers Association.

Submit short articles for publication. Offer to serve on highly visible committees or task forces. Edit the newsletter to get your name in front of the membership. Often, you will be referred to callers who seek training by calling the organization's main number. You may also learn a great deal from hearing others talk about their business or their industry. Keep a potential client file of the names of people you meet or listen to for a future targeted mailing.

Of all the ways to get the word out, networking is probably the best. Tell all of your friends in business - people have amazing networks. Professional organizations in communication may help you meet other consultants who are your competitors; they may share information but they won't often help you obtain clients. Join Toastmasters and display your skills, especially to local businesspeople. Civic groups, community organizations, and your social network are better avenues to spreading the word. Always be ready to tell someone, very succinctly, what it is you do. Practice the art of small talk, remember names, and be focused on the other person. Keep your business cards ready. It may be appropriate at the end of a lengthy conversation to offer your card. If they give you theirs, be sure to send a short note telling them that you enjoyed the opportunity to meet and that if they ever have a need for your services, you would appreciate hearing from them. Keep in touch with those contacts you think are important in order to develop a relationship (McDermott, 1992).

Let local convention centers, hotels, and civic organizations know that you offer training sessions and workshops on a variety of topics. You may be called by meeting and convention planners looking to round out a program or be referred by them to potential clients. Local radio and television stations may be interested in some aspect of your consulting practice on a community business report. Contact radio and television producers and see what interests them.

Offer short articles in local newspapers which tie into your area of expertise. Academic publishing will help to establish you as an expert in your field. When the time comes to publish a book to establish your name in business circles, consider that more than 1,000 titles are published each week and that there are numerous pitfalls (Hall, 1991). Some books emerge from training materials, some from your unique approach, and some from your experiences.

Above all, know that your reputation takes a long time to build and only seconds to destroy. When interacting, know that all are potential references and all are potential clients.

Set Up the Home Office

Should you work out of your university office, your own home, or rent office space. It is probably best to avoid working out of your university office; you have obligations to the university which necessitate availability to colleagues and students. If you generate income from the university office, the institution might rightfully claim a portion of the revenue for the use of space, telephone, secretarial services, and the like.

Renting office space can be costly and legally binding. Before you commit to a lease, remember that there are additional expenses: utilities (at corporate rates), telephone installation and service (at corporate rates), trash removal, common area upkeep (reception, office support, and rest rooms), business rental taxes, and the like. If your consulting practice doesn't fly, and especially if you did not incorporate, you are responsible for the balance of the lease payments.

That leaves us with the home office. 25 million Americans generate their income from home, 46 million are expected to do so by 1995, and 100 million by 1999 (Cohen, 1989; Lewis, 1993). Once the big-ticket deduction for independent practitioners, consultants, and professionals, home-office deductibility rules have changed. Recent Supreme Court rulings have made it harder to claim home-office deductions. No longer enough to claim that you prepared materials or client invoices in the office, you must now show that you provide the primary service there. This is especially bad news for communication consultants who deliver training at the client site (Black, 1993; Lewis, 1993).

Then there is the question of office equipment. I cannot imagine being in business with out a computer and a laserjet printer. Should you purchase or lease the equipment? That depends on your tax status and the advice of your accountant. Office equipment may still be a deductible expense even after the Supreme Court slashed the majority of home-office deductions. In general, you must be able to provide documentation that the equipment was used for a legitimate business purpose; exclusive business use is best if the claim is contested by the Internal Revenue Service (IRS) (Lewis, 1993).

In most cases, a special tax form (8829) will be prepared by your accountant to document your home office deductions. Taking a deduction for capital equipment, in particular the computer, can still mean substantial tax savings. For example, Section 179 of the tax code allows a home office deduction of up to $10,000 of the purchase price of equipment as a straight write-off against income, assuming that one earns at least as much as the claimed deduction (Lewis, 1993). Keep accurate records and document everything you think may become important (Rowland, 1993).

Low overhead is the key to staying afloat. You will certainly need to select business stationary (letterhead and business cards). A corporate identity may become more important as your practice gains visibility. You can retain a graphic artist to design your logo, to be used on all business materials, or you may want to work with computer graphics packages on your own. It is even possible to research whether or not a name or phrase that you are considering is already in use by using the forums and on-line services of Compuserve (Harris & Lyon, 1993).

One thing you definitely need is a very good telephone answering machine, or better yet, an answering service. When you begin to generate a lot of business, an 800 number can be had for very little a month and gives the impression that you more than a one-person shop. A fax machine has become a crucial part of my operation as I can send updated schedules, requests for audiovisual materials, and, most important, invoices into someone's hands immediately.

I write and desktop publish all of my training materials on my laptop computer and laserjet printer. I have had to learn to become computer literate as well as something of graphic artist. I have both a desktop 386SX and a laptop 386SX; both serve different functions. Because a large portion of what I do involves stand-up presentations, I had to learn to use presentation graphics for the creation of slideshows and overhead transparencies. Having used Aldus' Persuasion, the Software Company's Harvard Graphics, and Microsoft's PowerPoint 2.0, I must say I am most enamored with the last. It has a seamless interface with Microsoft Windows 3.1 and allows for a slideshow even if I use a computer on-site which does not have PowerPoint loaded on the harddrive. I purchased a laptop in order to continue to do business while on the road as well as run screenshows during seminars. Get the most powerful, best featured computer your budget can afford.

In addition, I use include The Word Perfect Corporation's Word Perfect 5.1 for word processing; Intuit's Quicken for Windows, which keeps my records and generates end-of-the-year financial statements for my accountant with the stroke of a few keys; Prisma's Yourway, which is like an electronic Filofax; and Aldus PageMaker for whatever desktop publishing isn't already done by WordPerfect. As software can be a major investment in time and money, compare features and cost. I find that *PC Magazine* offers very clear product comparisons to help you with your decisions.

There are training software packages to choose from but, for the most part, they are expensive and require a large volume of client activity. They can, however, do everything from scheduling, prepare letters and mailings, prepare training materials, and prepare trainee certificates.

I have a modem with which I can access Compuserve, America Online, Internet, Bitnet, and the Dow Jones News Retreival Services for company profiles. Access to such services allows me to access company profiles, business information, and transcripts of speeches and press conferences. I am also on the email system of one of my clients which I check often, even on the road.

If I have a longstanding relationship with a company that requests a seminar for a large number of people, I will ask them (or build into the original agreement) to make multiple training manuals from my set of laserjet-printed originals. Otherwise, I xerox, collate, and bind my own materials or send it out to a business printer franchise.

You will also need to purchase business attire, which may become your largest expense. It is important to buy quality, even if it means fewer outfits. Especially for women, nothing is more disheartening than the "bargain" suit you found being worn by every third woman who walks by the client site. Anything you can do to look as though you fit into the corporate world should be done. You cannot presume to tell someone else how to make a business presentation unless you at least appear to understand what it is like to give one yourself. To look as though you belong in a business setting and that you understand the corporate arena, you may need to take advantage of the advice of a professional image consultant who can help you make a few key clothing purchases until you get rolling. This is just part of the "personal packaging" element of marketing yourself (Elsea, 1984; McDermott, 1992; Molloy, 1975; Thompson, 1981). Thompson (1981) offers advice for women on total image projection, use of the voice and body language, and assertiveness. All of us know these communication areas but it is often helpful to have someone reframe all of this within the not-so-familiar business arena.

Because most of what I do is done on-site, I have no need for a formal office or training room. I use the company's training room or board room and bring my own training materials and, in some cases, video equipment. For presentation skills training, I knew that I wanted to conduct private sessions and videotape the presentations for playback and analysis. I purchased a basic system (camera, batteries, tripod, case) through American Express so that I could pay over time without interest, thus reducing startup costs. I will soon need to invest in much smaller, much more powerful video and playback equipment for use with clients, but the basic system has served me well for over six years.

The trainer's checklist at the end of this chapter may prove helpful. I carry with me a totebag with all of my training materials (markers, transparencies, pointers, flipchart tabs, etc.) I will ship the training bag to the client-site if I must travel by plane, carrying only the training manual I've developed and the overheads. Call me superstitious, but I know that the first time I check my training manual with my suitcase, it will go to an exciting city I hadn't planned on. I have learned not to depend on the support staff on-site for the many little things I need to conduct a training seminar.

Obtain Financing

If you decide to launch your consulting practice full-time, you'll need financial backing. One way to obtain start-up capital is to develop a business plan and seek a small business loan from a bank where you have an established relationship. The federal Small Business Association (SBA) may offer assistance by lending in conjunction with banks or by obtaining investors. Some states have pooled-loan programs which offer low-rate loans for small business start-ups. The Economic Development Authority in each state may provide a listing of available programs for which you may qualify (Freeman, 1993).

As a last resort, you may be tempted to use your lines of credit or a home-equity loan. When you incur that kind of debt, you may become locked into payments you cannot afford without the consulting income. That's when you make poor decisions about which clients to take on and how much work to commit to.

Stay This Side of the Law

Bernard Kamoroff (1993), CPA and author of *Small-Time Operator: How to Start Your Own Business, Keep Your Books, Pay Your Taxes, and Stay Out of Trouble*, suggest steps for start-up businesses. Of primary importance is the decision of how to structure the business: sole proprietorship, partnership, or corporation. If you don't incorporate, you are automatically a sole proprietorship where there is no legal separation between you and the business. If you are sued, your personal nonbusiness assets are at stake. If you work with a partner(s), you and your partners can be legally liable for all business debts and lawsuits. You may be responsible for the actions, loans, debts, and agreements of your partner(s), even if you did not sign the loan application or the letter of agreement. If you incorporate, you may find that it offers legal protection and tax breaks. There is also the option of forming an "S" corporation, which offers limited protection and pays no corporate income tax. All of these options require further clarification by qualified legal experts.

Additionally, Kammoroff advises that you obtain a local business license and understand zoning laws which may govern your ability to conduct business in some settings, add riders to your insurance policy to cover operating a business from it as well as cover any equipment in the event of fire or theft, and file a fictitious-name statement if you operate your consulting practice under anything other than your full, real name. When your business begins to generate revenue and your annual tax is estimated to be $500 or more, begin paying quarterly estimated taxes to the federal government.

Know about Copyrights, Trademarks, and Incorporation

When you have a great marketing angle to hook your practice onto or finally develop excellent training materials, know that there are others who may steal your ideas (and hard work) right from under your nose. Academics are expected to share and give freely of our knowledge in the classroom; not so in the world of business. While no form of protection is complete, there are some things you can do to protect yourself.

Evaluate the person to whom you disclose information and decide what level of detail is appropriate. Until you get a commitment from a client, you do not need to spell out every detail. More than one potential client has asked for a detailed proposal only to hand it to someone in-house to actually deliver.

Your training materials become part of the service you sell and they take a great deal of time to develop. In the preparation of those materials, you have distilled the pearls of the profession and given credit to, or received permission to use, the work of others. You should be able to rely on the ethical behavior of others. However, as this is often not the case, you should know about copyright law.

A copyright exists on your written materials automatically from the moment you write it; registration is not required under copyright law. Registration is often recommended, however, to substantiate the date the work was written and the right to obtain statutory damages should you have to defend yourself in court.

In addition, keep organized records and copies of important documents and training materials. Use regular mail to send yourself a copy of the materials you create and leave the envelope sealed. That will establish the date you created the materials should there be a first-use argument. Use express delivery services or certified or registered mail to prove that you sent proposals or documents to potential clients. Have a witness read the proposal and sign a statement. Label materials and documents proprietary and use nondisclosure agreements.

Should the heavens smile upon you and you need to hire associates, be sure to have them sign nondisclosure and noncompetition agreements before you open the candystore, only to have your former "employee" become your main rival using materials you developed (Gumpert, 1993).

While you will need to consult legal advice to be fully protected, there are many things you can do to begin to protect the name of your company, and its reputation, from infringement. Your name or trademark can be protected by attaching a symbol, such as "TM" for a common law or state registered trademark. The Patent and Trademark Office can register your trademark, but experts suggest using a trademark or intellectual property lawyer to navigate the system for you (Gumpert, 1993; Harris & Lyon, 1993).

There will be issues that lead you to consider incorporation; personal liability protection and potential savings in taxes and legal fees. Only you can make that determination after advice from your accountant and your lawyer. If you do decide to incorporate, it can be done in most states for a nominal fee and, often, over the telephone.

Determine the Cost

As an independent consultant, you have to determine what your time is worth. This includes your profit margin, development time, the cost of your materials, and the actual delivery time, all of which is filtered through the size of the client and what the market will bear.

You need to know what your billing rate is and approximately what how much of your time it will take to research, design, and deliver the training. Researchers in 1987 studied the cost of preparing self-study materials with instructor-led workshops. Estimates for the design of one hour of classroom training ranged from 28 to 315 hours with self-study materials requiring 80-345 hours (Hassett, 1992). Factors which help determine the range of hours are complexity of the task, relative simplicity of the design, the existence of support materials, and the available preparation time. As time goes on, you will become more accurate in the estimates you use to prepare cost figures for clients.

Kelley (1981) advocates the "Rule of Three" in determining the consultant's general billing rate: your salary, your overhead, and your profit. Each of these three equal parts when added together will give you an annual figure which can then be divided into a daily and/or hourly billing rate.

When I first started, I was shocked to learn what training cost. While some companies offer group seminars for $100 per person or less, most of the big firms charge roughly $1,000 per person for two-day group seminars. I sat down and thought about the time I needed for preparation, research, design and execution of training materials, and, in some cases, travel time. It became clear that training costs are not simply the time spent with the client and I began to realize that for each day of training, I spent three or four days preparing for a new client engagement. I did not think I could muster the courage to offer my services at $1,000 - $1,500 per day or even $2,500 per day but I have risen to the occasion and learned to charge just that. Amazing what assertiveness training can do. The other factor here is that even though I am a bargain at $2,500-$3,000 per day plus expenses for out-of-town travel, I am not the cheapest ticket in town. Coming from an academic setting, we seldom have a real idea of what our training is worth on the outside or what to charge for it. Executives do not respect what can be had cheaply and you need to charge enough to earn their respect. Remember that your advanced degrees (your training) cost you dearly and you are entitled to remuneration given your degree of training in the field. Just know that when you charge that kind of money, you'd better be worth it or start at a rate with which you're comfortable, even if it is much less, until you do feel comfortable with higher daily rates.

Know Your Audience

Identified by many names, director of human resources, management development specialist, director of training and development, director of organizational effectiveness, executive development specialist and by a host of others, they carry great responsibility: they must conduct, or arrange for, the training of all employees on a wide variety of topics. Not all training programs and initiatives can be handled by in-house staff, often "down-sized," and so the external consultant becomes a key player in the success of the overall training program. They key to success is to know what they look for, how they select consultants, how you will be viewed in terms of their own goals and obligations, and how you need to interact with them during the course of your association.

Consultants send thousands of sets of materials which cross the desks of corporate decision makers in the form of slick brochures, neon or oversized marketing pieces, videotapes of past seminars, and floppy disks of slideshows with instructions to " type > a:\setup." Many administrators will admit that the vast majority of the marketing pieces are never kept, much less looked at in great detail. Consultants cold call, perhaps leaving a message with the administrative assistant. Most administrators don't call back. If consultants do get through to the administrator, they are often met with what appears to be cold disinterest.

Getting in the door is tough. So, how can it be done? Here are a few tips on getting in the door (and staying inside) from the other side of the desk. Respondents include a management development specialist for one of the world's largest financial services firm, a regional sales manager, a director of marketing, a director of training for a manufacturing firm, and a director of human resources. Here are the qualities they find impressive and their thoughts.

Consultants who are persistent.

> "Don't be afraid of rejection. Ask if you can call again, if a large training cycle is coming up, if there are any other divisions which might need trainers. Each of the three top consultants I now use took three years to get in the door. They are the ones who didn't quit."

> "Cold calling can be successful if you are persistent. I may not have time to talk to you at the time that you call or I may not have a need for your services at the moment, but by putting your name in front of me often, you lay the groundwork for the time when I need a trainer yesterday and yours is the name that comes to mind."

Consultants who understand the bottomline and think like the client.

> "Skip the theory, skip the jargon, skip the research. Nobody wants to hear about it; they expect you to know it and translate it into how they will be more efficient, more profitable, more successful."

Consultants who charge enough to command respect.

> "I don't care how good you are, your low fee makes us think you aren't any good. A rate of $500 per day is lunch for us."

Consultants who sell themselves well and who are impressive.

> "You had better be pretty dynamic."

> "Don't sell the degree, there's not a lot of respect in the business world for a degree in communication. So educate them. Make sure you communicate to trainees what that degree means: expertise in

negotiation, sales acumen, conflict management, presentation skills, interviewing strategies - things that can make them better than their competitors. Sell your client list, your experience, and the benefits to the client."

"After all, we're all in sales. Don't sell the degree or the knowledge, sell the benefit for the client. Find a really good *selling statement*. Be succinct and be prepared to tell the client what this will add to the bottom-line."

Consultants who have very good telephone skills and convey a business-like demeanor.

"It's probably the hardest skill to master but the most important."

"Don't try to keep me on the phone long enough to hear your whole pitch. If I've got to run, let me go. I will love you for that."

"Call before 8 am or after 5 pm, that's when the support staff is gone."

Consultants who will offer a preview of a seminar or workshop or agree to do one when asked.

"I'm always amazed at the number of people who say 'no.' Don't they realize that if we like them, once they get in the door, we'll hire them again and again?"

"I put myself on the line when I have to sell a consultant's services to my in-house colleagues. I don't want to look foolish if you bomb. I need to know exactly what your programs look like."

Consultants who ask what the client wants or needs rather than simply prescribe the training.

"I can't tell you the number of times people have announced what I need rather than listen to what I say I need. Aren't these people in communication?"

"I hate canned programs. At least let me *think* I'm getting it customized."

Consultants who know the client's business, the industry and business trends.

"Of course, you've read the annual report, just don't spit it back up to me. Show me a broader base of knowledge."

Consultants who are flexible.

"I expect that the consultant will adapt to fit into our culture. Why should I change?"

"That's the nature of my business, very fluid. I need someone who understands that and who can change midstream without anyone noticing."

"With us it's feast or famine. Training crunches are cyclical. Stay in touch until you hit the boom period."

"Sometimes I ask consultants to commit to me six months from now without being able to give them exact dates or training specifics and yet that's all I have at the moment."

On the other side of the question, those interviewed found these qualities and attributes negative and, in many cases, too large a problem to proceed with any further discussion about being hired to conduct training:

Inappropriate business attire.
> "I've seen it all: Hush Puppies, polyester, cardigans. Let's face it, you only have thirty seconds to make an impression. Why would trainees listen to someone like that?"
> "A trainer came in to conduct a workshop of sales training wearing a silk shirt, gold chains, and slippered loafers. The trainees referred to him as "slick" and I think his attire was the only thing they remembered about the workshop."

Inability to speak the language of "business."
> "For God's sake, read the current business publications and the classic business books. Read the Wall Street Journal."

Ignorance of client and/or industry.
> "I'm not in the business of educating consultants."

Canned presentation about services without customization.
> "Why would I pay this kind of money for something off the shelf?"

Inability to make the shift from teaching to training.
> "They still don't get adult learners are different."
> "The lecture style all the time just doesn't cut it."
> "Don't patronize my trainees. Many of them are already pretty successful people."

Add to their comments the candor of the senior manager responsible for training at one of the Big 6 accounting firms who expects consultants to have professional expertise as a baseline. She looks for a consultant who establishes rapport, looks professional, has good references and a strong client list, and who demonstrates an understanding of the profession and its challenges. Equally as important, she needs to determine whether the consultant would be able to work independently or always need supervision. She identifies many red flags: poorly prepared written materials with errors, a poor professional image, and being "techniqued" during the sales call. As the engagement proceeds, breaches of trust, inflexibility, errors in judgement, and becoming socially involved with the employees could prompt termination.

Many who were interviewed indicated that it was, after all, sales and that consultants should know the first thing good salespeople know: it's all based on establishing rapport and trust and attempting to come up with a win-win situation. Many indicated the abhorrence of the "hard-sell;" just let them know you exist and what you can do. They'll call if there's a match.

If these people like the consultant who does a great job, chances are they will be asked back, and often. One training manager indicated that if the consultant worked out well the first time, they would be used again and again because it took too much energy to find a replacement. From the perspective of many, it made no sense to constantly change consultants after they have learned the corporate culture and mastered the initial resistance to a new trainer.

When asked about the choice of a consultant vs. a larger training firm, many responded that they preferred the more flexible design of programs and the comfort of knowing who the actual trainer was going to be rather than the person the large training company has available on a given day.

Training development people on the corporate side indicate that the types of communication-related training being offered most often include the "hot" topics of valuing diversity, gender, sexual harassment, mentoring and coaching, teamwork, and quality along with the tried and true topics of presentation skills, negotiation, conflict management, listening, interviewing, effective meetings, time management, and stress management; all adapted to the needs of different levels of trainee.

What are the current fees for consultants? At top corporations, the average consultant fee per training day is $5,000 plus first-class expenses, with fees reaching as high as $25,000 or more for a ninety-minute presentation by nationally known motivational speakers. Others use consultants whose fees are in the $1,500-3,000 per day range, plus expenses. Certainly, all fees are subject to market conditions, the area of the country, the industry, and the client's ability to pay as well as the consultant variables discussed earlier.

In addition to your effort to contact them, many are out there actively looking for you. Management and development specialists look for consultants at national and regional conferences, symposia, local chambers of commerce, and professional organization meetings. Invite them to hear you speak or attend your workshop. Once they have seen your work or heard you speak, the door is then open to discuss training for their firm.

Several suggested that because consultants are used in a variety of ways (stand-alone training, development and delivery of programs, workshop facilitation, simulation and feedback, and analysis), one way to get in the door is to show flexibility in what you offer. Contact regional or local offices of large firms who often bring in external consultants to give workshops on a variety of topics and that often serves as an entree to the larger firm.

When asked about making the career choice between in-house and external consulting, several offered this advice. For a career in in-house training, some companies look for a background in instructional design or corporate training but most take a varied approach - from a degree in the professional field to an advanced degree in an educational field. If you are just starting out, you may choose to go in-house for the experience, the structure, and the security. The drawback: companies rarely hire very young people because they cannot command the respect of advanced, successful trainees. There is greater respect to the external consultant who, over time, has built a practice, taken risks, and gained a business acumen that the consultant with in-house experience lacks.

The responses from my interviewees were reflected by research regarding the selection of consultants and the ensuing relationships. Learning International

(1992) surveyed 250 major corporations, finding that 77% of corporate buying decisions are based on three factors: a rapport with the service provider, the service provider's knowledge of the client's business, and the service provider's willingness and ability to respond to the client's needs.

When asked what they looked for when hiring consultants, corporate decision makers identified key areas: ability to listen and to communicate ideas clearly and succinctly; ability to prove an impact on the skills, knowledge and attitudes of trainees; honesty; integrity; expertise; the quality, quantity and timeliness of the initial proposal; response to mistakes and problems; willingness to admit deficiencies and a lack of expertise in an area; ability to stand their ground and stand by their professional opinions; ability to blend in with the corporate culture; and a commitment to keep confidences (Arnold & McClure, 1989; Rudolph & Johnson, 1985; Steinburg, 1992).

Lippitt (1972) discusses additional qualities which distinguish the professional consultant: displays professional respect for fellow consultants and training firms, even though they are the competition; clearly outlines the financial terms of the engagement; maintains loyalty to the client who made the initial introduction, even after other client relationships are formed; ability to sense the organizational climate and be diplomatic; and the willingness to have the training and/or services evaluated.

Assume that your efforts have paid off and you have been contacted by someone in search of training, try to get as much information as you can about what their needs are, what it is they say they want you to do, and the timeframe within which they need it done. Now, this may not prove to be the reality, but it is the place to start. Ask if you can prepare a proposal and meet to further discuss the matter. You should send your brochure or background materials to the potential client ASAP along with a cover letter that confirms the meeting and expresses your pleasure at the upcoming discussion. Hold your ground and be firm, direct, and businesslike. I had one client who was initially very curt with me on the phone. Later, she told me that she wanted to see how tough I was and whether she would do business with me. Her company is now one of my largest clients.

Over and over, the corporate clients with whom I spoke said the same thing: the key to success as an external consultant is to establish and maintain relationships with clients. It is not enough to be very good at what you do. It is the trust and respect that the two parties bring to the table that ensure a continuing relationship of mutual benefit.

Lawrence Tuller (1992), in *Cutting Edge Consultants*, provides insight into the mind of the client and suggests strategies for conflct resolution and negotiation. He offers these four "Cs" as qualities for consultant success: confidence, commitment, confidentiality, and chemistry (p. 71). Clearly, a great deal of the consultant's success is directly attributable to interpersonal communication competency.

Design the Training

After gathering information from the client, determining the trainees' current level of experience and expertise, conducting a needs assessment, or making your own assessments after research, you will need to determine the objectives of the training and the way in which you will accomplish those objectives through training. Trainees skills, knowledge, and attitudes are the elements which undergo change during training. You will need to determine what format(s) will be the appropriate choice given the objectives, the trainees, and the logistics. Formats include discussion, lecture, simulations (try not to call them role-plays as that is a turn-off for many trainees), and case studies. Principles of adult learning reinforce the need for trainees to demonstrate mastery of new skills and concepts by actually performing the new task of displaying the new skill in a simulation. Vary the format and give trainees ample opportunity to hear information in a variety of ways so that you increase the likelihood that they will master the material.

Write the Proposal

Arnold and McClure (1989) suggest three types of proposals: the needs assessment, the training proposal, and the executive summary. The needs assessment proposal would outline the proposed parameters and procedures such as the sampling plan, methodology, and means of analysis (p.58). In preparing the needs assessment proposal, gather as much information as you can about the industry and the company. Select a way to quantify the information you would be gathering at the client site. One of the best ways is to conduct interviews with the support of management. Using a standard set of interview or survey questions, you can get not only information about trainee attitudes and work experiences to be used in the training proposal phase but also examples and illustrations which directly relate to the client and which can be used during the actual delivery of training (Stoneall, 1991).

The training proposal, with or without information from the previous needs assessment, itself should be as clear, direct, and concise as possible. Proposals can be effective when presented in a variety of formats but there are several parts which should be included. The format below, which looks like an affirmative need-plan case, will serve a variety of initial proposal needs:
1. Overview of the client situation and/or background of the industry
2. Needs
3. Description of proposed training program, including objectives, strategies, format(s), implementation and evaluation
4. Benefits of the training program
5. Timeframe
6. Logistics (staff, location, equipment, etc.)
7. Fees

Of course, the proposal itself is desktop published on stationary that matches the rest of your business materials. A word of caution: don't give away the store. Determine how much information you are going to provide to a client who has not yet made a commitment to you. Additional details can always be added to the original proposal.

For relatively straight-forward training, an executive summary may be sufficient. This one-to-two page overview may be all that is required for the client to commit. When finished, send the proposal with a cover letter stating that you will call for their reaction after they have had a chance to review the proposal. Usually, this follow-up call is made within a week. I suggest that you give some thought to how the proposal will be delivered: by overnight mail, courier service, or regular mail, each of which sends messages about urgency and willingness to put materials in the client's hands in the shortest amount of time even if it costs a little more. After receiving the client's input, finetune the proposal, set up a time to meet, and brush up on the client's industry.

Make the Pitch and Close the Deal

Before you enter into a sales situation, be sure you understand how decisions are made in a particular industry and what clients look for in a consultant. We may not want to use the "s" word, but you are indeed in sales. You must learn how to promote your services not as great information to know but as trainee skills and behaviors tied to their bottom-line (Kramlinger, 1993; Miller & Heiman, 1985; Rowland, 1992; Shook, 1986; Ziglar, 1991). Gagliardi (1992) lists five factors which will determine your success in selling your services: the quality of your services, the nature of the customer, the comparative value of your services, your sales approach, and you demeanor during client service. Customer service is the key to sales (Power, 1992; Walther, 1992; Ziglar, 1991). Selling is an art, become an artist: use the latest research in neuro-linguistic programming, read bestselling books on the subject, and read the current research done in the communication field.

When you meet with the potential client, you present your training proposal using your best presentation skills. The format of the presentation usually follows this format - need, plan, benefit, action step. Sounds a great deal like Monroe's Motivated Sequence, doesn't it? Especially because communication is viewed as a "soft-skill," you will need to offer proof that training will actually affect the bottom-line . You can be sure that the client is asking, spoken or unspoken, these questions: How do we know that training affects the bottom-line? How do we measure the effects of training on trainee attitudes, behaviors, and performance? (Pine & Tingley, 1993) You need to have an answer more substantial than "good reviews" on the post-seminar "happy sheet" evaluation (also known as "euphoria ratings") that trainees fill out while still enthusiastic about their experience.

Several methods of determining the training return on investment exist

(Davidove & Schroeder, 1992; Hassett, 1992; Pine & Tingley, 1993). Tracking the performance levels of trainees over time and cross-checking the improved skills and behaviors against what was identified in the needs assessment is a good way to start. Observations, follow-up surveys, and formulas for determining the return on investment can also be used for documentation.

Negotiating the engagement may be uncomfortable at first but you needn't feel as though you are in uncharted waters. There are ways to negotiate that are in keeping with the "soft-sell" approach (Dawson, 1991; Fisher & Ury, 1981; Yeomans, 1985). Be sure that you know going into the negotiation what you can afford to offer, what you cannot, and when to opt out of a situation when it is not in your best interests.

After talking about the cost, answering objections and satisfying their anxiety about the process, you should suggest that you schedule the training sessions and clean up whatever details are necessary with the client. Get a commitment from him or her and say that you will send a letter confirming your discussion. This is also the part where you send the invoice for the first half or first third of the agreed upon fee. In the letter, you talk about how pleased you are that you will be working together.

Prepare for Training

Design the program using what models you find in your research that seem appropriate given the situation you now find yourself in. Whenever possible, visit the company and, if appropriate, meet some of the participants beforehand. You should do research on the company, the profession, and related areas. I do a great deal of work with two of the Big 6 accounting firms and I have had to learn about the profession, some of the issues that these executives face, and the types of business presentations they give. Call the professional associations affiliated with the industry and request information. You will need to become as well versed in the profession as you can. I once had, as a client, an author and graphologist who was to embark on a national speaking tour. I read several books on the subject in order to know what questions to ask during media training as I played the role of an antagonistic reporter, preparing her questions and responses.

Analyze adult learning behaviors and training techniques, design the program to meet the needs which have been identified by either yourself or your client. Line up all of your training materials, including your manual and the leave-behinds for the participants. Pack or ship everything well in advance and make extensive lists about what you will need to accomplish or handle prior to the training sessions. I always carry my training manual, overheads, and xerox masters with me in case the materials I send in advance never arrive. Better to be prepared than to tap dance in front of the client whose check you have already cashed.

Conduct the Training Program

Arrive early, check everything and assume nothing. Remember Murphy's Law? At no time in your life will you be more likely to experience its full effect. Because the pressure will be on you, the expert, to perform at a high level, your nervousness will increase. You will be more likely to overlook details and fail to follow through.

While training, be concrete and goal-oriented. Nothing frustrates participants more than to be forced by their superiors to participate in a training program which they believe has little value. You need to let them know right up front what they will get from this experience and how there will be a direct application to their working lives. Be flexible, draw them into the give-and-take of the training, and show them respect. Most of these people are fairly successful at what they do.

Upon successful completion of the training sessions or seminar, I give to each member of the small group sessions their graduation gift - a pointer. This may sound hokey, but everyone likes to be rewarded for their work and I give them a gift that not only helps them make better presentations and but also makes them think of me when they use it. I also give certificates that I print through the laser printer. Some companies even offer these graduates continuing education credits for the completion of my training.

Evaluate the Training Program

Always ask participants to evaluate the content and the delivery of the seminar. Have a formal anonymous evaluation device for them to use. You need to know where you are effective and where you need to rethink the process and revamp the program. Follow-up interviews and surveys can determine whether training has been effective over time. One of the best ways to learn that you have been effective is to be asked back to conduct additional training or when management indicates increased sales or improved employee performance. In addition to pre-test/post-test evaluations, Arnold & McClure (1989) suggest other ways to determine effectiveness: the time-series design, Solomon Four-Group, and the multiple-baseline design.

Continue the Relationship

The key to staying active is to keep a long-time relationship with clients. It is much easier to keep the faith with an existing customer than to build trust with new ones, although you must certainly explore new client service opportunities. More than one client has asked for help or advice in some way and I have offered it without thought of direct payment. Those small favors have resulted in continued consulting engagements. Customer service means that you adapt to meet the needs of your clients, you sometimes offer help without pitching your services, you sometimes honestly tell a client that you are not the best person to deliver what they say they need and then recommend a colleague, and you never let the customer know the time and effort it took to meet the deadline to which you committed.

Always conduct yourself in a businesslike manner. Document conversations and agreements in standard business letters. Remember to thank people for introductions, advice, and the opportunity to work for them. After being asked to conduct additional training at a particular firm, I ask the executive to lunch - power lunches get to be expensive but it is the cost of doing business. I order leather vestpocket calendars and have their initials and the name of my company imprinted on the cover. A little pricey, yes, but all year long, they see my name when they open the calendar. When someone recommends my training, I send them a letter of thank you and a gift. When I have an opportunity to give my clients business, I do. If I am asked to write an article and it's appropriate to quote them, I will. It's just part of the way I like to keep in touch with people so that when training needs arise, they think of me.

As Your Consulting Practice Grows

Sandroff (1992) highlights five critical turning points in the development of a consulting practice: turning down work; narrowing your area of specialization; hiring staff and acquiring office space outside the home; creating a network of support which includes hiring professionals to design marketing pieces, keep the general ledger, process invoices, or handle finances and investments; and changing the fast pace to allow you to enjoy the fruits of your labor. Perhaps nothing is more important than the last turningpoint; when it's not enjoyable anymore and the cost to your psyche is greater than the return, consider another path.

Develop a Code of Ethics

There are so many books about ethics, personal integrity, and values for you to choose from. Know that your clients are reading them and attempting to make changes in their lives as well. If you have time for only one or two books, consider those of Stephen R. Covey, *The 7 Habits of Highly Effective People* (1989) and *Principle-Centered Leadership* (1991). These two books may be helpful in framing the way in which you approach the client relationship as well as the way in which you conduct business.

In as much as there is no license needed to conduct a consulting practice and no professional organization which binds us to a set of standards and practices which it can then enforce, it is important for each of us, as consultants, to develop a personal code of ethics to which we adhere. Numerous organizations offer suggestions for inclusion. Below is part of the Code of Ethics of the American Society for Training and Development (ASTD 1992) for its

members:
1. Recognize the rights and dignities of each individual
2. Develop human potential
3. Provide ...clients and learners with the highest level quality education, training, and development
4. Comply with copyright laws
5. Keep informed of pertinent knowledge...
6. Maintain confidentiality and integrity in the practice of my profession
7. Conduct myself in an ethical and honest manner
8. Fairly and accurately represent my...credentials, qualifications, experience, and ability.

I have distilled a few thoughts about conduct as a trainer that you may find helpful:
1. Don't promise what you cannot deliver, even if the money is tempting, because you'll ruin your credibility
2. Don't spout theory and research - adopt a business attitude: if you can't show a direct effect on improving job performance, what's the point?
3. Remember that this is a service business - you need to be flexible, fair and willing to meet client needs (sometimes giving more than you originally agreed to if it means maintaining good will and your actions may engender additional business)
4. Keep confidences. Don't peddle your stories out on the street and certainly not to other clients. Use generic terms even though it may be tempting to drop names. Remember that it is, after all, a very small world
5. Work continually to enhance your own credibility - get your name in print, get published, give presentations, be quoted in articles, network
6. Once you have made a commitment to a client, stick to it - even if a more lucrative opportunity presents itself
7. Even if the name of the client and the fee is very tempting, if you cannot feel comfortable with the engagement, don't take it. I once turned down an opportunity to work for the largest cable company in the world because they wanted experiential training for forty people in the areas of presentation skills, conflict management and listening, all in one day
8. I truly believe that what goes around, comes around

(For a much broader treatment on the subject of ethics as a consultant, see the chapter, "Ethics and Communication Consulting.")

and finally...
Keep your sense of humor - you'll need it.

References

American Society for Training and Development. 1992. Who's Who in Training
    and Development Alexandria, VA: American Society for Training and
    Development.
Arnold, W. E. & L. McClure. 1989. Communication training & development.
    New York: Harper & Row.
Black, P. 1993. Making the most of those nickels and dimes. Business Week, 8
    March, 90.
Block, P. 1981. Flawless consulting: A guide to getting your expertise used.
    Austin: Learning Concepts.
Callahan, M. R. 1992. Tending the sales relationship. Training and
    Development (December): 31-36.
Cohen, J. 1989. Designing your home office. Home, September, 34.
Covey, S. R. 1989. The 7 habits of highly effective people. New York:
    Simon & Schuster.
Covey, S. R. 1991. Principle-Centered Leadership. New York: Simon &
    Schuster.
Davidove, E. & P. Schroeder. 1992. Demonstrating ROI of Training. Training
    and Development (August): 70-71.
Dawson, R. 1991. The secrets of power negotiating. Excepts read by the
    author. Cassette 474A. Niles, IL: Nightingale Conant.
Elsea, J. G. 1984. First impression, best impression. New York: Simon &
    Schuster.
Fisher, R. & W. Ury. 1981. Getting to Yes. Boston: Houghton Mifflin.
Foxman, L. D. & W. L. Polsky. 1988. Can you succeed as a consultant?
    Princeton: National Business Employment Weekly.
Freeman, C. 1993. What you need to know before starting a business. Bottom
    Line/Personal, 28 February, 7.
Gagliardi, G. 1992. The art of selling. Success, May, 32.
Gumpert, D. E. 1993. Protecting your business idea. Executive Female,
    Jan/Feb, 21.
Hall, K. 1991. The publishing journey. Training & Development (August): 31-
    38.
Harris, P. & D. Lyon. 1993. Making your Trademark. Compuserve Magazine,
    February, 26.
Kamoroff, B. 1993. Cut through the red tape. Home Office Computing, January,
    62.
Kelley, R. E. 1981. Consulting: The complete guide to a profitable career.
    New York: Charles Schribner.
Kramlinger, T. 1993. A trainer's guide to business problems. Training and
    Development, (March): 47-50.
Learning International. 1992. Profiles in customer loyalty. Stamford, CT:
    Learning International.

Lewis, P. H. 1993. In the home office, equipment may still be deductible. New York Times, 24 January, F8.

Levoy, R. P. 1966. The $100,000 practice and how to build it. Englewood Cliffs, NJ: Prentice Hall.

Lippitt, G. L. 1972. Criteria for selecting, evaluating, and developing consultants. Training and Development Journal, (August): 12-17.

McDermott, L. C. 1992. Marketing yourself as "me,inc." Training and Development, (September): 77-84.

Milano, C. 1992. How to start a business with just a home computer for less than $2,000. Bottom Line/Personal, 30 November, 9.

Miles, J. 1987. Design for Desktop Publishing. San Francisco: Chronicle Books.

Miller, R. B. & S. E. Heiman. 1985. Strategic selling. New York: Warner Books.

Molloy, J. T. 1975. Dress for success. New York: Warner.

Pine, J. & J. C. Tingley. 1993. ROI of soft-skills training. Training and Development, (February): 55-60.

Power, C. 1992. Smart selling. Business Week, 3 August, 46.

Rowland, M. 1992. On your own is a sales job, too. New York Times, 12 April, F23.

Rowland, M. 1992. Perils of small-business success. New York Times, 17 January, F17.

Rudolph, E. E. & B. R. Johnson. 1985. Communication consulting: Another career option. Annadale, VA: The Speech Communication Association.

Sandroff, R. 1992. The turning points of a consultant's life. Executive Female, September/October, 32.

Shook, R. L. 1986. The Perfect Sales Presentation. New York: Bantam.

Steinburg, C. 1992. The art of choosing a consultant. Training & Development, (January): 21-26.

Stoneall, L. 1991. Inquiring trainers want to know. Training & Development, (November): 31-39.

Thompson, J. ed. 1981. Image impact. New York: A&W Pulbishers.

Tuller, L. W. 1992. Cutting edge consultants. Englewood Cliffs: Prentice Hall.

Walther, G. R. 1992. Your secret opportunity. Success, May, 12.

Yeomans, W. N. 1985. 1000 things you never learned in business school. New York: Signet.

Younger, S. M. 1992. Sales savvy for the nineties. Training & Development, (December): 13-17.

Ziglar, Z. 1991. Ziglar on Selling. Excerpts read by the author.   Cassette. Nashville: Nelson Audio Library.

ETHICS AND COMMUNICATION CONSULTING

Michael Purdy

The ethical climate of today's organization demands that we enter the consulting situation wearing our principles on our sleeve. Ethical behavior is definitely "in." Political candidates must be squeaky clean to run for office. Congress and the president are called on the carpet for ethical breaches that would have gone unnoticed previously. The president's chief of staff is ousted for using government vehicles for personal travel. The director of the United Way is reprimanded for his excessive lifestyle. Organizational officials at all levels are experiencing a climate that dictates ethical behavior.

We are in the midst of a trend exacting ethical conduct from everyone in the public view. Faith Popcorn of the Popcorn Report (1991) which predicts social trends--and sets them--says efforts are going into making "the 90's our first truly socially responsible decade: the Decency Decade, dedicated to the three critical E's, Environment, Education, and Ethics" (86). She says "Doing good is no longer an option--it's a must" (87), and "Do right. It isn't enough just to 'do no wrong'" (92) Andrews observes in Ethics in Practice: Managing the Moral Corporation: "Public interest in ethics as a critical aspect of business behavior comes and goes" (1989, 1). Least we feel this is a brief fad, Popcorn's market research predicts most trends last a decade or longer.

To function ethically in today's market we must be proactive on ethics and follow through with impeccable behavior. This should to be our calling card. It will ensure our consulting reputation and help sell consulting in an era of ethics-conscious consumers. This chapter will explore what ethical behavior is and how to make decisions in the ethically troubling situations we encounter in corporate consulting. This chapter will also stress that ethics is not just a fad, but a crucial and determining factor of organizational life.

Before we can define ethics per se we must be clear about what ethics is not. To follow a line of behavior because it is prudent or the socially negotiated convention does not make it ethical. Frankena (1963) makes a clear distinction between prudence (in the sense of careful management, economy), force, convention, and ethical decision-making.

> It may be that prudence and morality dictate some of the same conduct, for example, honesty. It may also be that prudence is a moral virtue, however, it is not characteristic of the moral point of view to determine what is right or virtuous wholly in terms of what the individual desires or of what is to [her] his interest. [Convention] seems to rest largely on matters of appearance, taste and convenience. . . . Physical force and certain kinds of prudential considerations do not strictly belong to the idea of a moral institution of life (6).

Kohlberg (1980) makes similar distinctions between moral judgments and judgments that direct right behavior.

> Moral judgments are judgments about the right and the good of action. Not all judgments of "good" or "right" are moral judgments, however; many are judgments of aesthetic, technological, or prudential goodness or rightness (55)

Convention, prudence, or force are not adequate responses to the serious and complex ethical concerns of corporations. The essence of ethics is that we act based on rules and values (traits) that go beyond what is conventional or prudent. Trends, like clothes, go in and out of fashion, and behavior may be more or less prudent (and more or less ethical) depending upon the situation. Ethical behavior has a consistent rationality despite fashion or convention. To be ethical our actions should stem from moral awareness and include the greatest good for the greatest number, concern for long-term effect on others, empathy for others and their situation.

There are always skeptics who challenge the very possibility of ethical behavior. Lest anyone wonder if behavior based on more than self-interest is possible, a recent social-psychological study by Batson (1991) suggests that there is an individual motivation toward altruism: "we now have an affirmative answer, based on the evidence for the empathy-altruism hypothesis" (230). Ethical behavior is, therefore, a reasonable expectation -- people can feel for others and do act unselfishly.

Based upon current philosophical and practical research in ethics and consulting and my practical experience this chapter will discuss the nature of ethics and ethical behavior, present some of the major ethical issues for organizations, review ethical considerations for communication consultants, and set out directions for future ethical concerns in communication consulting. Overall, I intend to show the significance of ethical codes and the importance of integrating moral development into our goals for ourselves and corporate clients.

What Is Ethics?

Ethics . . . is philosophical thinking about morality, moral problems, and moral judgments (Frankena, 3).

Basically, ethics signifies a code of conduct or set of principles that are used to guide and explain one's moral life (Stroh 1979, xv).

The words "ethics" and "morals" are usually interchangeable. Ethics is defined in Webster's New World Dictionary (Third College Ed.) as "the study of standards of conduct and moral judgment." Webster defines Ethical as "having to do with ethics or morality, of or conforming to moral standards . . . conforming to the standards of conduct of a given profession or group." Johannesen observes that "Ethics denotes the general and systematic study of what ought to be the grounds and principles for right and wrong behavior" (1990, 1). This definitely fits the outlook of this book with its focus on the role and function of the communication consultant operating within the corporation. For our purposes we need to know what scholars of ethics say about ethics in the corporate environment because it will provide a foundation for clear thinking in confusing situations. This will lead to a discussion of "corporate ethics," as well as the standards of communication consulting professionals. As Drucker (1981) states, however, corporate or business ethics is not a special case of ethics, it is still ethics: "the right actions of individuals" (35).

From my experience any ethical direction that has meaning must be conducted on the micro level--as well as the macro--and include the small acts of daily life. We must be conscious of the little things in our business dealings and relationships. That implies giving full attention to a client when listening, taking time to talk to, and especially, to compliment people as we go about our job. It means telling the truth even when there is no obvious problem with bending the truth slightly. As Macklin (1980) states, it includes the decision of

> Whether to give someone time when our time is short, whether to object to small corruption's when silence is more expedient. . . . There is a need to cultivate an "ethics of the everyday," a morality of minor affairs, that translates respect for persons into small deeds of kindness, honest, and decency (131).

There are several ways to approach the problem of what guides ethical behavior, whether in everyday life or in a corporate climate. There are two distinct Western views of ethics:

> 1. "'Ethics as morality' treats ethics as being fundamentally concerned with rules of interpersonal conduct."

2. "'Ethics as the quest for the good life' is fundamentally concerned with values [traits] that are personal rather than interpersonal. . . . with determining the ends, or values, to be sought in a genuinely good human life and with the means of their realization."   (Gellermann, Frankel, Ladenson 1990, 41-42).

The first view argues that rules of conduct take precedence over all. Williams in Ethics and the Limits of Philosophy, concludes, however, that ultimately in a rule-based system one rule will be pitted against another and then rules (or some decision making strategy) will be needed to discriminate between the rules. For example, Frankena, quotes Sir David Ross, as observing: "That one ought to keep one's promises is always valid as a rule of prima facie duty; it is always an obligation one must try to fulfill. But it may on occasion be outweighed by another obligation or rule of prima facie duty" (24).

Further as Gellermann, Frankel and Ladenson (1990) suggest in Values and Ethics in Organization and Human Systems Development, the moral code (set of rules) is paramount over all other considerations; it is general, and it is rationally grounded (42). The authors define a code as having "to do with avoiding behavior that either causes harm to others or significantly increases its likelihood. . . . and one doesn't violate [the code] without moral justification for doing so" (46).

Making decisions about breaking or supporting the code doesn't mean falling back upon self-interest. Self-interest is an abstraction as much as any other social construct and not very meaningful in organizations where individuals cannot in any manner exist or operate alone. We need, at least, to recognize enlightened self-interest with empathy, altruism, and social role-taking operating as a baseline for individual behavior. Yet, these are not prescriptive demands or "shoulds". In the case of altruism, for example, Batson indicates that "it is a motivation, a desire. . . . not from duty, but from inclination" (230). It is a human propensity we may build upon in our corporate consulting.

Derry extends the question of ethical behavior beyond enlightened self-interest to advocate the concept of the "collaborative self" which for her "has two prominent features":

(1) It is based on a broader concept of self. . . . (2) It does not assume that self-interest in the standard sense is the primary motivator of women and men. Rather it draws on the motivations to encourage mutual growth, to combine efforts toward shared goals, to help others achieve their potential, to build relationships for the sake of relationships, to respond to the needs of others (126).

Derry's supplanting of self-interest with "support," "encouragement," and "reward" as aspects of human nature beyond self-interest dovetails nicely with Kohlberg's post-conventional level of moral development (discussed later in this chapter), which presupposes ultimate mutual respect between individuals. It stresses the ethical commitment corporations must make to the human factors of production if our nation is to be competitive. It emphasizes the need to adopt the more "feminine" (some would say) communication skills of "listening, responding on the basis of others' needs rather than on the basis of one's own needs, building strong relationships, making decisions on the basis of responsibility to others, giving feedback, nurturing, building cooperation rather than confrontation" (Derry, 127). It recognizes the importance the most important corporate resource: people. If we are people-centered we will of necessity require interpersonal skills to implement ethical action. Derry's supportive view is also close to Drucker's Confucian "ethics of interdependence" in which "there are only 'obligations,' and all obligations are mutual obligations. Harmony and trust . . . require that each side be obligated to provide what the other side needs to achieve its goals and to fulfill itself" (32).

In the real world needs and interest clash, however. Stoker (1992) provides the useful rhetorical tool of "public justification" for working with the judgments and choices we make in resolving conflicting interests. "What public justification requires is, instead, some account of how these interests are to be reconciled with the interests of others--some recognition of the requirements of community life" (372). So when the ethical codes (rules) within the corporation, or between the corporation and the consultant, conflict, the resolution should include a public justification that reconciles the interests of individuals and organizations involved.

This can be compared to the respect paid to standards and their public justification in professional organizations of lawyers, professors, therapists, or managers. When an individual (or group) challenges or violates an accepted canon the community judges the revision of the rules through peer review. The community as a whole operates to set norms which are more than intellectual exercises. They determine and refine practice within the field. Public justification sets out what is moral behavior for the community.

In the end, rules (codes) of ethics can provide essential guidance but not answers. We must often make decisions within specific, ambiguous situations and the problem of conflicting rules and their interpretation leads to the significance of the second Western view, the trait approach to ethics.

The cultivation of personal traits view dates to Plato and Aristotle and is concerned with "the cultivation of certain dispositions or traits, among which are 'character' and such 'virtues' . . . as honesty, kindness, and conscientiousness" (Frankena, 49). Traits are not inherited and therefore must be inculcated through education and training. However, traits or dispositions, as Frankena notes, need to be more than thoughts or feelings, they must be carried through to action (49). Many of these traits and related virtues come to us through our religious upbringing, though the basis of morality does not lie in religion alone (Kohlberg 1980, Williams 1985). Some moral principles are secular originating in civil documents such as the United States Constitution and Bill of Rights. Justice is one trait that is not fully developed in Christianity, and therefore must be "supplemented by the principle of distributive justice or equality" (Frankena, 44), which is strongly represented in our secular documents and practices.   If rules have their limitation in conflict with other rules in a situation, then the ground of ethical decision making and action rests on traits or dispositions already ingrained in the individuals involved.   If the traits such as character are lacking we are left with decisions most likely dependent upon a naive rendering of a rules approach, or a decision based upon convention or prudence.

Kohlberg's (1986) stages of moral development combine the two Western views of ethics into a principled "governance of moral judgment" (510) constructed from principles for moral action rather than a strict or absolute rule-governed approach. Kohlberg describes the stages of moral development and presents a principled ethics derived from the best thinking in ethical philosophy and current social research. Kohlberg's (1980, 1986) moral development scheme is divided into three levels of two stages each. His model effectively encourages consultants and corporations to enact training and construct environmental mechanisms that promote their member's moral growth.   In fact, Kohlberg concludes that moral conflict and its resolution promote the growth of individuals from one moral stage of his model to the next.   As an individual progresses through Kohlberg's stages his/her moral decisions become more aware and consciously directed. Kohlberg's Six Moral Stages are as follows:

Level I: Preconventional
"The child is responsive to cultural rules and labels of good and bad, right and wrong, but interprets [them] in terms of either the physical or hedonistic consequences of action (punishment, reward, exchange of favors), or in terms of the physical power of those who enunciate the rules and labels" (1980).

Stage 1: Heteronomous Morality (Punishment and Obedience Orientation)
Physical consequences of action decide its goodness or badness despite the human meaning or value of these consequences

Stage 2: Individualism, Instrumental Purpose, and Exchange
Right action consists of that which instrumentally satisfies one's own needs and occasionally those of others, human relations are viewed in terms of the marketplace.

Level II: Conventional
"At this level, maintaining the expectations of the individual's family, group, or nation is perceived as valuable in its own right, regardless of immediate or obvious consequences.   The attitude is one not only of conformity to personal expectations and social order, but of loyalty to it, of actively maintaining, supporting, and justifying the order and of identifying with the persons or group involved in it" (1980).

Stage 3: Mutual Interpersonal Expectations, Relationships, and
        Interpersonal Conformity
Good behavior is that which pleases or helps others and is approved by them.   "Being good" is important and means having good motives,

showing concern about others. Behavior is frequently measured by intention.

Stage 4: Social System and Conscience ("Law and Order" Orientation)
There is orientation toward authority, fixed rules, and the maintenance of the social order. Right behavior consists of doing one's duty, showing respect for authority, and maintaining the given social order for its own sake.

Level III: Post-Conventional, or Principled
"At this level there is a clear effort to define moral values and principles that have validity and application apart from the authority of the groups or persons holding these principles and apart from the individual's own identification with these groups" (1980).

Stage 5: Social Contract or Utility and Individual Rights
Being aware that people hold a variety of values and opinions, that most values and rules are relative to your group. These relative rules should usually be upheld, however, in the interest of impartiality and because they are the social contract. Some nonrelative values and rights like life and liberty, however, must be upheld in any society and regardless of majority opinion.

Stage 6: Universal Ethical Principles
Following self-chosen ethical principles. Particular laws or social agreements are usually valid because they rest on such principles. When laws violate these principles, one acts according to the principle. Principles are universal principles of justice: the equality of human rights and respect for dignity of human beings as individual persons.

This position is based on the assumption "that the function of moral reasoning, judgment and argumentation is to reach agreement where claims of interests conflict, most especially where the conflict is between two or more persons (raising problems of justice)" (Kohlberg 1986, 510). Further, Kohlberg claims that these stages have a universal component or form and "suggest that the same basic ways of moral valuing are found in every culture and develop in the same order" (1980, 33). Freeman similarly agrees that there are "fundamental human rights" so one doesn't necessarily have to do in Rome as the Romans do (7), one can take a stand on these basic ways of moral valuing.

Two implications can be drawn from the general cultural universalism of ethics. First, there is bound to be ethical conflict within an organization--a diverse "culture" with its own negotiated conventions. Sometimes the conflict will involve individuals in different stages of moral development, sometimes disagreement within a stage. Individuals need to recognize the social nature of the organization and balance self-interest with the interest of the community. Compromise and mutual agreement can be pursued as one way to strengthen the corporate community. To accomplish this each party adopts role-taking behavior--each party attempts to put itself in the shoes of the other--so as to understand the other's needs.

Second, Kohlberg's suggestion of "basic ways of moral valuing" denies the justification that ethics is all relative or culturally relative. Most moral philosophies conclude that there are some working principles we can function with, and indeed many corporations have ethical codes that make sense within their own community. This can, according to Kohlberg and Freeman, also be extended across cultures giving some moral authority to having principles that are functional in international offices. Again, the principle of "public justification" can operate in other countries to iron out cultural conflicts in a discursive framework.

The stages of Kohlberg's model offer consultants and corporate leaders a guide for thinking about ethical behavior. In particular, Kohlberg's stage 5 emphasizes the importance within organizations of universal rights "like life and liberty" that have strong implications for promoting cultural diversity. Stage 6 draws attention to the final significance of "respect for the dignity of human beings as individual persons." The consultant who is aware of the impact of Kohlberg's principled approach has a clearer vision of the role of ethics in the corporation. Ultimately our corporations are only as good as the moral community they foster.

Some Ethical Issues for Organizations

A. Thomas Young, president and chief operating officer of Martin Marietta Corporation when interviewed for an article on corporate ethics (Widder 1992) talked about how "Ethics and quality have a common characteristic. Both are attitudes--attitudes of doing things right." Young said that "If you do it right the first time, it's cheaper and faster." Martin Marietta was driven to institute quality by changing market conditions. They knew they needed to build quality products to be competitive. What they didn't realize at first was that unless they were ethical, unless their corporation embodied values such as honesty, quality was just a meaningless slogan. The ethical policies had to be observed in behavior that demonstrated ethical commitment. Young said "We went out on the shop floor and gave gifts to employees who stopped work rather than producing inferior products." Unit labor costs typically were cut in half. Government audit deficiencies dropped to zero. Young's point was that "ethics are a bottom-line issue." What's more Martin Marietta employees discovered they liked working for an ethical corporation.

In the same article the author noted that "Nearly one third of the 264 chief executives surveyed had issued a personal statement or formal discussion of ethics issues in the previous year" (Widder). Typically and historically attempts to promote corporate ethical behavior have been up to the individual, but it is now obvious that a new approach is emerging where the corporate community is taking more responsibility for an individual's ethical behavior. Brown (1988-89) observes that the obvious corporate effect of changing individual behavior is a change in the corporate community (1), and vice versa. There is also a trend across business schools and business associations to impose an ethical awareness on the business management community. An effective communication consultant will understand the ethical climate, work within it, and be supportive of corporate efforts to foster community values and develop ethical codes. An ethically astute consultant will take a leadership role in ethical issues.

Many corporations have changed their missions in the last decade to include a ethical dimensions such as support for individual growth and family well-being. IBM encourages their managers to have an open door and listen to both work and personal problems. What does this mean to the corporate communication consultant? What are some of the specific ethical issues that are being addressed in modern and post-modern organizations?

Democracy in the Corporation. Deetz raises a significant and overarching issue in Democracy in an Age of Corporate Colonization (1992). He describes how, at the same time that governments around the world are struggling for democracy, our personal lives have "increasingly come under corporate control" (ix). These corporations increasingly make decisions that affect every aspect of our social institutions, "but rarely are these decisions grounded in democratic process" (ix). Many communication consultants have held or hold positions in institutions of higher education which typically stress the role of persuasion, debate and argumentation as communication vehicles for an open and democratic process. Although we shouldn't be overbearing with missionary zeal, we may find opportunities to advance democratic values in the corporate world.

Quality. Quality was highlighted as a major issue at Martin Marietta but is an issue that is universal today. W. Edwards Deming has observed that quality control is a systemic problem in the organization. Kaoru Ishikawa, the guru of quality control, blends major elements of W. Edwards Deming with the work of others and concludes: "Fix the problem, not the blame" (qtd. in Bowles & Hammond, 1991). He says that we shouldn't blame people when it is the system of the organization--here the communication system--that needs revision. Communication consultants need to "fix" the communication systems so that people are respected, empowered and productive workers turn out quality products.

Ethics is inherent to issues of quality and empowerment, especially an ethical code that includes stages 5 or 6 ("the equality of human rights and respect for the dignity of human beings as individual persons") of Kohlberg's moral development model. Fixing communication problems so individuals are supported is essential to the total quality movement. There is a huge market here for communication consultants, as well as in Human Resource/Organizational Development which is essential to total quality management.

Human Resource/Organizational Development.

In contrast, one may view Organization Development not merely as a set of techniques to enhance the economic productivity of organizations but also-- and principally-- as a profession committed to making organizational life of all kinds more fully expressive of human values, such as autonomy, self-realization, fairness, cooperation, and concern for human well-being (Gellermann, Frankel, Ladenson, 49).

Organizational development should equally be human development. Most of what we do as consultants and trainers is (should be) aimed at human resource development. However, successful human resource development should mesh with the broader goals of the corporation. A corporation is made up of individuals and if the quality of an individual's behavior isn't supported and given shape by the policies of the corporation then development in the organization as a whole will not be as successful. As Andrews described in Ethics in Practice: Managing the Moral Corporation, the quality of the decision-maker is decisive and is "dependent on the experience, intelligence, and integrity of the decision-maker. That quality depends upon certain forces that do not diminish but educate subjective judgment--namely, information, experience, good intentions, and careful concern" (4). Therefore, ethics are necessarily a major part of human resource training and consultants need to emphasize the critical role of ethical awareness and growth in organizational development.

Cultural Diversity and Organizational Culture. Organizational climate has been inherent in each of the major corporate issues addressed above. Behavior and policy are given tone by the cultural character set by the organization and its leadership. My emphasis is the ethical imperative of dealing with it.

Ethics are shaped by the organizational culture and are subject to the conventions and morality of the broader culture. What do we do when there are conflicts between individual ethical standards and those of the corporation, or between the ethics of the corporation and the ethics of the broader culture (or a subculture)? Corporate members are more and more likely to also be members of the growing diversity of cultures within American society and to have ethical differences with the corporation. Gilligan (1982) for example, emphasizes the ethical divergence between the "cultures" of men and women. Because of distinct roles, expectations, and social relations there is an "observed tendency for girls to orient more toward the morality of care and boys toward the morality of rules and justice" (118). These tendencies carry over into adult life and determine different ethical stances for men and women.

> While an ethic of justice proceeds from the premise of equality--that everyone should be treated the same--an ethic of care rests on the premise of nonviolence--that no one should be hurt. In the representation of maturity, both perspectives converge in the realization that just as inequality adversely affects both parties in an unequal relationship, so too violence is destructive for everyone involved (Gilligan, 174).

Women and men (boys and girls) are exposed to different roles and expectations. How do we respect the integrity of these two disparate modes of experience. Gilligan argues we can because we are, in the end, all connected. A dialogue between fairness and care not only brings out a better understanding of relations between the sexes but also gives rise to a more comprehensive portrayal of family and adult work relationships--burgeoning and critical corporate issues. Such a dialogue can be instructive of how to promote the best of human potential in a culturally diverse environment.

Ethical Considerations for Communication Consultants

"Habit without reflection is adaptive only in a totalitarian climate" (Damon 1988, 145).

As consultant we must: (1) be aware of the ethical dimension, (2) be aware of our own ethics and sensitive to the ethics of our client, (3) be able to reconcile our ethical stance with that of our client.   To begin we have an obligation to stimulate our ethical imagination and become aware of significant ethical issues.   It is part of a consultant's responsibility to do the same for clients when and where appropriate: "part of preparing to be an ethical person in the real world is thinking about the contexts, the institutional settings, where ethical decisions will be made or not made" (Lickona 1980, 130).   Being an ethical professional means honing our analytical skills and testing our metal in real situations.

An equally important responsibility for a consultant is being well-prepared to consult.   The public should be spared idiosyncratic and erratic performance. We should strive for excellence within the organization as well as the discipline of our professional training.   We can use our own example to set a standard as we work, while simultaneously adapting to the standards of the organizations for which we work.   May (1980) also suggests cultivating aspects of character and virtue: perseverance, public-spiritedness (oriented to the common good), integrity (upright and integral or whole), veracity, and fidelity (232).   The consultant relationship is not just a contractual one, but emphasizes giving and receiving--talking and listening.   We not only teach but are constantly learning. We are students at the feet of our clients and not simply the ones with all the competence and knowledge.

Many professional organizations have codes of ethics.   Organization and Human Systems Development professionals have developed a code that covers: responsibility to self, responsibility to clients and significant others, responsibility to the profession, and social responsibility (Gellermann, Frankel, Ladenson, 34-40).   Johannesen in Ethics in Human Communication cites as an example the code of the International Association of Business Communicators (IABC).   The IABC code lists a consultant's responsibility to: Be honest and candid, to use information gotten responsibly and only with permission, to follow the spirit and letter of any laws covering their work, respect confidentiality of all parties related to a job, etc. With respect to honesty, a colleague was asked by a Chicago corporation to produce a video to introduce workers to new policies. He could have made a significant fee producing a video but explained that an audio tape and manual would be much cheaper and still accomplish the objective. Another major concern in many codes is the power and knowledge differential between consultant and client. Both power and knowledge are "lethal weapons" to be wielded only with full awareness of their effect on all parties concerned.

There are other codes, for example that presented by Gallessich (1982, 397-405), for those involved in the "profession and practice of consultation." The consultant's code of ethics stresses (among twenty-eight principles) that consultants: "place their clients' interests above their own," (397) safeguard "the welfare of their consultees and client organizations," (398) when they "perceive a consultee to behave in an unethical manner, they express their observations and the reasons for their concern to the person involved," (399) "avoid involvement in multiple roles and relationships that might create conflicts of interest . . ." (399). A specific code has not, as of yet, been adopted for communication consultants. Therefore, the codes of related professions can be useful in formulating a working code for the professional communication consultant.

There are also guidelines suggested for communication consultants. For example, Harrison (1982) proposes a beginning to a set of guidelines from a rhetorical perspective:

1. The consultant should invite and encourage the participation of all
   organization members potentially affected in the consulting process.
2. The consultant should communicate dialogically with clients (95-96).

These guidelines arise from the organizational developer's dilemma in trying to simultaneously improve "organizational effectiveness" and "quality of life," a situation that may include "contradictory goals" (Harrison, 89). These guidelines direct us to involve all affected parties and arrive at an ethical solution only after serious discourse with all parties. Ethical systems, in general, are not intended to provide all of the answers, they offer at best guidelines we can use to gauge our behavior as more or less worthy in any given situation.

Codes and guidelines, however, are useless if the consultant is not herself integrated. The consultant must recognize the value of ethical self-awareness, have character enough to stick to principles when appropriate, and courageous enough to listen to others when warranted. Self examination begins with an assessment of our own implicit and explicit ethical rules and the traits we find most critical for our personal life and professional work. If we do not have a firm grounding in ethics it is important to do some basic reading or attend a workshop or class on ethics. Having a grounding in ethics and having identified our own ethics we are better equipped to make decisions when we are faced with conflicts between what we know is right for us and what a client may feel is right. Most of us have been asked to train a group of employees in listening or interpersonal communication only to discover that the organization had more serious problems, such as trust, that fundamentally affected the relationship between management and workers.

Whose side do we take in such situations? It is best not to take sides if we can help it but to work as best we are able for the betterment of the corporation and the people involved. My own motto is "support people, attack the problem."

A good example of the complexity of an actual situation is provided by Browning (1982) in his article, "The ethics of intervention: A communication consultant's apology." Browning offers four questions (based on Kohlberg's work) to be used by the consultant in making ethical decisions: (1) "To what extent is the behavior self serving or giving?" (2) "To what extent is the behavior enough?" That is, did we do enough to resolve a situation or might we have done more? (3) "To what extent is the behavior independent versus dependent?" Were we dependent on the authority or the action of others, or were we able to act independently and not be influenced? (4) "To what extent is the behavior thought-out?" (103-107).

Browning continues by citing a hostile situation in a counseling firm with "high turnover, low morale, and low productivity" (107) where he had contracted to consult. Leadership in the firm was problematic but essentially everyone was at fault to some degree. Committees had failed to take action on important decisions, "administrative record keeping . . . was actively avoided" (108). He opted for a restructuring of the organization rather than a less-potent training strategy. In his discussion he reviews each of the four questions posed above and justifies his judgment call on each. Still, in the end, he confesses there was a conflict between his need to be open and learn from the unique situation and his belief that "principles (clear positions prior to event) be maximized" (115).

Conflicts are quite normal in consulting. We must be prepared to deal with conflicts between personal codes of ethics and those of our client. Generally, we must ask several questions: What is the culture of the organization? How is it different from our own? What are its values? How do they differ from our values? Do they conflict and undermine each other? Do they mesh and constructively reinforce each other? To what extent is the consultant justified in imposing his/her values on the client? Of how much importance is the client's consent?

When there are conflicts we should usually side with the client's wishes. In one consulting situation I found a lot of ill-will for the management of an organization. If I sided with the client, management, I would have suppressed the anger of the employees and continued with the training of interpersonal communication skills to better serve patrons. In this particular case I decided to help the employees express their issues and encouraged them to present them to their supervisor. In the long run I believe the relationship between supervisor and employees has greatly improved. Each incident is a judgment call.

Further we need to ask and seek clarification as to: What are the responsibilities of the communication consultant? What are the responsibilities of the organization? We need to evaluate: the aspects of a situation that we, as consultant, have control over; the aspects we can influence; and the aspects we have no control over at all. If we can clarify these in our own mind we have a better foundation for ethical decision making.

Gellermann, Frankel, and Ladenson raise a potentially sticky situation: "the consultant may recognize underlying problems of a sensitive nature that, in his judgment, the client requires further preparation to face." The dilemma involves informing the client early in the consultation and possibly imperiling chances for success, or waiting and destroying trust. How can such an action "best be reconciled with the value of openness in professional relationships? The above issue calls for striking a balance between competing values based on reflection, personal experience, and insights derived from the relevant experiences of other professionals" (57).

Finally, there are many, almost taken-for-granted, pieces of advice that may seem too obvious to mention: put all critical issues (goals, objectives, compensation, working relationship) into a contract, keep your client informed of anything unusual, maintain a daily log for legal purposes and future reference (such as research, with corporate permission), and always be courteous.

Essentially, we have a responsibility as professionals to think critically and to act in the public interest. As professionals we work not only for money and power, we also work to teach those with whom we consult and to use our critical skills for civic benefit.

Future Ethical Concerns in Communication Consulting

In thinking about professional ethics in communication consulting we need to go beyond the problems and challenges of individual situations. We have a role as communication professionals, and as citizens of the nation and the world. Our challenge as consultants should "include institutional and structural criticism, the clarification of professional character and virtue, and the enforcement of professional standards and discipline" (May, 212).

Institutional and structural criticism is a broad and sweeping challenge. I think one aspect of this is the democratization of corporate America as addressed by Deetz. We have an active role to play in this and other critical social movements as we conduct our daily business as corporate consultants. It is also an issue whose merits we need to study and debate in our academic conferences.

As consultants we are also challenged to focus on professional character, standards, and discipline. Professionals generally enforce their codes through self-discipline and voluntary adherence; they are taught their profession's code during training, and through peer consultation and review (Gallessich, 392). Johannesen (1988) sees a trend toward more concrete professional codes with the functions of: (1) educating new members about their responsibilities and the problems of the field, (2) narrowing the problematic areas with which a person has to cope, (3) helping the member to reflect on the profession's goals, and (4) minimize the need for outside regulation as a result of lax professional enforcement.

It may seem more difficult to have a code when practitioners come from varied disciplines, or orientations within a discipline--which I believe is to some degree true in corporate communication consulting. Yet, this is no excuse for not having a professional organization and a professional code to address these issues. A professional organization provides support for its members in following an approved ethical course of action. Public Administrators, for example, argue for a normative ethic which includes: " (1) an understanding of appropriate ethical principles. (2) an identification of virtues which are supportive of those principles, and (3) analytical techniques which may be employed in specific situations to interpret the principles" (Cooper, 1987, 321).

There are also basic questions other professions have addressed to varying degrees: how should consultants be trained? How can they develop their ethical acuity? How do we police ourselves? There are many professional organizations to look to for direction. There are also the exemplars or model teachers, the older, more experienced professionals who can work with younger consultants to teach them the ropes, and to help instill professional ethics. We have many experienced professionals now working in our discipline; we should use their knowledge.

Many organizations certify consultants to have better control over their training. Many organizations have professional codes of ethics. The communication discipline is not one of these organizations. The time has arrived to address these issues. We need a professional association. We also need to continue to dialogue about ethical issues in publications, at conferences, and in the broadest professional arenas.

References

Andrews, K. R., ed. 1989. Ethics in practice: Managing the moral corporation. Boston: Harvard Business School Press.

Batson, D. C. 1991. The Altruism Question: Toward a Social-Psychological Answer. Hillsdale, NJ: Lawrence Erlbaum.

Bowles, J., and J. Hammond. 1991. Beyond Quality: How 50 Winning Companies Use Continuous Improvement. New York: G. P. Putnam's Sons.

Brown, M. 1990. Ethics in organizations. Issues in Ethics 2 (1): 1.

Browning, L. D. 1982. The ethics of intervention: A communication consultant's apology. Journal of Applied Communication Research 10 (Fall): 101-116.

Cooper, T. L. 1987. Hierarchy, virtue, and the practice of public administration: A perspective for normative ethics. Public Administration

Review. 47 (July/August): 320-328.

Damon, W. 1988. The moral child: Nurturing children's natural moral growth. New York: The Free Press.

Deetz, S. A. 1992. Democracy in an age of corporate colonization. Albany, NY: State University of NY.

Derry, R. 1991. Institutionalizing ethical motivation: Reflections on Goodpaster's agenda. In _Business Ethics: The State of the Art_. ed. R. E. Freeman, 121-138. New York: Oxford University Press.

Drucker, P. F. 1981. What is "Business Ethics"? _The Public Interest_. 63(Spring): 18-36.

Frankena, W. K. 1963. Ethics. Foundations of Philosophy Series. Englewood Cliffs, NJ: Prentice Hall.

Freeman, R. E. 1991. Introduction. In _Business Ethics: The State of the Art_, ed. Edward R. Freeman, 121-138. New York: Oxford University Press.

Gallessich, J. 1982. The Profession and Practice of Consultation. San Francisco: Jossey-Bass.

Gellermann, W., M. S. Frankel, & R. F. Ladenson. 1990. Values And Ethics In Organization And Human Systems Development: Responding To Dilemmas In Professional Life. San Francisco: Jossey-Bass.

Gilligan, C. 1982. In a Different Voice: Psychological Theory and Women's Development. Cambridge, MA: Harvard University Press.

Harrison, T. M. 1982. Toward an ethical framework for communication consulting. _Journal of Applied Communication Research_ 10 (Fall): 87-100.

Johannesen, R. L. 1988. What should we teach about formal codes of ethics? _Journal of Mass Media Ethics_ 3(1): 59-64.

Johannesen, R. L. 1990. Ethics in Human Communication (3rd ed.). Prospect Heights, Illinois: Waveland.

Kohlberg, L. 1980. Stages of moral development as a basis for moral education. In _Moral Development, Moral Education, and Kohlberg_, ed. B. Munsey, 15-98. Birmingham, AL: Religious Education Press.

Kohlberg, L. 1986. A current statement on some theoretical issues. In _Lawrence Kohlberg: Consensus and Controversy_, eds. S. Modgil & C. Modgil, 485-546. Philadelphia: Falmer Press.

Lickona, T. 1980. What does moral psychology have to say to the teacher of ethics? In _Ethics Teaching in Higher Education_, eds. D. Callahan & S. Bok, 103-132. New York: Plenum.

Macklin, R. 1980. Problems in the teaching of ethics: Pluralism and indoctrination. In _Ethics Teaching in Higher Education_, eds. D. Callahan & S. Bok, 81-101. New York: Plenum.

May, W. F. 1980. Professional ethics: Setting, terrain, and teacher. In _Ethics Teaching in Higher Education_, eds. D. Callahan & S. Bok, 205-241. New York: Plenum.

Popcorn, F. 1991. The Popcorn Report. New York: Doubleday.

Stoker, L. 1992. Interests and ethics in politics. American Political Science Review 86.2 (June): 369-380.

Stroh, G. W. 1979. American Ethical Thought. Chicago: Nelson-Hall.

Victor, B., & J. B. Cullen. 1988. The organizational bases of ethical work climates. Administrative Science Quarterly 33: 101-125.

Widder, P. 1992. More corporations learning that ethics are bottom-line issue. Chicago Tribune. June 7, sec. 7: 1, 6.

Williams, B. 1985. Ethics and the Limits of Philosophy. Cambridge, MA: Harvard University Press.

Part Two: Communication Skills Training

LISTENING

Judi Brownell

Organizational communication consultants and trainers appear to be in the right field at the right time. In an information society, communication consultants are particularly valuable resources; consulting presents both an opportunity and a challenges to those who move from traditional educational settings to explore a more independent venture. The number of communication specialists who are entering the consulting field is growing steadily and, increasingly, consultants and trainers are held accountable for the results of their interventions.

There is little doubt that effective organizations are characterized by their emphasis on effective listening (Mundale, 1980; DiSalvo, 1980; Seibert, 1990). Well before listening became a subject in popular management books (Peters, 1988; Peters & Austin, 1985; Kanter, 1983), organizational leaders recognized its importance in both internal and external communication. If employees in the past have depended upon listening to accomplish their tasks, organizational members in the decades ahead will discover that listening ability is even more essential to perform well in turbulent, high-technology environments. As the workplace becomes more automated, accurate and timely communication becomes ever more vital. As organizational members and their customers become more diverse, the need to understand and respond appropriately to the human dimension becomes key to organizational effectiveness (Young & Smith, 1988). Rapid and continuous organizational change, whether as a result of strategic plans or random innovations (Zeira & Avedisian, 1989; Brownell, 1990), places new and complex demands on organizational members and their leaders. Most pressing among these is the need to listen.

Listening has historically been referred to as the "neglected" communication skill. In his work with Sperry Corporation, Lyman Steil noted that although managers spend more time listening than reading, writing, or speaking, few had had any significant training in this area (Steil, 1980). In fact, the emphasis in language arts education appeared to be in direct opposition to the frequency with which these skills were needed in the workplace. More recently, however, there has been a growing awareness of the essential role listening plays in all organizational processes, from customer service encounters to interdepartmental negotiations to top-level decision making. Listening, in fact, is often viewed as prerequisite to effective speaking. Organizations have responded to this need for better listeners with a commitment to training their employees in this key communication skill. Seminars designed for service employees, sales and marketing representatives, secretaries, managers, and numerous other groups have focused on the ways in which listening contributes to increased productivity, healthy employee relationships, and more satisfied customers.

Due to the vigor of this field, consulting and training opportunities have arisen in both public and private sectors. Communication specialists, as well as those whose backgrounds are in the behavioral and social sciences, are finding that expertise in listening prepares them for a wide variety of training and consulting opportunities. Listening experts are prepared both to enhance the skills of individual employees as well as to address larger issues of organizational development and change. In addition, listening as a content area supplements programs in related fields such as conflict management, interview skills, managing diversity, organizational change, presentational speaking, and other communication and human resources management topics.

This chapter provides consultants and trainers with a foundation for understanding the field of listening and its current research emphasis. The stages of program design and implementation are outlined, and a sample case study of an organization that benefitted from intensive listening training is provided. Finally, specific challenges in listening training and consulting are reviewed in light of both ethical and practical considerations.

Developments in the Field of Listening

Research in the field of listening is becoming more frequent, more informed, and more rigorous. Historically, insufficient listening research inhibited the development both of sound approaches to assessing listening competence and of clear, consistent instructional goals. Much early literature focused on prescription with little empirical evidence to support many of the generalizations on which listening training was based.

During the past few decades, however, a number of researchers have begun to examine both the listening process and its applications. Although definitions of listening vary widely (Glenn, 1989; Wolvin & Coakley, 1989; Lewis & Reinsch, 1988), most scholars agree that effective listening requires an individual's active engagement, both cognatively and physically. The debate regarding whether to approach listening as a covert mental process or a series of interrelated overt skills continues (Kelly, 1967). Models of listening (Barker, 1971; Brownell, 1986; Mills, 1974; Steil, 1983; Nichols, 1983; Wolvin &

Coakley, 1982) focus on such components as message reception, the assignment and interpretation of meaning, memory processes and, in many cases, the receiver's response. In each of these areas a body of research is steadily accumulating.

The growing volumes of literature on the subject indicate the need for increased dialogue among researchers and the integration of various approaches (Witkin, 1990). Several recent efforts (many initiated through the International Listening Association) have been made to examine the range of existing work and bring together ideas from different perspectives and different fields. Studies have also documented the growing interest in the teaching of listening in academic institutions (Coakley & Wolvin, 1990; Rhodes, 1985; Staley & Shockley-Zalabak, 1985) as well as in organizational settings (Wolvin & Coakley, 1991; Hunt & Cusella, 1983). Trainers will witness a growing number of listening resources in the next decades. Videos, assessment instruments (Watson-Barker Listening Test, 1984; The Kentucky Comprehensive Listening Test, 1978; The Brown-Carlson Listening Test, 1955), and books on listening (Steil, Barker, & Watson, 1983; Floyd, 1985; Montgomery, 1981; Brownell, 1986; Wolvin & Coakley, 1989; Wolff, Marsnick, Tacey, & Nichols, 1983; Purdy & Borisoff, 1991) are now widely available.

Behavioral Approaches to Listening

One recurring obstacle to those who seek to improve listening performance is the relative ambiguity of the subject. Trainers have difficulty focusing their efforts because concepts of listening tend to be general and vague. Covert cognitive processes are difficult to capture or to measure. Those involved in listening training and consulting, therefore, have generally elected to view listening from a behavioral perspective. They operate under the assumption that listening involves a cluster of skills that can be taught; that individuals become more effective listeners through deliberate interventions that modify or change existing habits and patterns of behavior. These specialists seek definitions of listening that can be readily operationalized and applied to organizational settings. A portion of this research has focused on defining the behaviors that organizational members use to make judgements about the effectiveness of their own as well as their colleagues' listening behaviors (Husband, 1987; Husband, Cooper, Monsour, 1988; Gilbert, 1989; Brownell, 1990; Smeltzer & Watson, 1985). A primary task of listening specialists, then, is to determine exactly what employees must learn to "do," not only to increase their listening effectiveness on the job, but also to be perceived by others as being a good listener.

The perception of effective listening is a vital concern to consultants and trainers because of the impact such perceptions have on individual satisfaction and morale as well as organizational climate and culture. In management training in particular, employee perceptions of a manager's listening affect a number of important organizational variables. Although the accomplishment of organizational tasks may depend exclusively upon an individual's ability to process the information he or she hears, strong interpersonal relationships require individuals to demonstrate their listening effectiveness through their verbal and nonverbal behavior.

One behavioral approach (Brownell, 1986), developed specifically for assessment and training purposes, is the HURIER model. This model was developed in response to the need for more precise information about individuals' definitions and perceptions of listening behavior. After careful examination of the existing literature and a review of the standardized tests most frequently used to assess listening competence, a list of specific behaviors used to make judgments of listening effectiveness was generated and a conceptual framework was then developed for clustering these behaviors into separate areas or components. The HURIER model suggests that these components, although interrelated, can be assessed and taught as separate skill areas (figure 1). Below, each of the six component areas is briefly described.

Hearing/Concentration. We know that the average person can listen and process information at a rate at least twice that of the normal speaker (Orr, 1964). This means that most listeners have a good deal of "unused" mental time--time that is often spend daydreaming, rehearsing, or anticipating events and activities unrelated to the communication event at hand. In organizational settings, listeners whose nonverbal behavior indicates that their attention is divided appear disinterested and rude. Speakers are likely to perceive these individuals as poor listeners regardless of whether or not their listening is effective when evaluated by other measures.

Motivation, too, plays an important role in the listening process. When speakers are interested in the information presented, attention is almost automatic. When listeners pre-judge information as irrelevant or dull, however, concentration will be a constant battle (Ostermeier, 1991; Bostrom & Bryant, 1980). Trainers seeking to increase effectiveness in this component focus on the ways in which listeners demonstrate their attention and interest and stay focused on the speaker's message.

Comprehension/Understanding. A number of studies examine listening comprehension, or the extent to which a message is literally understood. Several of these compare listening comprehension to reading comprehension; others isolate the variables that affect listeners' understanding of the messages they hear. With increased specialization and technical vocabularies, comprehension has become an increasingly vital component of the listening process in organizational settings.

Several standardized listening tests have been developed that measure aspects of listening comprehension (Brown-Carlson, 1955; Kentucky Comprehensive Listening Test, 1978), and numerous studies document their degree of validity and reliability (Shellen, 1989) Researchers and practitioners alike have been interested in the variables that affect listening comprehension and in the ways in which individuals can improve their understanding of the messages they hear (Carver, 1973; Beatty, Behnke, & Froelick, 1980; Tumma, 1980). Some of the most common methods include: learning effective organizational and notetaking systems, perception checking, and increasing vocabulary (Howe, 1970; Carter & Van Matre, 1975; DiVesta & Gray, 1982).

Memory. Most researchers agree that memory is a distinct cognitive activity, separate from listening (Sperritt, 1962; Bostrom & Waldhart, 1980). Still, the ability to remember and recall is so closely linked to listening effectiveness that almost all models of the listening process include memory as a key component. Every organizational member depends upon his or her memory to perform tasks effectively; poor memory almost inevitably results in lower productivity and inefficiency.

Bostrom's work in memory has had a significant impact on the field (Bostrom & Waldhart, 1988; Bostrom, 1990). In 1979 he developed a widely-used assessment instrument, the Kentucky Comprehensive Listening Test. His research suggests that significant individual differences exist in the degree of competence individuals demonstrate in short term (interpersonal) and long term (public speaking) listening situations. Others (Loftus, 1980; Thorndyke & Hayes-Roth, 1979; Goss, 1982) have also explored memory processes as they relate to human communication. Those interested in improving their listening would do well to focus on developing more effective memory techniques.

Interpretation/Empathy. An increasingly diverse workforce demands that greater emphasis be placed on interpreting messages, on going beyond understanding the substance of communications by taking into account the person speaking and his or her unique perceptions, attitudes, values, and experiences. Valuing diversity, a recurring theme for the decades ahead, requires listeners who attend to nonverbal cues and who are able to see things from another person's point of view. It encourages the listener to understand and to respect the person speaking before responding to the content of his or her message.

Those studying empathy (Bruneau, 1989; Basch, 1983; Broome, 1991; Howell, 1982; Stewart, 1983) emphasize the importance of this other-centered perspective to effective human communication. The Watson-Barker Assessment instrument, which includes tape recorded statements and dialogues, addresses issues of listening interpretation as well as other components of the listening process.

Evaluation. As employees become empowered to participate ever more actively in decision making processes, the quality of their judgments has a greater impact on organizational effectiveness. Although the first step in effective listening is to withhold evaluation until a message has been completely understood, making judgments regarding the value and validity of information is a critical organizational task (Kelly, 1977; Tutolo, 1975). Listeners must learn to put secondary factors into perspective when evaluating the merit of ideas.

Those trained in logic and reasoning will also be better able to make wise decisions. Individuals need to distinguish emotional appeals and propaganda from valid evidence and logical argument; they must consider a wide range of factors in making their decisions (Larson, 1989; O'Keefe, 1991). Although the critical listening process is complex, it lends itself more readily to assessment through paper and pencil measures than do other components of the listening process.

Speaker variables, such as mannerisms, indicators of powerless speech, eye behavior, and other factors must not interfere with judgments made about the value of the information presented (Bradac & Mulac, 1984; Johnson, 1989), nor must they be interpreted without regard to cultural and individual differences.

Response. Several transactional models of communication suggest that the speaker/listener dichotomy may be dysfunctional; that, in fact, individuals in communication encounters are simultaneously sending and receiving messages, processing incoming information as they formulate a response. Although researchers and practitioners are in disagreement as to whether or not response should be included in listening training, behavioral models suggest that individuals make judgments of listening effectiveness based largely on their partner's verbal and nonverbal response to their message. It is therefore useful, from a pragmatic standpoint, to focus on the quality and appropriateness of the listener's response as a key element in the communication process. This is particularly true when perceptions of listening behavior are assessed.

Listening Consulting: A Process Model

The accumulating body of knowledge about listening has directly and indirectly benefitted listening trainers and consultants, who must not only establish the importance of this skill but must also establish their own credibility in the field. Once a relationship with an organization has been secured, the consultant inevitably must explore issues related to the assessment of participant needs, the development of instructional programs, and the evaluation of training results. This section begins with an overview of the training and consulting function, and then addresses each of these key issues.

Training and Consulting. The terms trainer and consultant are often--and for good reason--used synonymously. Yet, experts on the subject believe there are also important differences (Eubanks, 1992; Bushe & Barrie, 1990). One recurring theme is that of control. While trainers can identify their specific task ahead of time, consultants often move into an organization to discover what is needed. The consultant role requires observation, assessment, and analysis in addition to expertise in the classroom. As Sprull (1986) notes, when moving from trainer to consultant you move "out of the contractor-doer role and into the facilitator role" (p. 21). Consulting in all fields has recently come to be viewed as a glorified activity. As one author notes:

> I remember how I viewed trainers and consultants; as glamorous,
> intelligent, worldly individuals who taught somewhere wonderful
> and different each week and made tons of money. (Russell, 1990, 126)

Although there may be more than a little truth in this perception for more than just a few consultants, those who have entered the field realize that training and consulting also take a great deal of energy, time, and continuous hard work.

Numerous specific consulting competencies have been identified. Clearly, consultants and trainers themselves must be active listeners in order to perform effectively. One list of training and consulting competencies, presented by Sprull (1986), is particularly comprehensive. She believes all consultants must possess:

1. Process skills
2. Interpersonal skills
3. Experience in human resource development
4. A commitment to personal growth
5. Risk taking ability
6. Client-driven motives
7. A business mind set   (pp. 20-21)

Each trainer or consultant, of course, brings unique contributions to the organizational setting. Two criteria that must always be met, however, are a solid knowledge of his or her field and a thorough understanding of organizations and how they function. Repeatedly, experts warn about the temptations of spreading yourself too thin. The most successful and effective consultants and trainers are those who have a specific, vertical market in mind, who carefully choose their area of expertise, and who stay up-to-date in their chosen field. Consultants, as one author writes, need to keep their skill level at "the leading edge" (Russell, 1990, 126). Those who choose to focus on the area of listening have much work in store, as this relatively new field is developing at rapid pace.

Needs Assessment: Listening for Individual and Organizational Development

Because listening is a multi-faceted, situational activity subject to individual interpretation, assessment is a particularly critical part of the consulting process. Unlike many other areas, listening trainers and consultants are concerned not only with an individual's skill but also with the way in which these behaviors are perceived by others. They are also directly concerned with the impact those perceptions have both on the specific individuals involved as well as on the organization's entire climate and culture (figure 1).

Individual Level. Although it can be argued that perceptions of listening may not reflect an individual's actual listening behavior as measured on standardized tests, perceptions of listening have usefulness to the extent that it is an employee's perceptions of being listened to that influence his or her attitudes, feelings, and subsequent behaviors. Although self-reports are helpful in diagnosing listening problems, respondents' self-perceptions do not always correlate closely to the perceptions others have of their listening ability. Repeatedly, studies confirm that individuals rate themselves as more effective listeners than do their colleagues (Husband, 1987; Brownell, 1990). This fact his potential significance for any training design, as motivation and perceived need become key elements in determining the success of training efforts.

In one study (Brownell, 1990), managers were asked to rate their own listening behavior, and then companion questionnaires were administered to each manager's subordinates, asking them to rate their manager on the identical items. Results indicated that managers did, in fact, over estimate their listening competencies on all dimensions of the HURIER model--attending, understanding, remembering, interpreting, evaluating, and responding.

In addition, studies (Brownell, 1990; Golen, 1990; Lewis & Reinsch, 1988) suggest that listening problems and definitions are organization-specific; the meaning of "doesn't listen" varies considerably from one department and one company to the next. There is little question, for instance, that while in one organization frequent meetings and memorandums may be perceived as time-consuming and tedious, in another case organizational members may interpret these activities as a means of facilitating employee involvement and information-sharing. An individual employee's background, goals, and expectations also play a role in determining how listening behaviors are interpreted. As the workforce becomes more diverse, consultants and trainers can anticipate greater challenges in identifying the most appropriate--and desirable--listening behaviors.

Individual needs assessment, then, can occur on three levels. On the one hand, employees can provide information regarding the areas of listening they believe need to be addressed. Through structured interviews and surveys, individuals in various departments or organizational groups can determine the focus of listening training by suggesting the type of instruction they feel would be valuable to them.

Since reasonably valid listening assessment instruments are available, consultants may choose to conduct a more traditional needs analysis by asking selected employees to take one of the several standardized listening assessment tests. Results of these instruments can then be used to focus training objectives and select appropriate methods and materials.

Another assessment strategy, particularly appropriate to management or supervisory training, is to ask individuals to assess their colleagues' listening. This data, based on perceptions of listening effectiveness, may reveal a very different picture of listening needs. Such an assessment can be conducted either within a single department or throughout the entire organization. The means of the ratings colleagues assign to an individual training participant can then be compared with the results of the individual's self-assessment. When such information becomes available to participants, it encourages them to consider the impact of their behavior on others and begins to bring their self-perceptions more in line with the perceptions their coworkers have of their behavior.

Organizational Level. Listening consultants have an obligation to consider the organization's culture and the degree to which it supports the training effort as he or she develops problem-solving strategies; otherwise, no lasting or meaningful results can be expected (Follert, 1980; Daniel, 1985; Lundberg, 1990;

Muchinsky, 1977). When an organization's culture appears to be in conflict with the skills a consultant has identified, further and more comprehensive interventions may be required. Not all problems can best, or first, be resolved through training, and it is the consultant's responsibility to determine the best strategies for positive organizational change.

Employees' collective behavior, particularly their listening attitudes and competence, has a significant impact on the organization's culture. Strong listening environments are characterized by a concern for the individual worker and his or her values, needs, and goals. Peters (1988) was among the first to use the term "listening environment" to describe an environment in which managers listen to their employees and teammates listen to one another.

Strong listening environments have been assumed to promote a free and open exchange of ideas and information among all organizational members (King, 1978). Signs of a strong listening environment range from managers' nonverbal cues to open office doors to active employee recognition programs. While specific employee behaviors and management policies contribute to the perception of the organization's listening environment, these perceptions, once established, influence employees' subsequent attitudes and behaviors (Lindley, 1984; Ashworth & Meglino, 1983). Assessing the organization's overall listening environment is a task consultants and trainers cannot ignore.

Common Problems Caused by Ineffective Listening. In summary, these problems are often found at the organizational level: low morale, low productivity, high absenteeism and turnover, lack of upward communication, and ineffective horizontal communication. At the individual level, these problems are common: misunderstandings, interpersonal conflict, ineffective meetings, and a lack of motivation.

Program Development and Design

The identification of listening skill deficiencies and an assessment of the organization's listening environment is only the first step of a consultant's job. Designing effective in-house training programs is a complex and challenging task. Behavioral models of listening are useful in that they enable trainers to select particular aspects of the listening process on which to focus, set specific goals, and develop organization-specific materials to meet those goals. In cases where listening behavior has been assessed in some structured manner, program development becomes a matter of designing instructional strategies to address the shortcomings that were found in the exploratory phase.

The importance of using appropriate examples, of knowing the names of key department heads, of understanding the organization's structure and the industry's relationships with its clients, cannot be over-emphasized. Consultants must know what the employees' attitudes are toward listening and toward communication skills training generally, as well as the degree to which upper level management supports the recommended interventions.

When a company makes a commitment to train its people, it expects improved performance. That's the bottom line. The consultant and trainer's primary task, therefore, is to facilitate lasting behavioral change--change that will have an impact on the employees and that will affect the organization's performance as well. The goals must be clear, the payoff must be visible.

Training that focuses on skill development over the acquisition of knowledge requires a design different from that associated with traditional classroom instruction. Research has clearly demonstrated that clarifying objectives and providing an overview of the program content and format are essential to all training settings (Latham & Wexley, 1981). Effective listening trainers often begin with a description of a specific problem (a tailored case study, for instance) and then vividly demonstrate how the listening skills covered in the program are necessary to solve the problem or rebuild the relationship. Participants must be stimulated to want to know what to do, and be convinced that there's a better approach than the one they've been using. The results of any pre-program assessment, especially those that compare participants' self-assessment to their colleagues' ratings, may also serve as a motivating device. Such information demonstrates to participants that their colleagues do not perceive their current listening behaviors as positively as they do and gives them personal, concrete objectives.

Since the primary goal of skills training is transfer, it is also helpful to look at some of the ways in which this might best be accomplished. Trainers must do whatever possible to simulate the organizational environment in which listening behaviors will be practiced. Research reveals that three factors encourage the transfer of skills to on-the-job situations:
(1) the use of relevant examples and illustrations to make points clear
(2) maximum similarity between the training and job environments
(3) a sufficient amount of practice in each skill area
Another important factor, once again, is the listening environment and organizational culture into which participants will be returning. No amount of skills training will enable one individual to overcome a negative communication environment. As mentioned earlier, consultants must be address both individual and organizational aspects of the situation. They must also implement measures to assess the effectiveness of their strategies.

Assessment of Training Results

Happiness sheets have long been standard measures of program effectiveness, and the immediate feedback from participants can be helpful in modifying program content, pacing, and other aspects of the design. Immediate program evaluations, however, are but one assessment measure. Most trainers have difficulty demonstrating that their instruction has the intended effects. Back in the same office, working with the same people, participants often fall into the very habits they had hoped to correct.

Thorough assessment of listening training incorporates participants' opinions of the session after they have had time to experiment with new listening behaviors on the job. It also incorporates feedback from those who deal directly with the participants, including their assessment of the participant's progress toward specified listening goals (Brownell, 1989). The use of a pre-program assessment instrument as a follow-up evaluation tool solves many common problems related to accountability. If outcomes have been specified in behavioral terms, using relevant portions of the pre-training assessment questionnaire as a guide and then comparing participants' pre and post-training performance against established goals is one valuable measure of program success.

In addition, periodic informal feedback sessions can be held, perhaps monthly, to hear participant's concerns and to provide on-going support as employees work together to change long-established behaviors. Participants' self reports concerning their progress appear, too, to be a reasonably reliable source of information regarding their progress. Both participants and their supervisors can be interviewed to determine whether progress is being made toward meeting personal and program goals. Whatever the specific design for generating information regarding program effectiveness, it is essential that comprehensive and long-range evaluation methods be built into the initial training design in order to ensure maximum goal accomplishment and to firmly establish the program's effectiveness.

From a senior management standpoint, however, the "real" training results pertain to the impact listening programs have on organizational performance. Although progress is being made (Sypher & Zorn, 1986; Weinrauch & Swanda, 1975; Sypher, Bostrom, & Seibert, 1989), far too little research has been done to substantiate claims that listening training translates directly to the bottom line. Even when consultants are confident that their training strategies are effective, it is essential to present as much proof as possible that better listening has a significant impact on organizational effectiveness.

An example of the type of research needed is a case study regarding the introduction of new technology where Papa and Glenn (1988) concluded that listening ability has a direct impact on productivity levels. They discovered that when tasks were routine, listening behavior had only a slight influence on productivity. When tasks were novel and changing, however, listening ability had a significant impact on performance. Similarly, Papa and Tracy (1987) found that effective listening directly contributed to more effective problem solving. As such research accumulates, it should become difficult to dispute Spyher, Bostrom, and Seibert's (1989) conclusion that listening ability is directly related to success at work.

Listening Training and Consulting: A Case

The range of opportunities and the types of organizations in which listening consultants find themselves vary widely. More and more frequently, however, consultants will be challenged to design interventions that consider long-range implications and which address issues affecting the entire organization. The consultant's range of responsibility increases as he or she initiates programs and policies that affect both individual and organizational performance. Although the rich detail and thick descriptions of organizational life available to a consultant are not possible to reproduce in a short case, the following example of a consultant's role at HighTec may give you some idea of the scope of consulting activity.

HighTec Corporation, a mid-sized manufacturing company in New York State, found itself in a highly competitive market. Its culture was production-based; management focused on efficiency and promoting high levels of technological skill. Those who were particularly successful and on the "fast track" advanced competitively, "beating out" their colleagues for a few select positions.

Gradually, however, HighTec was losing its market share. Turnover was on the rise, and employees generally lacked the commitment corporate executives believed essential to keeping pace with a rapidly-growing field. Repeatedly, key employees were joining HighTec's competition for only slight increases in salary.

The Training and Development Department was healthy and unusually innovative. Employees received an extensive orientation, regular training in their areas of expertise, and experts in the field were brought in periodically for special programs. If asked, almost all employees would say that they were receiving a fair salary, that their working conditions were satisfactory, and that they had a high level of job knowledge. Still, the company itself was losing ground.

Senior management expressed a growing concern with the problem as they realized that immediate intervention was essential. A member of the Training and Development Department recommended that a communication consultant be brought in to assess the problem and, in a "what have we got to lose" framework, the Board agreed.

The communication consultant first conducted interviews with senior level managers and key opinion leaders at all organizational levels. These conversations were followed by a more extensive communication audit, a survey designed to provide information on all aspects of communication activity. Findings of this two-month effort revealed that while employees were generally not dissatisfied with their jobs, neither did they feel any sense of identification or company loyalty. The prevalent attitude appeared to be, "I do my job--that's what I get paid for." When managers were asked for information about their employees, they had considerable knowledge of their levels of productivity and their performance measures, but knew little about their personal concerns, attitudes, or aspirations. In addition, many employees had little trust that the organizational would treat them fairly.

The consultant, after studying the available data, concluded that organizational problems stemmed in large part from an organizational culture characterized by a weak listening environment. Clearly, here was an organization where employees perceived that their voices were seldom heard, where they often felt isolated and disengaged. Although well-qualified for their jobs, employees were reluctant to put forth the extra effort that would have made a significant different in HighTec's performance.

The communication consultant recommended that strategies be implemented on both an organizational and an individual level. At the organizational level, policies and procedures were developed to create a stronger listening environment (Brownell, 1992) so that all members would have a greater sense of belonging and also feel that their contributions were heard and recognized. Employee input and participation were encouraged through suggestion boxes, open door policies, and increased walk-around management practices.

The consultant realized that changes in organizational policy alone, however, would be ineffective if not accompanied by individuals who practiced more effective listening on a daily basis. Managers, especially, were needed to serve as role models of good listening practices. A focused listening assessment instrument was administered to all employees to determine the precise type of listening training required. As suspected, the results of the survey revealed that employees' listening behaviors were poor in a number of areas.

Based on a behavioral model, assessment instruments revealed that the most relevant components were concentration and interpreting messages. Much thought was given as to the most appropriate program design. Ultimately, a twelve-hour tailored training program, using company-specific examples, was developed and implemented. The program was delivered in four, three-hour modules. Beginning with senior level managers, employees were given opportunities to attend listening seminars and to improve their listening behavior.

After the first program sessions were run and evaluated, a team of carefully screened volunteers from all divisions within the organization were trained by the consultant to conduct the program for their fellow employees. Optional follow-up sessions were also offered on a regular basis so that participants could discuss any problems they were having in implementing the listening strategies taught in the seminar. A listening resource room was established to encourage employees' independent learning. As new employees entered the organization, they were immediately placed into the listening program.

In addition to program evaluation forms that were administered immediately following each session, a three-month and six-month assessment was also conducted to determine whether employees' perceptions of their listening environment, and their own listening competence, had improved. Records of absenteeism and attendance were monitored carefully, and feedback was continuously solicited from all employees. At the end of nine months the consultant met with senior level managers to determine the overall effectiveness of the intervention. It was determined that the strategies implemented to improve listening effectiveness had been highly successful. Employee morale had significantly increased, as had productivity. The consultant, who was now intimately familiar with all aspects of the organization, outlined a two-year training plan that would involve a variety of communication topics focused specifically on the needs of various organizational groups. At this point, employees recognized the value of communication training and were anxious to improve their personal and professional competence.

As you can see from the HighTec example, the most powerful listening training is delivered as part of a larger program that considers organizational as well as individual dynamics. At HighTec, comprehensive, preventative listening training was accompanied by changes in organizational policies and practices. Upper level management remained directly involved in the process throughout. Until HighTec employees began listening to one another, almost any other type of communication training would have been ineffective and short-lived.

Listening consulting, then, often involves more than the ability to deliver high-quality programs. It also involves the ability to conduct needs analysis, set agendas, and assess the overall effectiveness of the intervention. Those companies unwilling to invest the time and commitment to an extensive and integrated program are unlikely to enjoy significant or lasting results.

Challenges and Future Directions

In their enthusiasm to demonstrate the importance of effective listening, consultants must keep sight of some of the basic ethical concerns and must consider the responsibilities and challenges that are inherent in consulting practice.

Perhaps the most recurring ethical question in listening training pertains to its emphasis on perceptions of listening and its focus on teaching overt behaviors while often neglecting the more humanistic aspects of the subject. When trainers tell loan officers to nod and maintain eye contact while listening to a customer's tragic story, do they also talk about what it means to express true empathy? As participants in a program for counselors are advised to lean forward and reflect feelings verbally, are they also sensitized to the feelings and experiences others portray?

The prescriptive approach, so often representative of listening programs, is also subject to question in light of growing multiculturalism. Although almost all cultures value listening, effective listening is expressed behaviorally in culture-specific terms. How can trainers be sensitive to and accommodate an increasingly multi-cultural workforce? Clearly, a number of ethical issues will follow us into the next century. Those pertaining to listening consulting are particularly problematic because they influence the very fabric of our organizations.

The information explosion has taught us many things, among them that flexible, adaptable individuals are in demand. Employees at all levels must be prepared for an uncertain and rapidly changing environment in which communication breakdowns are inevitable. The way these problems are handled, the sensitivity and ethical concern with which they are addressed, is a crucial factor. Effective listening is essential for individuals to cope with and resolve many of the difficulties created by uncertainty and organizational change.

The approach listening consultants take must be holistic and preventative. Consultants must consider the larger organizational context when diagnosing and recommending action plans. Providing individuals with tools which help them make decisions, handle conflict productively, and facilitate information sharing cannot help but promote organizational health and individual well-being. Few competencies make more difference in an individual's ability to carry out the tasks that lay ahead than effective listening.

Employees who listen effectively create an environment that contributes both to healthy interpersonal relationships and to high performance. Few skills have such high leverage; that is, few other communication behaviors have the degree of impact for the resources invested. While topics such as assertiveness training, conflict management, presentational speaking, or effective interviewing are situation-specific, listening is a key component of all communication encounters. Its pervasiveness places it at the heart of individual and organizational performance.

Carol Pearson, a human development consultant, has remarked that "Everyone is on a hero's journey" (Adams, 1990, 46). Her observation is that, if given the opportunity and the tools, all organizational members have something important to contribute. Listening trainers and consultants, if they do their job well, can create organizational heros--employees who have a solid, personal code of ethics and who confront daily challenges with both knowledge and sensitivity. This business of listening consulting and training requires dedication and hard work. Consultants in the business of helping people reach both higher performance and greater personal satisfaction, however, must surely discover that they, too, are on an endless hero's journey--one that will take them to new and exciting organizational frontiers.

References

Adams, M. (1990). She makes you feel so Jung. Successful Meetings, 39(8), 46-50.

Ashworth, D. M., & Meglino, B. M. (1982). Organizational climate and employee performance. Mid-Atlantic Journal of Business, 21(1), 1-8.

Basch, M. F. (1983). Empathic understanding: A review of the concept and some theoretical considerations. American Psychoanalytic Association Journal, 31, 101-126.

Beatty, M. J., Behnke, R. R., & Froelick, D. L. (1980). Effects of achievement incentive and presentation rate on listening comprehension. Quarterly Journal of Speech, 66, 193-200.

Birnbrauer, H. & Tyson, L. A. (1985). How to analyze needs. Training and

Development Journal, 39(8), 53-55.

Bostrom, R. N. (1990). Listening behavior: Measurement & Application. New York: The Guilford Press.

Bostrom, R. N. & Waldhart, E. S. (1988). Memory models and the measurement of listening. Communication Education, 37, 1-13.

Bostrom, R. (1983). The Kentucky comprehensive listening test. Lexington: Listening Research Center.

Bostrom, R. N. & Waldhart, E. (1980). Components in listening behavior: The role of short-term memory. Human Communication Research, 6, 211-227.

Bostrom, R. N. & Bryant, C. L. (1980). Factors in the retention of information presented orally: The role of short-term listening." Western Journal of Speech Communication, 44, 137-145.

Bradae, J. & Mulac, A. (1984). A molecular view of powerful and powerless speech styles. Communication Monographs, 51, 307-319.

Broome, B. J. (1991). Building shared meaning: Implications of a relational approach to empathy for teaching intercultural communication. Communication Education, 40(2), 35-249.

Brown, J. I. & Carlson, G. R. (1955). Brown-Carlson listening comprehension test. New York: Harcourt, Brace, and World.

Brownell, J. (1992). Listening environments. Perspectives on Listening, A. Wolvin & C. G. Coakley (Eds.), New York: University Press.

Brownell, J. (1990). The symbolic/culture approach: Managing transition in the service industry. International Journal of Hospitality Management, 9(3), 191-205.

Brownell, J. (1989). The RADIAL model: An integrated approach to in-house communication training. ABC Bulletin, 52(1), 3-11.

Brownell, J. (1990). Perceptions of effective listeners: A management study. Journal of Business Communication, 27(4). 401-416.

Brownell, J. (1990). A listening questionnaire. In A. Wolvin & C. G. Coakley (Eds.), Experiential Listening: Tools for Teachers and Trainers. Auburn, Alabama: Spectra, 5-10.

Brownell, J. (1986). Building active listening skills. Englewood Cliffs, New Jersey: Prentice-Hall, Inc.

Bruneau, T. (1989). Empathy and listening: A conceptual review and theoretical directions. Journal of the International Listening Association, 3, 1-20.

Burnke, R. J. & Weir, T. (1978). Organizational climate and informal helping processes in work settings. Journal of Management, 4(2), 91-105.

Bushe, G. R. & Barrie, W. G. (1990). Predicting organizational development consulting competence from the Myers-Briggs type indicator and stage of ego-development. Journal of Applied Behavioral Science, 26(3), 337-357.

Carter, J. & Van Matre, N. (1975). Note taking vs note having. Journal of Educational Psychology, 67, 900-904.

Carver, R. (1973). Effect of increasing the rate of speech presentation upon comprehension. Journal of Educational Psychology, 65, 118-126.

Coakley, C. G. & Wolvin, A. D. (1990). Listening pedagogy and andragogy: The state of the art. Journal of the International Listening Association, 4, 33-61.

Daniel, T. L. (1985). Managerial behaviors: Their relationship to perceived organizational climate in a high-technology company. Group & Organization Studies, 10(4), 413-428.

DiSalvo, V. S. (1980). A summary of current research identifying communication skills in various organizational contexts. Communication Education, 29(3), 283-290.

DiSalvo, V. S. & Larsen, D. C., & Seiler, W. J. (1976). Communication skills needed by persons in business organizations. Communication Education, 25, 269-275.

DiVesta, F. & Gray, G. (1982). Listening and notetaking. Journal of Educational Psychology, 63, 8-14.

Eubanks, P. (1992). Consulting careers: The myths and realities. Hospitals, 66(6), 62.

Floyd, J. J. (1985). Listening: A practical approach. Glenview, IL: Scott, Foresman and Company.

Follert, V. (1980). Communication climate: A theoretical framework for accessibility. Journal of Applied Communication Research. 8, 91-100.

Gilbert, M. (1989). Perceptions of listening behaviors of school principals. Paper presented at the ILA Convention, Atlanta, Georgia.

Glenn, E. C. (1989). A content analysis of fifty definitions of listening, Journal of the International Listening Association, 3, 21-31.

Golen, S. (1990). A factor analysis of barriers to effective listening. The Journal of Business Communication, 27(1), 25-37.

Goss, B. (1982). Listening as information processing. Communication Quarterly, 30, 304-306.

Howe, M. (1970). Notetaking strategy review and long term retention of verbal information. Journal of Educational Research, 63, 284-288.

Howell, W. S. (1982). The empathic communicator. Belmont, CA: Wadsworth Publishing Company.

Hunt, G. T. & Cusella, L. P. (1983). A field study of listening needs in organizations. Communication Education. 32, 393-401.

Husband, R. L., Cooper, L. O., Monsour, W. M. (1988). Factors underlying supervisor's perceptions of their own listening behavior. Journal of the International Listening Association, 2, 97-112.

Husband, R. (1987). Assessing manager and subordinate perceptions of managerial listening behavior. Paper presented at the convention of the International Listening Association, New Orleans.

Johnson, C. (1989). Ethical implications of powerful and powerless talk. Texas Speech Communication Journal, 14, 7-11.

Kelly, C. M. (1967). Listening: A complex of activities--and a unitary skill?

Speech Monographs, 34, 455-466.

Kelly, C. M. (1977). Empathic listening. in Bridges not Walls, J. S. Steward (Ed.). Reading, MA: Addison-Wesley, pp. 221-227.

King, C. P. (1978). Keep your communication climate healthy. Personnel Journal, 57(4), 204-206.

Larson, C. U. (1989). Persuasion: Reception and responsibility. Belmont, CA: Wadsworth Publishing Company.

Latham, G. P. & Wexley, K. N. (1981). Developing and training human resources in organizations. New York: Scott, Foresman, and Company.

Lewis, M. H. & Reinsch, N. L., Jr. (1988). Listening in organizational environments. The Journal of Business Communication, 25(3), 49-67.

Lindley, C. J. (1984). Putting "human" into human resource management. Public Personnel Management, 13(4), 501-510.

Listening in everyday life: A personal and professional approach. (1991). M. Purdy & D. Borisoff (Eds.). Fort Worth, TX: Holt, Rinehart, and Winston.

Loftus, E. (1980). Memory. Reading, MA: Addison-Wesley.

Lundberg, C. C. (1990). Surfacing organizational culture. Journal of Managerial Psychology, 5(4),

Montgomery, R. (1981). Listening made easy. New York: American Management Association.

Moss-Kanter, R. (1983). The change masters: Innovation for productivity in the American corporation. New York: Simon and Schuster.

Muchinsky, P. M. (1977). Organizational communication: Relationships to organizational climate and job satisfaction. Academy of Management Journal, 20(4), 592-607.

Mundale, S. (1980). Why more CEOs are mandating listening and writing training. Training, 17, 37-41.

O'Keefe, D. J. (1990). Persuasion: Theory and research. Newbury Park, CA: Sage Publications.

Orr, D. B. (1964). Note on thought rate as a function of reading and listening rate, Perceptual and Motor Skills, 19, 872-886.

Ostermeier, T. H. (1991). Fast talkers and speeding listeners: Television/Radio commercials, Journal of the International Listening Association, 5, 22-35.

Papa, M. G. & Tracy, K. (1987). Communicative indices of employee performance with new technology. Paper presented at the International Communication Association, Montreal.

Papa, M. G. & Glenn, E. C. (1988). Listening and performance with new technology. The Journal of Business Communication, 25(4), 5-15.

Peters, T. (1988). Thriving on chaos. New York: Alfred A. Knopf.

Peters, T. & Austin, N. (1985). A passion for excellence: The leadership difference. New York: Warner Communications Company.

Rankin, P. T. (1926). The measurement of the ability to understand spoken language. Unpublished PhD dissertation, University of Michigan,

Dissertation Abstracts, 12, 847-848.

Rhodes, S. (1985). What the communication journals tell us about teaching listening. Central States Speech Journal, 36, 24-32.

Rhodes, S. C., Watson, K. W., & Barker, L. L. (1990). Listening assessment: Trends and influencing factors in the 1980s. Journal of the International Listening Association, 4, 62-82.

Rhodes, S. C. (1985). Specific listening skills important in organizations. Communication Research Bulletin, 7(4), 1-2.

Rhodes, S. C. (1985). What the communication journals tell us about teaching listening. Central States Speech Journal, 36, 24-32.

Roberts, C. (1986). A validation of the Watson-Barker Listening Test. Communication Research Report, 3, 115-119.

Russell, L. (1990). Secrets of my success. Training, 24(40), 126.

Schlesinger, L. & Balzer, R. (1985). An alternative to buzzword management: The culture performance link. Personnel, 62(9), 45-51.

Seibert, J. H. (1990). Listening in the organizational context. Listening Behavior: Measurement and Application. R. Bostrom (Ed.), New York: The Guilford Press.

Shellen, W. N. (1989). Some evidence that listening tests measure "normal" listening. The Journal of the International Listening Association, 3, 62-71.

Smeltzer, L. R. & Watson, K. W. (1985). A test of instructional strategies for listening improvement in a simulated business setting. The Journal of Business Communication, 22, 33-42.

Snyder, M. (1974). The self-monitoring of expressive behavior. Journal of Personality and Social Psychology, 30, 526-537.

Sperritt, D. (1962). Listening comprehension: A factorial analysis. Melbourne: Australian Council for Educational Research.

Spruell, G. (1986). How to be an internal consultant. Training and Development Journal, 40(2), 19-21.

Staley, C. C. & Shockley-Zalabak, P. (1985). Identifying communication competencies for the undergraduate organizational communication series. Communication Education, 34, 156-161.

Steil, L., Barker, L., & Watson, K. (1983). Effective listening: Key to your success. New York: Addison-Wesley.

Steil, L. K. (1980). Your personal listening profile. Blue Bell, PA: Sperry Corporation.

Stewart, J. (1983). Interpretive listening: An alternative to empathy. Communication Education, 32, 379-391.

Sypher, B. D. & Zorn, T. E. (1986). Communication-related abilities and upward mobility: A longitudinal investigation. Human Communication Research, 12, 420-431.

Sypher, B. D., Bostrom, R. N., & Seibert, J. H. (1989). Listening, communication abilities, and success at work. Journal of Business

Communication, 26(4), 293-303.

Thorndyke, P. A. & Hayes-Roth, B. (1979). The use of schemata in the acquisition and transfer of knowledge. Cognitive Psychology, 2 82-106.

Tumna, M. C. (1980). A comparative review of reading and listening comprehension. Journal of Reading, 23, 698-703.

Tutolo, D. (1975). Teaching Critical Listening. Language Arts, 52, 1108-1112.

Watson, K. & Barker, L. (1984). Watson-Barker listening test. New Orleans: Spectra, Inc.

Weinrauch, J. D. & Swanda, J. R. (1975). Examining the significance of listening: An exploratory study of contemporary management. The Journal of Business Communication, 13, 25-32.

Witkin, B. R. (1990). Listening theory and research: The state of the art. The Journal of the International Listening Association, 4, 7-32.

Wolff, F. I., Marsnick, N. C., Tacey, W. S., & Nichols, R. G. (1983). Perceptive listening. New York: Holt, Rinehart, and Winston.

Wolvin, A. D. & Coakley, C. W. (1989). Listening. Dubuque: William C. Brown Company.

Wolvin, A. D., Coakley, C. G., & Disburg, J. E. (1991). An exploratory study of listening instruction in selected colleges and universities. Journal of the International Listening Association, 5, 68-85.

Wolvin, A. D. & Coakley, C. G. (1991). A survey of the status of listening training in some Fortune 500 corporations. Communication Education, 40(2), 152-164.

Young, J. & Smith, B. (1988). Organizational change and the HR profession. Personnel, 65, 44.

Zeira, Y. & Avedisian, J. (1989). Organizational planned change: Assessing the chances for success. Organizational Dynamics, 31-45.

PRESENTATIONAL SKILLS

Leigh Makay
and
John Makay

There is a widely shared view that America is entering a new economic order which is driven by competition, quality, customization and timeliness (Carnevale, 1991). This new economy is shaping the role of people at work. Where workers used to be specialized and job responsibilities were narrowly defined, today's worker faces responsibilities and skill requirements which are less job specific, more flexible and overlapping. Interaction between workers and teamwork is becoming increasingly important as workers are forced to take responsibility for the quality of final goods.

Organizations in today's global economy not only face the challenges stemming from new technologies and the emphasis on quality in order to remain competitive, but they also face a new constraint which centers in the nature of the workforce. A decline in the 16 to 24 year old population forces employers to seek out and retain older workers for entry level positions. In order to remain competitive, employers are replacing the old view that people are expendable or superfluous with a goal to assist current and future workers in achieving workplace competency (Carnevale, Gainer & Meltzer, 1990). As a result, training budgets are growing. In 1992, U.S. organizations with 100 or more employees spent $45 billion in order to train 40.9 million workers. This figure represents a four percent increase in money spent on training from 1991 (Training, 1992). While several types of training programs are reflected in the increase, there is consensus in corporate America that strong communication skills are needed by workers in order to succeed in the global economy (Carnevale, Garner & Meltzner, 1990). Unfortunately, American schools offer minimal instruction in oral communication and listening. Therefore, the task of training workers in effective communication falls to corporate America.

A survey conducted by Training (1992) revealed that 84% of the organizations sampled offered training in basic communication skills. One type of communication skill which is growing in demand is presentational speaking.

This growth is evidenced by the fact that 59% of the corporations surveyed incorporated presentational training into their 1992 training budget. Given the demands placed on corporations by the new economy, this trend towards increased training in presentational skills is likely to continue. Therefore, the purpose of this chapter is to provide direction and details about consulting with corporate clients who recognize the need to have their supervisors, managers, and higher level executives develop presentational skills. Consulting, in the sense we use the term here, includes not only the offering of authoritative opinions but training in presentational speaking as well. In preparing to engage in presentational consulting, there are several questions that are often asked.

What is the difference between a "Presentation"and "Public speaking"? Howell and Bormann (1988) offer perhaps the clearest distinction between public and presentational speaking and, in their comments, explain the essential characteristics of a presentation. These authors note that a considerable number of books talk about business and professional communication but not to the extent of providing exclusive attention to "designing, building, and delivering powerful presentations." (p.6) Presentations are usually formal oral messages delivered to reasonably small and selected audiences to serve a purpose that involves change.

The presentational speaker in the corporate setting is "primarily - first, last, and always - a change agent" (Howell & Bormann, 1988, p.8). For instance, the corporation may be one which depends ultimately on sales presentations to achieve financial goals. Obviously the presenters are asking outside or external audiences to make a decision that brings about change in the organization the audience represents. On the other hand, a corporation may have made a decision to change a policy or internal procedures and presentational speakers are asked to address in-house audiences to brief listeners about what is involved and required of them to bring about this change.

The presentation is a message that may be largely informative in nature or largely persuasive. The actual line between making the traditional distinction between informative and persuasive speaking is blurred as the purposes are blended in order to manage the message and achieve the response the presenter wants from her or his audience (Makay & Fetzer, 1980). Suppose for example, a corporation has decided to genuinely reduce the amount of paper used in the organization by putting all employees "on line" to receive electronic mail. The decision was made by upper management and the equipment has already been purchased and is about to be installed. At this point a number of managers have been asked to meet with employees in their unit to make several presentations about the reasons for the change and how everyone is expected to operate in order to bring the change about. It is important that each worker fully cooperate in the introduction a cost-saving and most efficient way to receive and exchange information electronically. While explicitly the managers are to construct and deliver informative presentations, implicitly they are to persuade their workers to accept and support this endeavor. *The presentation can be a powerful form of organizational rhetoric - strategic speech designed to achieve a precise response from an intended audience.* It is important to recognize that presentations should be defined according to the responses the speaker needs from the intended audience. Therefore, in order to obtain the desired responses, messages are designed and presented with the potential for both persuasive and informative results. The organizational communicator, however, should have a clear persuasive or informative response in mind as she or he chooses from the alternatives of speech-craft to prepare, deliver, and assess the presentation.

What sort of audience does the Presenter usually face? Earlier we stated that presentations are usually designed for reasonably small and selected audiences. Certainly when the President of the United States addresses a national television audience he is not making a presentation but rather he is delivering a public address. The presentational speaker is usually located in a corporate board room, training room, or similar setting speaking to a handful of corporate employees who are either charged with the responsibility of making a recommendation for a decision to be made or else have the power to make the decision themselves. On other occasions, as we suggest above, the speaker is presenting in order to brief her or his audience with necessary information in order to work successfully. While a presentational speaker may speak to an audience of 100 people, this is usually not the case. For example, a chief executive officer could be required to make a presentation to a room filled with stock holders and other audience members which may reach a considerable size. The most typical presentational audience is considerably smaller in size.

How important are audio/visual/video aids? When delivering presentations to small, selected audiences in order to effect some type of change, the oral message is often enhanced through the use of visual aids or audio/visual/video means. Corporations usually have departments or units within the organization equipped to produce visual or audio/visual supporting material. Increasingly, organizations turn to production companies that specialize in the production of industrial, corporate, or other kinds of professional videos to be used by presentational speakers. We will discuss audio/visual/video support later in our chapter because the proliferation of equipment to support presentational technology is considerable.

What types of time constraints occur in the organizational setting? A presentation must conform to a variety of time allotments but usually the speaker is asked to speak for 25 - 30 minutes and allow 15 minutes, more or less, for a question and answer period. Admittedly we have worked with individuals who were responsible for 15 minute proposals and 45 minute proposals as well. How much time is allotted for a presentation is not nearly as important as how the time is used by the speaker. Competition in the corporate world fuels the metaphor "time is money". Therefore, every minute of the speaker and the audience's time is crucial. One of the goals of the corporate trainer is to help employees accomplish the most with their audiences in the short time-frames they will face.

What is the role of corporate presentational training? Employers frequently rely on one or two person consulting firms to conduct presentational training (Carnevale, Gainer, Villet & Holland, 1991). As a corporate communication consultant in a business or other professional setting who is also a communication educator, you may find yourself designing and implementing a training program to teach presentational skills to an audience of clients ranging from front line supervisors to middle managers to top management vice presidents. While certainly there are those individuals in the corporate setting who have had some sort of a speech course at one time or another in their lives, there are a considerable number of persons who completed either a high school program if not one or more college programs while managing to avoid a speech communication course altogether. Even those with modest training in public speaking find that once "on the job," the task of confident and effective speaking seems enormous. Thus, they are quick to admit that further training is not only desirable but necessary.

If you have an opportunity to provide consulting and training to enhance the presentational skills of a corporate client or clients, what are you likely to do? The suggestions we make in the rest of our chapter are largely based upon our own experiences and the success we have enjoyed in working with a number of corporate clients.

Developing the Training Seminar

The term "training" includes both the development of a skill and learning for a specific purpose which is associated with the goals of the organization (Mayo & DuBois, 1987). Most training in general is a three-prong process involving problem assessment, training and evaluation. Therefore, we will look at each component of the training model.

Assessment. Frequently the consultant and trainer in communication is required to demonstrate both a need for a service and how the need can be effectively minimized if not eliminated through training. However, the need for training in presentational skills is usually recognized by those who either are called upon to make successful presentations or who must supervise others who are to make presentations to serve organizational goals. Presentational skill deficiency may also be detected through a formal corporate needs assessment or a communication audit. Also, because giving speeches is a public activity, many people perceive the experience to be threatening and are therefore eager for instruction which will reduce this threat. The task of the presentational training consultant, then, is to assess the extent of the need as quickly as possible and to follow the assessment with a training program that can significantly satisfy the clients within a time-frame determined by the organization.

Usually the assessment can be made through several interviews between the consultant and managers such as a director of training or public affairs, or a person in a similar position. We have conducted assessment interviews with corporate clients who have held positions ranging from director of employee communications to senior vice president for corporate affairs. The common concern of each of them is the obligation to provide quick, efficient, and high quality training for employees who genuinely acknowledge a need for fresh and effective training in presentational skills.

In the assessment interview we have encountered a variety of needs which have helped to shape specific training seminars. One client called upon us to train company scientists to make effective presentations to external audiences who were not scientists but needed to learn about the corporation's scientific efforts. The training here was to teach clients how to prepare and present informative presentations that were understandable to a specific type of audience. Another corporate client asked us to train both sales representatives and designers who would go to customers and make joint presentations with the ultimate aim of persuasion - getting sales! We would design and present training programs to serve the particular needs of these clients and, at the same time, recognize that common needs were shared by everyone who sought our training. For example, almost always we found clients who continued to struggle with "speech tension" or "performance anxiety" so we could always plan to work on minimizing stage fright and offering an effective psychology for having speakers make their nerves work for them rather than against them. We continually found that speakers needed a keener sense of their audiences and several "short-cut" routes to audience analysis and adaptation. Another common theme we encountered is that corporate speakers (unlike many college or university freshmen who enter a basic course in speaking) usually have more information than they know how to handle. Training must be designed to help them sort out and use their information both economically and effectively. Finally, all of our clients have been concerned with how they use their voice, bodies, and total physical appearance to the best of their abilities in front of an audience.

In addition to assessing the need for presentational speaking training within the organization and the time-frame available for the trainer to conduct the seminar, in the initial interview or interviews it is important for the consultant to identify information about the organization that will later facilitate in the creation of rapport with the employees enrolled in the seminar. When developing examples used in the lecture/discussion section of the seminar, it is helpful to be able to use material that participants can relate to directly. A carefully conducted in-depth interview can provide the consultant with useful illustrative material. In addition, the consultant will often incorporate impromptu speaking exercises to give participants short, non-threatening periods in which success may be experienced. The topics for these impromptu exercises may be identified in the assessment interview.

While many of the ideas and principles necessary to meet these concerns can be drawn from the fundamentals of public and presentational speaking, the information to be used by the consultant must be chosen with care and presented in a fashion that makes it not only interesting but useful to the corporate speaker as well. If you are to serve as a corporate consultant/trainer, there are a variety of ways to meet the corporate needs and several available time-frames which have been successful in presentational speaking training seminars. However, whether a consultant markets herself or himself in order to find clients or whether the consultant is fortunate enough to have clients seek their services, the consultant needs to have several optional presentational speaking programs available.

Designing the Training Seminar

Perhaps the most prominent constraints on helping individuals with presentational skills in organizational settings are two: time and approach-avoidance conflict. When a representative of an organization considers ways to help associates improve their skills in preparing and delivering presentations, she or he must first figure out how to provide the assistance within the structure and the schedule mandated by the organization. Some employees travel a great deal and are not "in the shop" for any length of time while others have crowded schedules that allow little time to work in additional meetings or training classes. Most often, the client expects the consultant to suggest several options for packaging services so that one may be selected as the program most likely to meet the needs of the organization.

The seminar or programs that are most likely to be attractive to clients in search of help with presentational skills are those that provide basic instruction with ample opportunities for making presentations and receiving meaningful feedback. While college and university professors have the luxury of teaching courses in business and professional speaking over ten to sixteen week periods, the organizational setting only allows for relatively short time periods. Clients ask for equivalent college training in periods ranging from one-half day to two or three day sessions. We have provided training to organizations over a five-day period and we have packaged the same program for two-day sessions as well. When five days were allowed, the program lasted mornings from 8:00 a.m. to noon while the two day meetings brought people together from 8:00 a.m. to 4:00 p.m. Once the consultant determines what the basic program in presentational speaking is to consist of, she or he works out ways to offer the training in several time periods so that the client can select the format most appropriate to the organization's situation. The following examples demonstrate how presentational training can be offered according to different available time periods.

Option One - Two Day Seminar in Presentational Speaking

Most organizations can provide two days for consulting and training for "on site" training for their employees or to send them to two day programs in which participants are enlisted from a variety of organizations through a process of general subscription. The sessions are offered back-to-back to provide an intensive and practical learning opportunity. If two days are not available, then Option Two, a one day session, may be equally useful. Both options devote most of the time and training to actual video taped presentations prepared and delivered by participants. A typical two day program may look like the following:

<u>Seminar in Effective Presentations</u>

First Day

8:00 to 8:15   Coffee and Conversation.

Even if participants know each other, and even if they have had some sort of breakfast before arriving for the session, some coffee or tea with pastries available provides a gradual entry into a session faced with initial apprehension about having to speak in front of an audience.

8:15 to 8:30   Ice Breaker Introductions

To continue to ease apprehension, the consultant can get the participants on their feet shortly into the morning to introduce themselves to others in the seminar. We have often asked participants to include any bizarre events in their lives in their brief introductory comments. This request brings out information that everyone can laugh or chuckle over. Laughter often helps to reduce tension. The point to keep in mind is that once participants say a few words to others in the seminar, they usually relax more which allows them to listen to what the consultant has to say about presentational speaking. The initial anxiety is over and the participants realize that nothing disastrous is likely to happen to them when they stand before peers or other associates to say a few words.

8:30 to 9:30   "Essentials of Presentational Speaking"

Most of the morning in a two-day seminar will be spent giving the participants information through lecturing, discussion, and the distribution of "hand-outs" as instructional material. The first hour is devoted to center the purpose of the seminar: to work on presentational skills in terms of genuine communication. The presentation is one important way to create and manage meaning in an effort to obtain a specific response from an audience.

Participants in an organizational setting are usually more eager for advice and prescription than the traditional college student. The reason for this desire is that they have gone beyond the setting of formal education and have discovered that training in speech communication is particularly important to them in order to succeed in their work. The level of motivation coupled with the desire for practical knowledge is considerably intense.

We usually begin our first lecture/discussion by talking about the essentials of a good presentation communicator. The terms which the consultant chooses to use to label as "essentials" may vary, but we focus on confidence, knowledge, integrity, and skills. The degree of **self-confidence** participants bring to a seminar often varies but more often than not, the business and professional inexperienced speaker musters up a considerable amount of tension, if not anxiety, upon facing the task of making a presentation.

For example, at one extreme we had a vice president of development for a huge corporation tell us that he could converse with the mayor and the governor and that he was a sky diver, but he was terrified each time he was required to stand before an audience to make a presentation. At the other extreme, we recall the corporate executive whose hobby was "magic" to the extent that he appeared at school assemblies and other social events to put on a magic show; he certainly did not lack self-confidence when facing an audience. In between these extremes are bright, educated, interested professionals who have both a recognition of their need for presentational skills and some apprehension centered in their own lack of confidence about being "good at speaking to an audience."

Knowledge is introduced as an essential characteristic because while most participants are considerably knowledgeable about their expertise and their career field in general, they have difficulty in translating their knowledge into 25 - 30 minute presentations that communicate to their audience that they do know what they are talking about. This topic lays the groundwork for subsequent information about framing core ideas, selecting supporting material, choosing language, and organizing information in meaningful ways.

Integrity is an element that needs to be discussed with caution. Participants view themselves as persons of integrity and their character is not to be questioned in a seminar. At the same time, they needs to understand that the concept of "ethos" or "credibility" or "image" is crucial in many presentational settings. We know, for instance, that in addition to our integrity, when we represent an organization or a profession to an "outside" audience, we bring not only our own personal or professional integrity to the situation but also the audience's perception of the organization we represent as well.

Skills make up the primary principles offered in presentational training because they include self-management and the management of ideas in meeting the challenge of making an effective presentation. We always remind clients that skills also are instrumental in portraying to an audience one's confidence, knowledge and integrity. An initial lecture discussion may, to the experienced communication educator, seem like an obvious list of "things to do," but to the professional asking for basic guidance in presentational skills, the information is likely to be quite useful.

Consider the sample outline below as practical guide for the first lecture/discussion:

Essential Qualities of a Good Presentational Speaker
1. Confident
2. Knowledgeable
3. Trustworthy

4. Skillful

Essential Guides for Presentational Effectiveness
1. Content of the Presentation
    a. Determine the specific response you want from the audience.
    b. Design a core idea and subordinate points for the audience.
    c. Select supporting information the audience will understand.
    d. Select clear, concise, even vivid language that is meaningful.
    e. Select an organizational format that meets your needs.
2. Delivery of the presentation
    a. Project your voice naturally with appropriate emphasis.
    b. Observe your audience directly to receive feedback.
    c. Maintain confident posture and use meaningful gestures.
    d. Express yourself with enthusiasm and sincerity.
    e. Become involved with your audience; involvement reduces tension.

The level of sophistication or abstraction a consultant chooses to operate at will vary of course, but our experience suggests a word of caution. In preparation for conducting seminars for a particular corporation or other organization, once again we must emphasize that the trainer should devote part of her or his preparation to gathering illustrations and examples from the frame of reference of participants. We are reminded of a hostile question directed at us midway through out first of more than a dozen seminars for first-line supervisors in an automobile manufacturing plant: "Hey professor!" one youthful participant shouted from the back of the room. "Don't you have any examples about cars?" he questioned. We can assure you that by the beginning of the second seminar we **did** have automotive illustrations worked into our lecture discussions and we continued to pick up more as the sessions continued.

The consultant's topics for lecture/discussion may vary depending on the needs and interests of the client. After an initial interview about conducting a seminar, the consultant is likely to have good idea about what the organization expects to have included for participants. We find certain topics continue to have value for most clients interested in increasing the presentational skills of employees. For example, consider the list of lecture topics below:

1. Essentials of a Good Communicator
2. Confidence - How to Make Your Nerves Work for You.
3. Supporting and Organizing a Presentation to Help Your Audience
4. "Visuals" - How to Get the Most from your Visual Aids.
5. Delivery - Finding you Best Voice and Mastering Body Language
6. "Q-A" Moments - How to Effectively Deal with Questions.

Whatever your choices are for a two-day seminar, remember that all of the lecture discussions with "hand-outs" should be finished by noon of the first day. The consultant must manage the time carefully to allow everyone to speak and receive feedback by 4:00 p.m. This allows thirty minutes for a "wrap-up" session and to make an assignment for the next day.

9:30 to 10-15   Speech Tension: What it is and What to Do About It

Studies reveal that speech tension or performance anxiety is one of the most important concerns of the inexperienced presentational speaker (Motley, 1988). Therefore, there is usually enough interest and concern about this phenomenon in corporate audiences to warrant spending 45 minutes to an hour explaining the basic information about making "your nerves work for you" (Makay, 1992, p. 39).

10:15 to 10:30   Coffee Break

10:30 to 11:00   Effective Use of Audio/visual/video Materials

Presentations almost always are supported by visuals, videos, or audio aids. The most frequently used visual is, of course, the transparency which is used with an overhead projector. Increasingly, business and professional speakers are using multimedia equipment to make the information on their computer screen visible to their audiences. Therefore, some time should be spent advising the participants in ways to use these aids effectively.

11:00 to 11:20   The Question and Answer Period

Quite often the greatest apprehension of the presentational speaker is handling the question and answer period with confidence and clarity. Speakers find working with an outline or other forms of notes somewhat threatening, but they are even more concerned about having to respond to members of the audience without the guidance of their notes. "What do I do if someone asks me a question I can't answer?" is perhaps the most frequently asked question of the consultant. So, near the end of the morning session, special time needs to be devoted to the Q&A period.

11:20 to 12:00   Speech Preparation

At this point, blank 8 x 5 cards should be distributed to the participants so they can outline their notes for a two minute speech. The topic for this speech is to be some aspect of their job. The speech outline is to be completed during the lunch period so that participants are ready to begin speaking at 1:15. The audience, how to analyze their needs and motives must be central to comments throughout the morning session.

12:00 to 1:15   Lunch

1:15 to 3:00   Presentations, discussions, video replay

After each speaker delivers their presentation, the consultant facilitates discussion and makes use of the video replay for instructional purposes.

3:00 to 3:15   Coffee Break

3:15 to 4:00   Continue presentations, discussions, video replay

4:30 to 5:00   Summary

During this period the objective is to review the principles of presentational speaking discussed earlier in the day and to demonstrate how they were, or were not applied in the afternoon presentations. If the seminar is for two days, part of this time is spent discussing what can be done differently the second day. The consultant then assigns the following speech:

Select a presentational situation you are likely to face in the future and this evening prepare a six minute presentation to be delivered tomorrow. Make certain that you incorporate some type of visual aid. When you arrive back at our room, sign up for your place in the speaking order and we will begin at 8:30 a.m. Coffee and rolls will be available by 8:00 for those of you who wish to get here early and relax in the room before we begin.

If the seminar is one day only, then the consultant summarizes with advice for the participants to consider for their presentations in the future.

Second Day

Day two of the seminar is devoted entirely to completing the assignment. The participants will each have their turn, the consultant and participants will complete written analysis/evaluation forms, and everyone will be encouraged to comment. Each presentation will be video-taped for the discussion periods as well. During the "wrap-up" session of the first day, participants can be invited to bring in a blank tape to use when they make their presentations. This allows them to take a tape of their presentation home with them once the seminar is finished. The quality and value of this seminar for teaching presentational speaking skills is determined by the quality of the performance of the consultant and how motivated the participants are. Our experience is that participants in corporate seminars are always highly motivated so that a great deal of learning can take place in two days and the experience can be enjoyable for everyone.

Since most corporate presentations are conducted with visuals, it is important to discuss the speaker's use of visual aids in their presentation. The assignment on the first day is one we make without any expectation that visuals are to be used. The assignment for the second day, however, is different and we ask that everyone use some sort of visual that represents what they are likely to use elsewhere in order for speakers to receive feedback on this important component of presentational speaking. Most participants will elect to use transparencies with an overhead projector or a flip chart that can be mounted on an easel. Even with only the night to prepare, other visuals can be assembled or obtained, such as mock-ups, models, charts, posters, or video segments.

Option Two - The One Day Seminar

Some organizations simply cannot afford or schedule a seminar in presentational speaking for two days. If this constraint is apparent in the initial assessment interview conducted with the client, the consultant must be prepared to offer a one-day version of the seminar. Option Two is a less intense "Day One" of the two-day seminar with some additional speaking experience. The consultant carefully selects what to talk about, what "hand-outs" to distribute, and has every participant speak at least three times during the day:
(1) the morning "ice-breaker" introductions
(2) an impromptu talk based on topics prepared in advance by the consultant which were obtained during the assessment interview
(3) a three minute presentation about a career related topic (prepared before lunch and delivered after lunch).

If the seminar is to be presented "on site" for a particular organization, the consultant can prepare a couple of dozen impromptu topics in advance that relate to the business or other professional activities of the organization. If the seminar attracts participants on a general subscription basis, then topics of general interest or current events must be available to use with the participants. A well prepared intensive one-day seminar in presentational speaking skills can be quite effective for corporate participants.

Option Three - Seminars Without Practice

Communication consultants are asked to provide information about presentational speaking skills to corporate clients who want the information in an afternoon or an evening session. In this situation the client's company either does not have the time for option one or two, or the company believes that providing essential information at an evening session will provide participants with information sufficient enough to guide them in both the preparation and the delivery of corporate presentations. We have offered a number of three to four hour seminars that have taken place either in the late afternoon or early evening.

When a potential client indicates that their company is interested in only one session to offer new or review information to employees, the consultant must provide a list of between four to five topics that might be presented and ask the client which three or four are most appropriate for meeting the organization's needs. These topics are selected from the lecture topics discussed above. Using hand-outs, transparencies, slides, or a flip chart, the consultant can provide her of his seminar participants with practical information that can genuinely help them to develop and polish their presentational skills.

Option Four - Individualized Consultations.

There are a number of executives who prefer to work with a consultant on a one-to-one basis. In this sort of situation, the consultant completes and in-depth initial interview with the client and maps out a concise program tailored to her or his needs. Some individuals do not have time for seminars even if they have a strong need for the information and practice. Other individuals are either too self-conscious to appear in front of a group to make presentations or they need an intense educational experience that can be achieved by having the consultant's exclusive attention. The consultant assesses the client's needs, shares appropriate information with her or him and, works with the client using video-tapes and careful analysis to help them improve their presentational skills. While there are certainly advantages to this sort of arrangement, the disadvantage for the client is the lack of an audience (beyond the consultant) to address and who will provide additional feedback.

If the corporation is located near the consultant so that a number of visits can be made over a one, two, or three week period, the information the seminars can be arranged in a variety of time segments agreeable to both corporation and consultant. Some organizations prefer having two 90 minute meetings a week for three weeks while others find five meetings for three hours a day to be suitable. The consultant ought to be flexible and prepared to adjust to the schedule most attractive to the client.

Evaluation

An important component of the training process is evaluation of the effectiveness of the training program. Not only does this give the consultant an opportunity to improve the presentational seminar, but it also may provide the trainer with an opportunity to continue to work with the client to develop advanced skills. The type of evaluation is dictated by the client. Minimally, a seminar evaluation sheet is provided following the seminar in which participants are asked to respond to their learning experience. A more useful evaluation, however, can be arranged during the initial assessment interview in which a contact person is identified and a program of evaluation is designed. For example, when conducting a presentational seminar for a public utility company, the Director of Speaker Services provided presentational speakers with self evaluation forms. The purpose of these forms was to allow the speaker to reflect, with a criteria, about their own perception of the strengthens and weaknesses of their presentations in the workplace following the seminar. The forms were then shared with the consultant and future training was designed to meet the needs identified in the evaluation forms. If the consultant is retained by the corporation, then assessment can be conducted on a regular basis.

Consulting in the area of presentational speaking is an exciting endeavor. What we have tried to do in this chapter is to clarify what presentational speaking is, why it is important in the corporate setting, and how a consultant/trainer can conduct seminars in presentational skills. It is important to remember that training includes both assessment and evaluation.

References

Carnevale, A. P. (1991). America and the new economy. San Francisco, CA: Jossey-Bass Publishers.

Carnevale, A. P., Gainer, L. J., & Meltzer, A. S. (1990). Workplace basics: The essential skills employers want. San Francisco, CA: Jossey-Bass Publishers.

Carnevale, A. P., Gainer, L. J., Villet, J., & Holland, S. L. (1989). Training partnerships: Linking employers & providers. Washington, D.C.: U.S. Department of Labor; Alexandria, VA: American Society for Training and Development.

Howell, W.S. & Bormann, E. G. (1988). The process of presentational speaking. New York: Harper& Row.

Industry report, 1992. Training, October 1992, 10-25.

Makay, J. J. (1992), Public speaking: Theory into practice. Fort Worth,TX: Harcourt Brace Jovanovich.

Makay, J. J. & Fetzer, R. C. (1980). Business communication skills: A career focus. New York: D. Van Nostrand Co.

Mayo, G. D. & DuBois, P. H. (1987). The complete book of training: Theory, principles, and techniques. San Diego, CA: University Associates, Inc.

Motley, M. T. (January, 1988). Taking the terror out of talk. Psychology Today, 46-49.

INTERPERSONAL CONFLICT MANAGEMENT

Deborah Borisoff

The Image of Conflict

One definition of the word "consult" is "to advise." The consultant is "one who gives professional advice or services." For many who provide communication skills training to an organization, the communication consultant is a welcome adjutant. His or her advice is sought after. Whether it is to provide presentation skills training, programs to enhance listening, sensitivity training regarding crosscultural communication, or training to enhance writing skills, the subject matter itself -- that is, public speaking, listening, crosscultural communication, and writing -- are not regarded negatively in our culture.

What distinguishes conflict training from many other areas of corporate consulting is society's negative attitude towards conflict and the reluctance to deal with problems. Ask any class or seminar group to write down the terms they associate with "conflict," and invariably a preponderance of negative associations emerge. Such words as "war," "battle," "problem," "differences," "dispute," "anxiety," "aggression," "loss," and so on, are typical responses. Rarely do some of the more positive associations with the term "conflict," such as "opportunity," "challenge," "change," or "collaboration" appear.

From the negative associations with the term conflict, we witness a seemingly natural predisposition in our culture to want to avoid conflict at all costs. Many individuals erroneously assume that to engage in a conflict reflects negatively on themselves, on their ability to control themselves, their interactions, and, their environment. We know, however, that this is not possible. So long as individuals come to any encounter with their own perspectives, experiences, and unique backgrounds, then conflicts over beliefs, ideas, attitudes, and resources will, quite naturally, persist. Moreover, such conflicts will occur in all contexts:

in the home; in the workplace; in social settings.

Before addressing how the communication consultant can approach conflict skills training in the organization, it is important first to understand what we **mean** by the term conflict. This term has been variously defined over time. Coser introduced the conflict perspective into American sociology with his definition of conflict as "a struggle over values and claims to scarce status, power, and resources in which the aims of the opponents are to neutralize, injure, or eliminate their rivals" (1956, p. 8). Cross, Names, and Beck define it as "differences between and among individuals" that are created by competing or incompatible goals, values, motives, ideas, resources, etc. (1979, p. v). Thomas (1976) provides a process definition of conflict -- a process that originates when one individual perceives that another party has frustrated, or, is about to frustrate some goal or concern of his or hers. Deutsch maintains that conflict exists "whenever incompatible activities occur .... An action which is incompatible with, or injures, or in some ways makes it less likely or less effective" (1971, p. 51). Finally, Hocker and Wilmot provide a communication perspective for the term conflict. They view conflict as "an expressed struggle between at least two interdependent parties who perceive incompatible goals, scarce rewards, and interference from the other party in achieving their goals" (1985, p. 23).

A look at the above definitions of conflict informs our reaction to the term itself: "incompatible," "frustration," "interference," "perception," and "interdependence." Part of the problem our culture has in dealing with conflict "stems from the pejorative connotation any type of discord conveys in a society that values harmony, compatibility, satisfaction, and independence. Because of these values, there has been a tendency...to avoid conflict" (Borisoff and Victor, 1989, p. 2). As a result of such avoidance, organizations often find it difficult first, to admit to basic problems with communication, and, second, to then go outside of the organization to ameliorate these problems. Part of the role of the outside consultant is to be extremely sensitive to how the individuals within the organization regard the differences that affect them.

This chapter integrates some of the theory on conflict management with practical approaches to conflict training. It is divided into five basic sections: the pressing need for conflict training in our culture, the practical steps the conflict trainer must pursue are explored, the need to assess the climate prior to training, some typical cases whose problems are fundamental to our understanding about how the conflict trainer can work effectively within an organization, post-training analysis, and ethical considerations that may be of special interest not only to the conflict trainer but also to any communication skills trainer who has been invited to run a program or to conduct a workshop.

The Need for Conflict Training

The need for organizations to address conflict management is compelling. The organizational setting, studies tell us, is rife with conflict. The American

Management Association reported more than 15 years ago that CEOs, vice-presidents, and middle managers spend nearly 25% of their time at work dealing with interpersonal conflict deriving primarily from communication failure, personality clashes, and value differences (Thomas and Schimdt, 1976). For school and hospital administrators, the figure was nearly 50% (Lippitt, 1982). At the time these studies were reported, management was largely male territory in the U.S. As women, minorities, and members from other cultures have entered the professional ranks, it would seem that the percentages would be even higher today because the more diversity introduced into an environment, the greater the likelihood for misunderstandings and miscommunications to occur (Deutsch, 1991).

Similarly, because individuals do not walk unfettered into the workplace but carry with them their personal problems and concerns, dealing with conflict in the professional arena can also have a positive impact on personal relationships. Studies indicate that the major factors in couples' dissatisfaction are the inability **to listen** and **to resolve conflict productively.** According to Harold Markman of the University of Denver, "what keeps couples together or breaks them up is not how much they love each other or whether they have good sex, but how they handle conflict .... " (1992, p. 33). In fact, "the early stages of a relationship can predispose or predict the later stages." Researchers report, according to Duck, "that the style and amount of conflict that occur in premarital relationships are accurate predictors of conflict and distress in subsequent marriage" (1991, p. 98). Too, the American Association for Marriage and Family Therapy has increased from 9,000 to 19,000 within the last decade with varying approaches to resolving differences between couples being a primary focus of therapy (Hoban, 1992, p. 32).

Relationships in personal and professional environments, therefore, are not mutually exclusive. The factors that affect the way individuals learn to deal with conflict will have an enormous influence on interpersonal interaction. Moreover, this interaction is fundamental to relationship satisfaction. While the chapters in this text on Gender and Communication (Herndon), Listening (Brownell), Crosscultural Communication (Victor), and Communication Styles and Predispositions (Rancer) explore more fully how we acquire the communication strategies we employ in the workplace, it is important to examine, albeit briefly, some of those factors that influence as well our conflict-handling behavior.

Socialization in the family. Rahim reports that conflict is ranked fifth among the 65 topics addressed in MBA courses (1981). However, by the time students enroll in graduate school, their own style for dealing with conflict has become well-entrenched. In class after class, students indicate that they had no formal conflict-management training during their education. Whether they see themselves as compromising, accommodating, avoiding, collaborating, or competing, is largely influenced by how they learned to communicate within the family. The number, age, and gender of siblings, the style of communication in familial role models, and attitudes of the family toward managing differences were instrumental, they felt, in shaping their own attitudes toward conflict and in developing their own conflict style.

Socialization of gender. Integral to how we learn to communicate within the family is how we learn "appropriate" gendered communication. Gilligan argues that through play, young boys learn behavior required for the highly competitive organizational culture: "By participating in controlled and socially approved competitive situations, they learn to deal with competition in a relatively forthright manner - to play with their enemies and to compete with their friends - all in accordance with the rules of the game" (1982, p. 10). Girls, it is argued, learn the art of affiliating, nurturing, and attending to the needs of others (Gilligan, 1982; Maltz and Borker, 1982; Tannen, 1990). Regardless of several recent studies that argue that psychological rather than biological behavior may be more salient for how women and men behave in organizations (Harlan and Weiss, 1987; Powell, 1988; Rancer and Dierks-Stewart, 1987), sex-trait stereotyping remains prevalent. Williams and Best (1982) in their 30 pan-nation study-report that the adjectives "adventurous," "dominant," "forceful," "independent," "masculine," and "strong-willed," were assigned to men; the terms "emotional," "sentimental," "submissive," and "superstitious," were used consistently to describe women. If acceptable gender behavior for men and women is divergent, then how each gender will **regard** conflict itself as well as the strategies they use to ameliorate differences, may reflect a gendered orientation rather than the actual reality and needs of the members within an organization.

Socialization of culture. Gender affects styles of communication and attitudes toward conflict. Equally significant is the dimension of culture. Sumner has characterized ethnocentrism as the "view of things in which one's own group is the center of everything, and all others are scaled and rated with reference to it .... Each group nourishes its own pride and vanity, boasts itself superior, exalts its own divinities, and looks with contempt on outsiders" (1906, pp. 12-13).

The ethnocentric perspective to which Sumner alludes is, according to Deutsch, "conducive to the occurrence of conflict but not conducive to its constructive resolution" (1991, p. 33). For a conflict trainer to be effective, especially in a multicultural organization, not only must he/she be knowledgeable about the communication behaviors, values, an attitudes for managing differences of the diverse cultures reflective of the environment. Perhaps more importantly, the trainer must suspend his or her **own** values and attitudes to accomplish the training best-suited to the organization's needs.

Who we are -- our experiences in our families, our gender, our culture -- are but a few of the important factors that shape our capacity to communicate. Additionally, our background helps us to formulate our attitudes toward conflict and to develop competence in understanding and managing differences. For trainers to be effective, they must continually scrutinize their own behavior. Lest they risk being ethnocentric themselves, and dogmatic in their own assumptions and assertions about what is right within an organizational climate, they must be especially sensitive to their own perspectives and to how they relate to the organization. Only by being accepting, understanding, and open can they be effective communicating with others.

Assessment: Understanding Self-competence and the Variables that affect Organizational Conflict

Before conflict trainers can hope to be successful, they must first ascertain the nature of the problem about which their expertise is being sought. Of equal importance, trainers need to examine the organizational climate in which they will be conducting training. To do this, the trainer must begin with the self.

Understanding self-competency. The literature on conflict management stresses that conflict is a matter of perception, and, of course, perceived differences (Borisoff & Victor, 1989; Coser, 1956; Deutsch, 1971; Hocker & Wilmot, 1985; Thomas, 1976; etc.). Wedge reminds us that "perceptions have exceedingly little to do with what actually exists, but they are nevertheless of great importance, particularly in conflict situations, because they influence out actions. We act," he goes on to say, "in terms of what we believe to be true, of what we think the other side may be doing and why it many be behaving the way it is and we may be horribly wrong" (1987, p.284). While Wedge is addressing here parties engaged in conflict, the perspective of the trainer may have considerable influence on how he/she even views or defines the problem. Thus, two trainers, depending in part on their own backgrounds and experiences, may have divergent views on what constitutes a hostile environment in an organization or whether a situation is solvable.

Attitudes toward how we regard and manage conflict reflects individual orientations. The conflict trainer, therefore, must monitor carefully his/her own biases, assumptions, and attitudes. Earlier it was mentioned that until recently, conflict was regarded negatively - as something to be avoided. Today, we include opportunity in out outlook toward conflict, and we view conflict as a means to articulate or clarify our views as well as to ascertain and comprehend the views of another. There is, consequently, greater emphasis on collaboration and cooperation than was previously prescribed when conflict was considered as a struggle where one party wins and the other party loses. As a result of this change in outlook, not only must the conflict trainer overcome his/her own negative attitudes about conflict but also address these attitudes as well in the minds of the individuals receiving training. That is, if one is working with individuals who strongly perceive conflict resolution as an either/or, win/lose prospect, these individuals are likely to resist strenuously the more cooperative orientations of compromise and collaboration.

Understanding the variables that affect organizational conflict. For a conflict trainer to be effective, he/she must also be cognizant of the variables that contribute to organizational conflict. Putnam and Poole (1987, p. 555) posit the following four general aspects of the organizations that interact with communication in organizational conflict:

actor attributes -- the members of the organization and the factors and attributes that make them individuals (personality, culture, race, religion, gender, experience, education, etc.);

conflict issue -- or the nature and source of the conflict which may result from scarce resources., incompatible beliefs, goals, and/or attitudes;

relationship variables -- or the extent to which individuals within an organization feel they can interact and relate to one another in an atmosphere conducive to communication; and,

contextual factors -- or the organizational norms, climate, and procedures that influences the way problems, procedures, and communication are handled.

From a practical standpoint, the trainer can begin by asking several questions to ascertain important information related to the variables presented above. The trainer might first ask, what barriers exist to assessing accurately the source and nature of the conflict? Sandole (1987) distinguishes between the observable dimensions or symptoms of a problem (the phenotypic characteristics of a conflict), and, the invisible, underlying processes of a problem that are not always apparent (the genotypic traits of a conflict). "What most of us cannot see, and indeed, have some difficulty conceptualizing," Sandole warns, "are the underlying processes, the genotypic phenomena; and it is at the genotypic level that I believe cross-level commonalities exist" (p. 289).

In order for the conflict-consultant to be effective, s/he must get at the source of the problem. To do so, s/he has to rely on the accurate attributions of the organization's sources. Unlike the medical doctor who can directly observe symptoms (such as a cough, red throat, fever, etc.) and with a high degree of accuracy link these symptoms to some cause (flu, virus, strep, etc.), the conflict trainer often does not have the opportunity for much direct observation. Nor does the trainer have a *Gray's Anatomy* for conflict resolution that links symptoms and-causes. Moreover, the same symptoms or problems may, in fact, have different causes. To illustrate, low morale may be evident in different offices within the same company. In one instance, morale may be affected by the physical nature of the environment - by such factors as color, air circulation, spatial delineations, and so forth. In another instance, morale may be affected by the emotional climate -- by such factors as different personalities of co-workers by the supervisor's style of management. And, in a third case, the task environment may influence morale -- through constant 'crises,' through highly repetitive or unchallenging assignments, etc. Unless the conflict trainer can adequately link the cause and effect aspect of the problem(s), managing differences will be difficult. One way to gain this information is by talking to as many members of the organization as possible. The manager's viewpoint, the secretary's perspective, the executive officer's insights will provide layers of information that will undoubtedly influence the trainer's understanding of what kind of training is needed moreover, if training can be beneficial.

A second question the trainer might ask is, what dimensions of the organizational climate can or cannot be changed? Typical problems or conflicts in organizations stem from sources that may or may not be mutable. Deadlines, for example, may be fixed. The pressures created by the tasks themselves (i.e., too frequent, insufficient notice, always changing, etc.), and, by the physical environment (i.e., too cramped, too noisy, too hot, etc.), can result in stress, low morale, high turnover, increased absenteeism, in-fighting, etc. The physical plant may be inadequate for the size or function or a particular unit. While certain aspects of the climate may not be within the purview of the trainer to alter, the trainer should seek strategies to implement small, manageable changes within the framework of the organization's operating procedures and budget.

A third question that might be asked is what dimensions of the emotional climate facilitate or impede conflict training? A company may have seemingly all the resources in the world, and yet individuals working within the organization may regard it as a hostile environment. Conversely, a fledgling company struggling to make it in a competitive marketplace may foster in their employees a sense of loyalty and commitment. Adequate resources alone do not solely define the emotional climate of an organization. Without a sense of emotional support, employees are likely to feel thwarted, frustrated, suspicious, or angry.

In his seminal work on group conflict, Jack Gibb (1961) defined and distinguished between the defensive and supportive communication climate. One type of climate he describes as defensive and threatening. Such a climate is characterized by communication that is evaluative, controlling, manipulative, neutral, superior, and certain. The other climate Gibb presents is supportive and provides an atmosphere conducive to mutual trust, openness, and cooperation. In contrast to the defensive climate, the supportive climate is characterized by communication that is descriptive, problem-oriented, spontaneous, empathic, equal, and provisional. (See Table 1 below).

TABLE 1

CONTRASTING COMMUNICATION CLIMATES
IN INTERPERSONAL COMMUNICATION

Evaluative vs. Descriptive Communication

Evaluative (Defensive): "You're falling down on the job!
Descriptive (Supportive): "I've noticed you've had difficulty meeting deadlines the past two weeks. Let's talk about it."

Controlling vs. Problem Orientation

Controlling (Defensive): "I'm the boss. I'll decide who takes lunch when!"

Problem Orientation (Supportive): "We need to make sure the office is covered. Let's see what kind of schedule can be worked out.

Manipulative vs. Spontaneous Communication

Manipulative (Defensive): "We've already spent too much time talking about evaluations. There are other agenda items we've got to get to."

Spontaneous (Supportive): "I'm aware the topic of evaluations is more important than I had first realized. I'd like to call a special meeting and make this the only agenda item."

Neutral vs. Empathic Communication

Neutral (Defensive): "I realize you have family problems, but I have an office to run and you'll just have to deal with it."

Empathic (Supportive): "I know how difficult this period is for you. Let's see if there are ways we can adjust your schedule so that you can be there for your family."

Superior vs. Equal Communication

Superior (Defensive): "I've been here longer than anyone, and I can tell you that trying it your way simply won't work!"

Equal (Supportive): "We've not been successful using your approach in the past. I'd be interested to hear why you believe it will work at this time."

Certainty vs. Provisionalism

Certainty (Defensive): "I know your plan won't work. There's no sense even trying it!

Provisionalism (Supportive): "I'm willing to try out this new procedure. We'll meet periodically to see how it is working and make adjustments accordingly."

If we were to summarize the major distinction between defensive and supportive communication, defensive communication tends to stifle interaction. It is hard to speak when one feels ignored, put down, or, believes that one's own assertions are being trivialized. Supportive communication, in contrast, confirms. It is far easier to interact when one feels listened to.

The fourth question the trainer might ask is what dimensions of conflict training are realistic or feasible? This question is related both to the resources available for training and to the emotional climate of the organization. First, the resources. A director of personnel contacts a conflict trainer and indicates that there is a great deal of tension in the company stemming from the cultural differences of the employees. The director wants the trainer to conduct a two-hour workshop for the employees so that they can learn how to get along. While Stephan (1985) indicates that such workshops and sensitivity training programs may have short-term positive effects, Deutsch (1991) cautions that the positive benefits may be qualified by the fact that "most such studies do not have long-term follow-up and have not included behavioral data" (p. 35).

The conflict trainer must ask, it seems, if management really wants to improve or resolve the situation and has adequate resources to commit to such an undertaking, or, if instead lip-- service is being paid to the problem. The conflict trainer must also address the emotional climate as well as to the employees who would participate in training. Do the individuals targeted for training **want** to be involved in training, or are they being ordered to participate? Furthermore, what can they gain from training, that is, what's in it for them? The more positive the attitude **of** the participants, the more likely they will comply with the training process.

An understanding of the conflict trainer's own competencies and attitudes, of the organization's problems, resources, and emotional climate will inform the kind of conflict training the consultant can best implement. These steps comprise the action phase and form the core of the next section.

Action: Expected Outcomes

Once the consultant has assessed the climate and needs of the organization, she can develop the appropriate exercises, cases, presentation, etc. for the actual training. Conflict training is a highly individualized process. The conflict trainer must be flexible and able to adapt to the needs of the group or individuals receiving training. To acclimate to the needs of the trainees, the trainer may need to assure confidentiality, may need to establish with the group the value of training, and, will need to identify the nature of the conflict.

Confidentiality. Confidentiality may be an especially thorny issue. In an open and supportive communication climate, the individuals hiring the consultant and the participants in the training process may welcome the opportunity to discuss problems, concerns, and areas for change, If, however, the trainer is working with individuals or groups who feel theirs is a pressured or hostile climate and trust is low, the trainer may need to assure participants that comments made or examples provided will remain confidential. The ability to make this assurance must be negotiated by the trainer ahead of time. (The issue of confidentiality is regarded as part of the ethical considerations and is examined further later in this chapter.)

What's in it for them? A conflict trainer can only be effective if the trainees are willing to participate fully in the program or workshop. Part of helping to find solutions to problems may emerge from first ascertaining **why** the participants remain in the organization - especially in a climate characterized as volatile, hostile, difficult, stressful, etc. If a company or office is beset by so many problems, the trainer might elicit from the group what are the benefits for remaining in the workplace? Placing side by side the benefits and the problems, the group can begin to identify which problems areas can or cannot be controlled or altered. From a discussion, the group can gain a sense of perspective about their own climate. They can begin to seek potential areas of change and look for mechanisms to achieve such change. They can begin by becoming involved in improving the work environment.

Defining the underlying conflicts.   In order to address conflicts, individuals first must be able identify the source of the conflict. Sandole, as mentioned before, cautions that the genotypic traits of a conflict must be ascertained before they can be ameliorated (1987, p. 289). The following sample cases illustrate how the phenotypic (or observable) traits of a conflict may in fact indicate a problem but not its source.

Case: The 800 Room

Consider the following: A company has an 800 room with six operators who have high-school educations and who come from diverse ethnic backgrounds. The operators must field all incoming callers are individuals with questions or problems. Calls come in all day long. The 800 room is located in a basement. There are no windows.   Attached carrels provide the workspace for each operator. Operators' performance is determined by how many calls are handled, and, by how few 'problem' callers are referred to the supervisor. Turnover is high and morale is low. The consultant is brought in to "make the group more articulate" because in the eyes of the supervisor **this** is the source of the problem. In fact, the trainer found that articulation and enunciation were **not** creating the stress. Rather, stress was linked to two other sources. The trainer asked the operators to bring in examples of the typical problems or conflict they had to deal with at work. By talking about the conflicts, and by allowing the staff to vent their frustrations in a supportive climate, the following concerns emerged as the root of the low morale.

Many of the callers, it was learned, were themselves under pressure. Often they would expect the operators to have information beyond their expertise, or, to be able to resolve issues beyond their responsibility and training. Outside callers would sometimes take out their frustration on the operators. The operators had not learned how to manage these conflicts. To develop conflict handling strategies and to learn the language appropriate to allay the callers' concerns, the operators and the conflict trainer actually role-played "problem" calls. Responses such as "I understand your concern, and I will have the appropriate supervisor get back to you as soon as possible", and, "I realize that you haven't heard about your loan yet. Let me give you the number of the office that processes these applications" became a part of their repertoire. By enabling the operators to empathize with the callers, they were able to be more helpful and found that the number of conflicts they experienced diminished over time.

The task environment was not the only source of conflict for the operators. The physical quarters in which they worked was also stress-provoking. Housed in a small room without ventilation or windows with phones literally ringing all day long did not provide a pleasant setting. They used such terms as "suffocating," "dying," and "boring" to describe the office. While impossible to re-locate their office, a couple of recommendations could be implemented immediately. First, to improve the aesthetics of the room, it was suggested that posters or pictures of outdoor scenes be rotated in the room seasonally. Second, to allow the operators to physically remove themselves from the incessant ringing, it was recommended that a small table and coffee machine be placed in the copying room. These small steps to address the complaints of the staff were repaid many times over because for the first time staff members felt they were being listened to, and that they were being taken seriously. Most importantly, they felt they were valued members of the organization.   There was an immediate change in their attitude toward the workplace, and a willingness to continue working toward making small improvements over time.

Case: An Engineer in a Man's World

Consider the following: a woman engineer contacts a consultant and asks for listening skills training. Her boss has singled her out (there are 120 employees; five are women) and has indicated that her listening skills are wanting. This is affecting her evaluations, her raises, and her overall morale. She is convinced that the criticisms are gender-based and wants also to confront her supervisor.

The client worked one-on-one with the communication consultant for a total of three meetings. Important for the consultant to ascertain was the contexts in which the supervisor accused the employee of not listening. The employee was encouraged to meet with her supervisor and indicate that she-appreciated his evaluations and had, as a result, hired a communications trainer to work with her on enhancing her listening skills. Moreover, she wanted to know from the supervisor what specific behaviors had led to his assessment of her as an "ineffective listener." Upon review of his assessment of her (i.e., she didn't display the affect of listening that he expected from women such as head nodding, smiling, paralinguistic cues like "I see," "un huh," etc.), it became evident that he was attributing poor listening habits to her in part because her behavior did not conform to the feminine sex-trait and sex-role stereotypes for listening. In fact, she claimed she deported herself more like the men so that she would not stand out. She wanted to fit in. Moreover, she performed exceptionally well on all listening assessments measuring comprehensive listening which was the kind of listening required of her position. The trainer reviewed the verbal and nonverbal behaviors advocated by -researchers in the area of, listening that **convey** active listening **regardless of gender** (Borisoff and Purdy, 1991; Steil, Barker and Watson, 1983; Wolvin and Coakley, 1991).

Understanding how her own behavior was perceived enabled her to monitor her affective display of listening. A follow-up meeting several weeks later revealed that not only did she feel more comfortable as a communicator (she was no longer trying to act "like one of the guys"), but her supervisor discerned a major difference in her behavior. Her evaluations improved and she felt much more at ease not having to conform to masculine communication strategies.

Case: The Reluctant Trainees

This case illustrates conflict prevention by reviewing how a trainer handled a program when the trainees, themselves, did not want to be "trained." The commissioner of a government agency in a major urban city wanted the deputy commissioners to be trained to make presentations to community groups and agencies, and, to be able to "handle themselves during interviews with the media." The group of 12 deputies consisted of 11 men and one woman. The men had held their positions an average of 20 or more years and felt they were competent communicators who did not need an eight session training program, let alone, a program conducted by a woman who was considerably younger. The consultant was informed of their resistance ahead of time and knew she would be entering a less-than-welcoming environment.

To address the issue of their discomfort working with a younger woman, the trainer hired a male colleague to co-conduct a couple of the training sessions. To address the issue of their own self-assessment as competent communicators, the trainer informed the group that because of their considerable expertise and experience, rather than begin with techniques on making presentations, they would start right away at a more advanced level by videotaping each commissioner. When the commissioners had the opportunity to see themselves on tape, they realized they could benefit enormously from the training and their attitude toward the training program and toward the female consultant changed dramatically. What began initially as a potentially difficult consultancy turned instead into a productive program for all involved. In fact, evaluations of the training program indicated that additional communication skills training would be welcome.

Case: Empowering Others with the Language of Effective Conflict Management

A government agency handles the dockets for a city. An office of 40 staff members (12 supervisors and 28 support staff reflecting diverse ethnic backgrounds), process each and every docket that goes through the system. They deal with the judges who hear the cases (at the top level); a clerk who is responsible for making sure work flows properly and on time; lawyers for clients who must file papers with specific guidelines; the public at large whose cases are being heard. Deadlines exist outside of the staff; the staff is woefully small to meet these deadlines effectively. Tempers often flare up and individuals resort to personal attacks and to stereotyping others as a means of coping. The morale in the office is low. The supervisor wants to provide a series of workshops to help the staff deal with these issues as effectively as possible in an environment that is supportive. Funds for training and time to allow for staff training are limited, so the consultant is hired to conduct two half-day workshops.

The consultant learned that neither the deadlines nor the number of staff members could be changed. Moreover, discontented staff could not be relocated. The consultant felt that within the limited time afforded to training, emphasis would be put on creating a more positive attitude and improving communication between staff members. Because the supervisor and manager of human resources were wonderfully supportive, the consultant believed that any change, however small, would be reinforced.

There is considerable material to support the use of clear, "I-centered" messages as-opposed to leveling accusations at others (Borisoff and Victor, 1989; Deutsch, 1991; Folger and Poole, 1992; Gibb 1961; Hocker and Wilmot, 1985; Knapp, 1980; Mehrabian, 1981; Putnam and Wilson, 1982, etc.). For the first session, the participants were asked to discuss typical conflicts that occurred and how they felt. (For example, "I'm in charge of processing dockets. If Lenny doesn't give them to me totally checked, then I get backlogged and the lawyers are furious with my group. Lenny goofs off a lot! He should be working harder.") It became apparent that the jobs performed were both routine and highly pressured. Since the group was so quick to point out the problems with working in the department (i.e. "The supervisor's nice but even he gets pressured and can't do anything about it!"), the consultant examined with the group why they stayed in this environment. Were there benefits to working for the agency?

Once the group saw the list of positive and negatives side-by-side, the trainer reviewed the negatives and tried to find strategies with the group to change some of the negatives. For example, could the group processing dockets create a simple check sheet so that when the next unit received the dockets, they could see at a glance that all work was complete. Also, some tasks could be easily shared by employees. Could some sort of rotation-system be introduced to alleviate the boredom experienced by many. Regular staff meetings at which time employees could vent their frustrations and discuss problems or ideas were implemented. For the first time the employees felt they were given some control over their professional lives. Feeling empowered was regarded positively. Finally, the trainer had the members role-play some of the interpersonal conflicts and the group looked at how communication influences conflict. The second meeting, scheduled several weeks later, served as a followup.

Certainly many of the problems such as stress, deadlines, routine tasks, etc. persisted. However, attitudes toward the job and a spirit of cooperation was highly evident -- especially when members had the opportunity to work in another member's position. The group had become more cohesive and supportive. Although Deutsch (1991) cautions about the sustained effect of workshops and brief seminars on organizations, in this instance it was learned that five years after the initial workshops, the overall climate of the unit remained significantly improved.

Clearly, change cannot occur without cooperation. For the communication consultant to introduce effective programs that require conflict training, a positive and realistic attitude on the part of **all** levels of the organization are critical to assure successful training.

Analysis: Solutions or New Problems?

As the aforementioned cases demonstrate, conflict training can entail challenging and dynamic sessions. While many training programs or workshops are limited, it is important that the trainer not be constrained by the time designated for training. Consideration should be given to two major issues: debriefing and follow-up, and, confidentiality.

Debriefing and follow-up. After training, the consultant leaves an organization. The group or individuals, however, remain, and the potential for the continuation of problems, unresolved issues, or misunderstandings persists. The positive aspect of obtaining and providing feedback in a communication exchange is posited in nearly every text in the speech communication discipline. The trainer needs to ascertain if the training was appropriate, understood, /and useful. The participants in a workshop need to feel they can have access to someone especially if continued problems, special needs, or concerns about the training emerge.

Of equal importance, a follow-up session(s) allows the trainer to determine with the group if unarticulated issues have developed as a result of training. If so, how can these issues be relayed to the appropriate parties? Therefore, while one-shot training sessions may appear economical initially, in fact, it may be a far more prudent investment to allow minimally for one follow-up session.

Confidentiality. The conflict trainer may feel torn between the trainees who opened themselves up, and the individuals in management who have hired him or her, especially if the trainer has not clarified initially with either group what he/she feels can and cannot be divulged. One consultant, for example, makes clear to the participants in training sessions that to be able to be effective, it is important that the group can trust the trainer. What is said within the group, therefore, remains confidential. Moreover, problems or suggested solutions may be brought to the management's attention in general terms only. These suggestions would be formulated with input from the group itself.

Regardless of the topics to be addressed, the attitude of management is the key to implementing an effective training program. If employees sense a feeling of frustration, powerlessness, or a lack of trust, it is difficult to engage them in productive training. If, however, they sense that there is a real commitment on the part of management to listen to and to respond to their concerns, they are far more likely and actively participate in the sessions provided.

Thus there are certain expectations the consultant, the agent hiring the consultant, and those being trained must share to assure effective training. While there is no published ethical code for the conflict trainer to abide by, important ethical considerations should be acknowledged. These considerations are explored in the next section.

Ethical Considerations: Coming to Terms

Ethics in conflict management training appears to be a contradiction in terms. In fact, it is a seemingly impossible contention. One definition of ethics in Webster's 3rd New International Dictionary is "the principles of conduct governing an individual or a profession: standards of behavior." Another definition includes "the discipline dealing with what is good and bad or right or wrong or with moral duty and obligation." This section examines four extant problems in conflict management training in organizations that impede establishing ethics in this type of training.

The meaning of standards. The first problem concerns the "standards" portion of the definition of ethics vis a vis "a profession." Wedge (1987, p. 284) contends that individuals who study conflict management bring the orientation of their own discipline to bear on the subject. The social psychologist, for example, may emphasize perception. The anthropologist may look at culture. The political scientist considers power politics and power balances. Deutsch (1991, p. 26) in a later work adds to this list: the sociologist stresses social, role, status, and class conflicts; economists emphasize game theory and decision-making, economic competition, labor negotiations, and trade disputes. There are, it appears, apparently as many different perspectives on the study of conflict as there are disciplines that study it. If we are seeking standards, then, which perspective prevails? Do all receive equal import? Furthermore, how does an individual acquire the mantle of specialist in conflict resolution? What criteria or curricula determine these norms? To what standards may one aspire? Are these standards free from one's own biases?

The hiring agent: what's "in it" him or her? The second major problem confronting the conflict management trainer are the ethics of the individual(s) who hire the consultant. We would like to assume that others share our beliefs, values and attitudes. Therefore, when the conflict trainer is contacted by the organization to assess or to institute training, one assumes the individual employing the consultant wants to do everything possible to resolve and/or to improve the existing situation. For the most part, this assumption is accurate. Yet, this may not always be the case. Let us consider two circumstances that point to compromising situations.

The first is the **quick fix.** Typical of this kind of situation is when a problem exists and a supervisor directs a subordinate to "handle it." For example, an office deals with deadlines beyond their control so that everything is a 'crisis' that must be dealt with 'yesterday.' The workers who must cope with this pressure perceive the supervisor as irascible and unsympathetic to their stress. They have a negative attitude toward work, yet, because it is a government job, it would be extraordinarily difficult to fire them. To deal with the unrest, the supervisor instructs her personnel manager to bring in a consultant to provide conflict training and stress management techniques for the staff. Thus, the consultant can deal with the phenotypic traits of the problem as previously defined by Sandole. The important genotypic aspects of the problem, however, may not be addressed.

A second example of a compromising condition under which a consultant may be hired is when the person doing the hiring has a **hidden agenda** or **motive.** To illustrate this point, consider the manager who is aware that due to personality and/or cultural differences, for example, members of the organization do not get along. He is aware that most likely no amount of outside intervention will rectify the situation. Yet, to give-the appearance of 'taking steps' to improve the communication environment, he invites a trainer to conduct sessions on effective communication strategies. The consultant, therefore, may prepare a very helpful program that is destined to fail precisely because of the irreconcilably negative attitudes of the participants.

The conflict trainer must take steps to assure that his/her time is not wasted; that the company's money is not wasted; that the reputation of the communication consultant remains positive. The aforementioned steps of assessment, action, and analysis can facilitate such assurance.

When the academic makes the transition to consultant. Because the academic consultant may have succeeded in the classroom, it is possible to assume erroneously that what works in academic will translate into the corporate setting. While knowledge of theoretical constructs may, in fact, qualify the academic to conduct corporate training, most worker being trained want skills and practical application rather than the names and dates of prior studies. It is important, therefore, for the academic to be able to move comfortably in the corporate setting. Relatedly, the academic must be able to transfer what works in the classroom to a different context. Factors of time, of resources, of the size of the group being trained, and most importantly, of what kind of training can be achieved within the company's constraints must be acknowledged honestly and accurately by the trainer.

A matter of outcomes. The final ethical issues confronting the consultant relate to outcomes. First, have unarticulated issues emerged in the training session about which management was unaware? How can these issues be communicated to the appropriate parties? What issues of confidentiality emerge? And, second, what kind of feedback can be ethically provided to the individuals who have hired the consultant? What kind of support are they willing to allocate in order to follow-up? Will training be supported from the top?

Conclusion

It is impossible to ascertain with absolute certainty the underlying motives of each individual who hires the communication consultant. However, the trainer can scrutinize carefully the information gathered during the Assessment stage. This information can be highly instructive and useful to the trainer. The more experience the conflict trainer has negotiating the Assessment, Action, and Analysis phases of the training process, the closer he/she is moving toward arriving at certain principles or guidelines that may influence the behavior. We are, by induction, moving toward an ethical consideration of conflict management training in the field. While there is some comfort in recognizing and encouraging patterned behavior, it is important for the communication consultant to acknowledge the potentially numerous variations of acceptable and appropriate behavior within a communication environment. It is important to consider from both a practical and ethical perspective the viability of instituting a successful training program.

References

Bernard, J. 1981. The female world. NY: The Free Press.

Borisoff, D. & M. Purdy. 1991. Listening in everyday life: A personal and professional approach. Lanham, MD: University Press of America.

Borisoff, D., & D. Victor. 1989. Conflict management: A communication skills approach. Englewood Cliffs, NJ: PrenticeHall.

Coser, L. A. 1956. The functions of social conflict. NY: The Free Press.

Cross, G. P., J. H. Names, & D. Beck. 1979. Conflict and human interaction. Dubuque, IA: Kendall Hunt.

Deutsch, M. 1991. Subjective features of conflict resolution: Psychological, social and cultural influences. In New directions in conflict theory, ed. R. Vayrynen, 26-56. Newbury Park, CA: Sage Publication, 26-56.

Deutsch, M. (1973). The resolution of a conflict: Constructive and destructive processes. New Haven: Yale University Press.

Duck, S. 1991. Understanding relationships. NY: Guilford Press.

Fisher, R. & W. Ury. 1981. Getting to yes: Negotiating agreement without giving in. Boston, MA: Houghton Mifflin.

Folger, J. P. & M. S. Poole. (1984; 1992). Working through conflict: A communication perspective. Glenview, IL: Scott, Foresman & Co.

Gibb, J. 1961. Defensive communication. Journal of Communication 11 141-148.

Gilligan, C. 1982. In a different voice: Psychological theory and women's development. Cambridge, MA: Harvard University Press.

Harlan, A. & C. L. Weiss. 1982. Sex differences in factors affecting managerial career advancement. In Women in the workplace, ed. P. A. Wallace, 59-100. Boston, MA: Auburn House.

Hoban, P. 1992. He said, she said: Couples therapy is the flavor of the month. New York, 15 June, 31-36.

Hocker, J.L. & W. W. Wilmot. 1991. Interpersonal conflict. Dubuque, IA: Wm. C. Brown.

Jablin, F. M., L. L. Putnam, K. H. Roberts, L. W. Porter. 1987. Handbook of organizational communication: An interdisciplinary perspective. Beverly Hills, CA: Sage Publication.

Knapp, M. L. 1980. Essentials of nonverbal communication. NY: Holt, Rinehart, Winston.

Lippitt, G. L. 1982. Managing conflict in today's organizations. Training & Development Journal, (July): 67-74.

Macoby, E. E., & C. N. Jacklin. 1974. The psychology of sex differences. Stanford, CA: Stanford University Press.

Maltz, D., & R. Borker. 1982. A cultural approach to male-female miscommunications. In Language and social identity, ed. J.J. Gumperz, 196-216. Cambridge, ENG: Cambridge University Press.

Mehrabian, A. 1981. Silent messages: Implicit communication of emotions and attitudes. 2nd ed. Belmont, CA: Wadsworth.

Powell, G. N. 1988. Women and men in management. Newbury Park, CA: Sage Publications.

Putnam, L., & M. S. Poole. 1987. Conflict and negotiations. In Handbook of organizational communication, eds. Jablin, et.al., 549-599. Newbury Park, CA: Sage.

Putnam, L. L., and C. E. Wilson. 1982. Communicative strategies in organizational conflicts: Reliability and validity of a measurement scale. In Communication Yearbook, ed. M. Burgoon. 6. Beverly Hills, CA: Sage.

Rancer, A., & S. Dierks. 1987. Biological and psychological gender differences in trait argumentativeness. In Communication, gender, and sex roles in diverse interaction contexts, eds. L. P. Stewart & S. Ting-Toomey, 18-30. Norwood, NJ: Ablex.

Rahim, M. A. 1981. Organizational behavior courses for graduate students in business administration: Views from the tower and the battlefield. Psychological Reports 49: 583-592. Quoted in L. Putnam, & M. S. Poole, Conflict and negotiations. In Handbook of organizational communication, eds. Jablin, et.al., 549-599. Newbury Park, CA: Sage.

Sandole, D. J. D. 1987. Conflict management: Elements of generic theory and process. In Conflict management and problem solving: Interpersonal to international applications, eds. J. D. Sandole and I. Sandole-Staroste, 289-297. Washington Square, NY: New York University Press.

Steil, L. K., L. L. Barker, & K. W. Watson. 1983. Effective listening: Key to your success. New York: Random House.

Stephan, W. G. 1985. Intergroup relations. In The handbook of social psychology, eds. G. Lindsey & E. Aronson, 599-658. New York:

Random House, 599-658.

Stockard, J., and M. M. Johnson. 1980. Sex roles: Sex inequality and sex role development. Englewood Cliffs, NJ: Prentice-Hall.

Sumner, W. G. 1906. Folkways. New York: Ginn Press.

Tagiuri, R. 1968. The concepts of organizational climate. In Organizational climate: Exploration of a concept, eds. R. Tagiuri & G.H. Litwin, 11-32. Boston, MA: Harvard University Press.

Tannen, D. 1990. You just don't understand: Women and men in conversation. New York: William Morrow.

Thomas, K. W. 1976. Conflict and conflict management. In The handbook of industrial and organizational psychology, ed. M.D. Dunnette, 889-935. Chicago, IL: Rand McNally.

Thomas, K. W., & W. Schmidt. 1976. A survey of managerial interests with respect to conflict. Academy of Management Journal 19 (2): 315-318.

Wedge, B. 1987. Conflict management: The state of the art. In Conflict management and problem solving: Interpersonal and international application, eds. J. D. Sandole & I. Sandole-Staroste, 279-288. New York: New York University Press.

Williams, J. E., & D. L. Best. 1982. Measuring sex stereotypes: A thirty nation study. Beverly Hills, CA: Sage Publications.

Wolvin, A. & C. G. Coakley. 1991. Listening. 4th ed. Dubuque, IA: William C. Brown.

CROSS-CULTURAL COMMUNICATION

David A. Victor

This chapter discusses the opportunities available to the communication consultant in the area of cross-cultural business communication. These opportunities extend to both international business communication and to domestic cross-cultural diversity management. This chapter addresses only the area of cross-cultural communication as it affects business and professional settings. Cross-cultural concerns admittedly affect a wide range of other areas in communication studies, ranging from bicultural family relations to cultural influences on theology to name but two. This self-imposed limitation to business communication has more to do with the author's own experience as the president of the Human Resources Advisory Council consulting firm and professor of management and international business communication at Eastern Michigan University. Still, on a less personal basis one might argue that a focus on business and professional applications may prove the most productive and relevant for the somewhat more narrow needs of the communication consultant.

This chapter is divided into four parts. The discussion begins by defining the term "culture" and what the term means in the context in which we use it here. After we have defined the terms, we discuss the two main approaches to cross-cultural training. Next, we describe the relatively recent increase in demand for cross-cultural communication training, and some of the factors contributing to this increased interest among business and professional practitioners in the subject. Following this, the chapter addresses the nature of providing cross-cultural communication training in a business setting. In particular, possible delivery methods and program approaches are suggested.

Definition of Culture

Before we can proceed, it is necessary to define exactly what is meant by the term "culture." While most people use the term culture without giving it a second thought, the term itself is remarkably difficult to define. Indeed, Alfred Kroeber and Clyde Kluckhohn in their now-classic book, *Culture: A Critical Review of Concepts and Definitions* (1954), came up with well over 300 different definitions. Since the 1950s, as interest in the field has grown, even more working definitions of the term culture have come forth.

Part of the reason that culture is so hard to define is precisely because the boundaries between cultures are so unclear. As the anthropologist James Clifford has observed, living as we do in an -ambiguous, multivocal world makes it increasingly hard to conceive of human diversity as inscribed in bounded independent cultures (1988, p. 23).

Still, we need to develop a definition of culture if we are to discuss it in any useful fashion. With this in mind, among the best definitions for a consideration of the effects of cross-cultural differences in a business setting is that of the Dutch management researcher Geert Hofstede, who has defined culture as "the software of the mind" (1991, p. 4). Employing the analogy of computer programming to human behavior, Hofstede calls the -patterns of thinking, feeling, and acting mental programs," although he is careful to note that people are not as thoroughly programmed as a computer so that a person's behavior is only partially predetermined by her or his mental programs: "(s)he has a basic ability to deviate from them" (1991, p. 4).

For our purposes, we can focus on three key attributes of culture that will directly affect the delivery of training. First, culture is learned and not in-born. Thus, in cross-cultural situations, no such thing as normal or correct exists. If I may be allowed to quote myself from my book, *International Business Communication*, what is right in one culture is not necessarily right in another culture. In cross-cultural matters, behavior is not inherently right or wrong, only different" (1992, p. 6).

Second, culture does not exist in isolation. Culture always acts as a function of the group in which it takes place. When people of different cultures begin to work and live together, they begin to form a new culture. Thus, culture is constantly changing to adapt to the individuals it affects. Still, culture as a collective phenomenon does point to the fact that certain things (if not indeed most things) are comprehensible only within the boundaries of the culture as a whole. Consequently, certain behavioral variables remain constant throughout a given culture regardless of the nature of the subgroups to which individuals belong within a greater shared culture. This is important for the trainer because values and behavior that seem to remain constant within a single culture are likely to shift dramatically when transferred to another culture.

Finally, culture is inextricably intertwined with communication. Our culture determines how we communicate and we convey the cultural attributes of our culture almost exclusively through communication. As John Condon and Fathi Yousef put it, "we cannot separate culture from communication ... (although) it is possible to distinguish between cultural patterns of communication and truly intercultural or cross-cultural communication" (1985, pp. 34-35).

Approaches to Cross-Cultural Training

Two main approaches to cross-cultural training compete currently in the marketplace: the catalogue of do's and don'ts and the broad-based foundational approach.

Generally speaking, many consultants tend to focus on the do's and don'ts of cross-cultural communication. These individual issues of communication protocol are often amusing but not particularly valuable to business professionals who must face a whole host of situations and react immediately. Ironically, the consultant is likely to find that the clients themselves mostly demand precisely such a checklist of cross-culturally acceptable behavior and a catalogue of amusing anecdotes. The average clients seeking cross-cultural training may indeed be unaware of what they need to know in cross-cultural dealings, which is precisely why they have hired the consultant in the first place. What they do know is that they need a format that is readily accessible and generally not particularly time-consuming. Checklists, from a client's point of the view, are simple, allow easy categorization of another culture, are readily verifiable and can be delivered in a very short timeframe.

Moreover, the anecdotes that go along with lost catalogues of do's and don'ts are themselves likely to leave an impression on the client because they tend to enliven the consultant's training style. The stories, in short, can be amusing. To the extent that a consultant should give the what they want, it is -- at least practically speaking -- advisable to provide some sense of these stories. Thus, no real harm is done by sharing with a U.S. audience that most Saudis find the handing documents with the left hand to be offensive or that most Greeks will tend to stand closer together than their U.S. counterparts. Anecdotes taken by request directly from the participants in a training program are particularly valuable for reinforcing the importance of cross-cultural communication training in a very real and immediate way.

The consultant should take particular care, however, not to limit his or her training to recounting of a series of quaint tales. The consultant does the client little good by reducing cross-cultural understanding to simplistic protocol suggestions regarding the opening of gifts or when to show up for a meeting.

Unfortunately, the do's and don'ts catalogue approach has several advantages to the consultant more interested in earning a few extra dollars rather than in helping his or her client. First, this approach is the easiest to deliver in a short timeframe. Since many businesses may make an unrealistic demand to provide in an hour or two "all you need to know" about whichever culture concerns them, little real foundation can be provided; the catalogue approach fills the void because it gives the illusion of substance in a short speech while actually not imparting any useful knowledge to the person so trained. If the person fails in his or her cross-cultural assignment, however, the consultant has an excuse for the client's failure since the examples given seem to prove that crosscultural communication is beyond the reach of the average business person.

A second questionable benefit of the do's and don'ts catalogue approach is that it is easier to learn and deliver for the consultant with little background. Anecdotes abound and, as mentioned earlier, are by their nature amusing. A good speaker can keep an audience rapt with attention to the stories. At the same time, the trainer in such a situation need have no greater understanding of crosscultural differences than the stories themselves.

In the end, though, if the training focuses primarily on mistranslations or cultural faux pas, the consultant risks frightening the client away from the cross-cultural exchange altogether. Similarly a list of twenty or thirty do's and don'ts are likely to lull the client into a false sense of security. Even when clients retain a fairly comprehensive list of so do's and don'ts for another culture and most clients, by the nature of the training, will not retain the entire list -- the material is of questionable value since the number of individual crosscultural differences the average business person is likely to face may well range into the 1000's each day, none of which may be specifically on the consultant's do and don't checklist. In the end, such lists give an illusion of knowing more about another culture than impart and, at least in my personal experience, even tend to promote the notion that people from other cultures are somehow amusing or quaint.

By contrast, the cross-cultural communication consultant is most likely to serve the client best by focusing on those factors affecting communication that are most likely to shift across cultures in a business or professional setting. Even if the consultant chooses to liven up the program with anecdotes and selected checklists of the type just discussed, these underlying' behavioral factors should be the major focus of the cross-cultural communication consultant.

Generally speaking, the consultant would do well to give clients a series of questions to ask themselves in any cross-cultural situation. These would be questions regarding the impact on communication across cultures of language, place, thought-processing and nonverbal communication behavior.

Language

For most U.S. audiences, the issue of language is crucial and very visible. In fact, it may be necessary for the consultant to emphasize the relative unimportance of linguistic barriers simply because U.S. audiences tend to over-rate their importance.

Generally speaking, most U.S. audiences tend to categorize people by language group. Thus in domestic multicultural situations, many business people and even U.S. federal government agencies tend to lump all Hispanics together, as if Hispanic were a cultural rather than a linguistic group. It is thus important to point out that Cuban-Americans, Mexican-Americans and other Spanish speaking groups are all quite different cultures. The reverse of this is the assumption on the part of many U.S.-born international business beginners that other English-speaking cultures are very similar to the United States. They are not, as many business people have learned too late in dealing with such varied cultures as the English, the Australians, the South Africans, the Irish, or the New Zealanders. A variation of this mistake when the business person abroad assumes that a speaker of English as a second language is somehow culturally similar simply because they can speak the same language.

More pertinent questions often arise in long-term training situations. These concern questions of which language is best to study or the desire to receive a survival list of phrases helping the client to order food in a restaurant or secure a room in a hotel. These are useful but are better left to the language tutor. The consultant should encourage the interested client to study another language (any other language) as a means of increasing cross-cultural awareness. The consultant, however, should be careful to point out that language training is quite different from cross-cultural communication training and require a long-term commitment on the part of the language student.

So, the question arises, what aspects of language should the consultant address in intercultural settings? Probably the most fruitful discussion of language would, be to discuss four issues: 1) cultural attachment to a language, 2) problems with people who pretend to be more fluent in a language than they are, 3) methods for speaking and writing for those speaking English as a second language and 4) practical matters such as how to choose an interpreter or proofread a language the client does not speak. Several works exist addressing these issues (Ricks, 1983; Seelye, 1984; Borisoff and Victor, 1989; Victor, 1992), and the consultant should refer to these works since the intention here is to provide the direction rather than the specifics of such training. The consultant should train the clients to ask themselves to what extent each of these factors may be playing a role in a given cross-cultural exchange.

Place

Cultural values regarding place affect communication primarily in two ways. First, communication is affected by the work and living environment in which people find themselves. Second, people are affected by their views toward technology.

The effect of environment shapes the world view. Thus, an office is set up to communicate the status of its owner in ways that often do not translate across cultures. For example, a big desk speaks to the-status, of the owner in one culture while its placement in the room carries the same message in another.

Similarly, the consultant must keep the client abreast of the technological differences from culture to culture. For example, dependable phone systems are not a given even in relatively industrialized countries. Even when present, facsimile machines, videoconferencing devices, photocopiers and other technological devices may differ in their availability and operation all of which affects communication. Indeed, technology itself may seem suspect in some cultures where technological intervention may be seen as interfering with God's will or as a threat to a central authority.

Thought-Processing

The cross-cultural communication consultant should most likely devote most of his or her training time to an issue that is, arguably, beyond the range of many communication specialist: cross-cultural differences in thought-processing. While it may arguably be more formally in the realm of anthropology, psychology or sociology, cross-cultural differences in thought-processing is clearly the biggest impediment the average business person in a multicultural setting faces.

Thought-processing can be roughly divided into four key areas: contexting, authority conception, social organization and the conception of time.

Of the four areas, contexting is most clearly in the field of communication. The term was coined by the communication theorist Edward T. Hall in his groundbreaking 1959 book The Silent Language to describe the manner in which one chooses to communicate something as opposed to the actual words used. Hall has gone on to refine his theories of contexting in as series of books (1966, 1976, 1983), and his works should be fairly well known to most communication specialists. Still, to summarize briefly, contexting refers to the information surrounding a communication exchange (or the context) which combines to provide a meaning based on what is not given in words that directly affects what is said or written. The degree to which people rely on context for understanding the full meaning shifts drastically from culture to culture. Those cultures -- such as the Japanese or Arabic -- whose members rely heavily on context to understand the overall meaning are said to be High Context cultures. High context cultures rely less on what a person actually says than on how what is said should be interpreted in the light of the surrounding events and background knowledge one has of the communicator. High context cultures, in short, are not particularly literal and read in between the lines of a message. Those cultures -- such as the U.S. or German -- whose members do not rely heavily on context to understand the overall meaning are said to be Low Context cultures. Low context cultures rely more on what a person actually says or writes than on how the communicator delivers that message or the events surrounding the communication exchange. Low context cultures, in other words, are comparatively literal and tend to take words more at face value than do high context cultures.

Authority conception, the second of our thoughtprocessing factors, deals with how people deal with authority. While this issue extends far beyond the parameters of communication as a field, at least two key issues directly bear on cross-cultural communication: formality of communication and communication flow. The French researcher Andre Laurent (1983), among others has empirically shown a marked differences based upon culture regarding the informality or formality of communication between subordinates and their superiors. Geert Hofstede, in turn, empirically proved that power distance or -the measure of interpersonal power or influence" (1984, p.72) between a subordinate and superior (as perceived by the subordinate) -is to a considerable extent-determined by ... national culture" (1984, p. 72). All of this, in turn, directly affects communication flow and the nature of upward or downward communication within an organization or between members of different organizations of different ranks.

Social organization, our third thought-processing category, is a broad area primarily in the arena of the sociologist. Still such issues as kinship and family links, gender roles, class differentiation, the actual view of work and occupational institutions, educational ties and educational stratification and even the day-to-day effect of religion on daily life all affect the way in which individuals view the world around them and, as a result, how they communicate. For example, men in a given culture often are expected to employ different lexical choices than women. Similarly members of cultures with clearly delineated class differences have access to and are expected to employ a different vocabulary and syntax according to their class. Since each of these areas is exceptionally variant across cultures, they merit the attention of the communication consultant's clients.

Finally, our last area of cross-cultural thoughtprocessing is the conception of time. Time in itself is not directly linked to communication, and it is not the physical nature of time per se that should concern the average individual conducting business across cultures. Yet how we use time itself sends a message. As Leonard Doob has put it, "The value of an activity is positively correlated with its temporal priority, the objective time devoted to it, and the frequency with which its duration is judged" (1971, p. 63). In other words, while time itself may remain constant, the order in which one approaches tasks communicates a message, how long we spend with any given activity sends another message, and finally how often we consider time to be a factor in a given situation communicates yet another message.

Doob's three correlations themselves shift across cultures. Thus, while behavior toward any one of the three correlations may remain constant within the confines of a single culture, the behavior toward that same correlation may vary in a different culture. For example, a business executive may have two messages on the desk both marked URGENT. One is from the boss; the other, from the executive's daughter. In one culture, the prioritization will favor the boss' urgent request by placing it first. In a second culture, the family tie will prove stronger and so the daughter's request will receive the priority. In both culture's the choice may well seem so clear-cut that the executive could easily assume that such prioritization would be universal. The way in which the two requests are prioritized, however, are directly a function of the executive's culture.

Edward Hall (1959, 1983), in fact, has postulated that the entire conception of time is culturally learned. Hall divides cultures into monochronic and polychronic approaches to time. In monochronic cultures, interpersonal relations are subordinate to preset schedules making time inflexible. In monochronic societies, tasks in organizations are measured by output in time and work time is clearly separable from personal time. Polychronic cultures, by contrast subordinate preset schedules to interpersonal relations so that interpersonal relations coordinate activities, making appointment time flexible. In polychronic societies activities tend to be measured not as output over time by as part of a general organizational goal of which any individual's activities are integrated as part of a greater whole. Relatedly, no clear distinction exists between work time and personal time precisely because work time is directly affected by personal ties and relationships. While Hall's theories on monochronic and polychronic societies are generally well-known by most communication experts, they remain generally unknown to most business people calling on a cross-cultural communication expert for training. Indeed, the cross-cultural variability of time often proves to be the most eye-opening material the consultant can provide his or her client.

Nonverbal Communication

Probably no area of cross-cultural communication is more fully addressed in the university curriculum than the cultural variability of nonverbal communication. As one might expect with so much attention devoted to it, a similarly corresponding degree of awareness exists among the consultant's likely clients. In general, most business people conducting business across cultures if they have received any preparatory information at all have run across the fact that nonverbal behavior is different with whatever group they are going to deal with. At the very least, if the client has already dealt with people from another culture at all, they can generally recognize readily whatever the consultant is likely to address in this area.

Because the knowledge of nonverbal variation is so widespread, the consultant **may** be tempted to rely heavily on the do's and don't catalogue. Indeed,' culling examples of nonverbal difference from the clients does represent a good way to introduce the subject. The use of videotapes for even foreign films and commercials may go a long way to reinforce the clients' observations or to provide a basis for discussion among clients with little or no contact with the culture or cultures in question.

In general, though, the consultant will provide the greatest service by explaining the basic ways in which nonverbal behavior is likely to shift. In other words, the consultant should train the clients on how to observe differences than in what the differences specifically might be. Thus, the consultant should train the clients to pay attention to that nonverbal behavior most likely to shift across cultures: 1) appearance and general dress, 2) proxemics or physical distance, 3) oculesics or eye motion and eye contact, 4) haptics, tacesics or touching behavior, and 5) kinesics or body movement. Time permitting, the consultant might also touch on such passive nonverbal communicators as common symbols, color, and smell.

Demand for Cross-Cultural Communication Training

Until relatively recently, executives and training directors in the United States considered cross-cultural communication to be a field with little direct application to business. While the field has always existed as an area of theoretical interest in scholarly fields as diverse as linguistics and anthropology, or theology and sociology, it is only in recent years that cross-cultural communication has emerged as an area of intense interest in non-academic settings.

Two factors can account for the seemingly sudden relevance of cross-cultural communication issues in business and professional situations. The first is the awareness on the part of U.S. executives of the increasingly integrated global economy as an influence on their own business concerns, whether domestic or international in nature. The second major contributing factor is the importance of managing cultural diversity in response to the marked demographic shift in the U.S. domestic work environment.

International Business Communication

The means to compete in a globally integrated economy is probably the most well-accepted cross-cultural concern today. Decisions made in Frankfurt immediately affect not only businesses in Germany but their counterparts in New York and Kyoto or wherever that area of enterprise holds sway. Until fairly recently, however, the United States had not particularly felt affected by the global economy. Even today, with its overall industrial strength greatly diminished and the level of its exports greatly increased, the United States remains more insulated from the effects of the global economy due to the enormous size of the U.S. domestic market, which remains the largest in the world. The size of the U.S. market relative to the rest of the world's domestic economies continues to have its influence. It is extremely rare for a non-U.S. company to succeed while limited exclusively to its own home market. Most French companies export a considerable percentage of their product or service outside of France, for example, as do most German, Japanese, Korean or any other nation's companies. By contrast, it is still possible (though increasingly less so) for a U.S. company to succeed while limiting its activities to the United States; the size of the U.S. domestic market allows it. What it is not possible to do even if the company limits itself to the United States is to avoid foreign competition. Thus, even those companies that limit themselves to the United States have a need to understand the competitors facing them from other cultures.

On the whole, the hegemony of the United States in global business has in recent years undergone a serious diminishment, and most U.S. businesses are aware of this. Following World War II, the United States was essentially the only industrialized economy left intact. At first, businesses considered the appearance of foreign competition surprising. Indeed, U.S. executives and business professors alike talked of the German economic miracle of the 1960s, and then the Italian economic miracle of the early 1970s. By the time of the unpredicted rise of the Japanese competitors of the late 1970s and the 1980s, the realization that these events represented patterns of reindustrialization rather than economic miracles became clear. As other nations reindustrialized, U.S. companies that paid no attention to international business communication increasingly found themselves losing their share of world market to companies that did pay attention to such matters. As a result, by the end of the 1970s and beginning of the 1980s, even parochial U.S. companies began to pay attention to international business. And of the issues they considered important in international business, none has outranked communication. Thus, by 1979, David Ricks and Michael Czinkota found in a survey that U.S. firms ranked communication as the number 1 problem area among 33 options (1979, p. 99).

The types of clients the consultant or trainer is likely to find for international communication training in my experience has divided into two categories. First is the group who deals regularly with many foreign customers or foreign suppliers. This group is generally very cross-culturally aware. However the people in this group, despite their sophistication, may be lacking a system for integrating what they have experienced so that they can use that experience to predict likely future behavior and situations. This group is usually interested in a culture-general framework that would help people dealing with a multitude of cultures rather than a culture by culture approach.

The second group is the client dealing with one or two specific cultures. For this group, the culture-general approach is interesting but, in their assessment, likely to be considered tangential. In such a case, a culture-general model is recommended but only when applied point by point to the culture that concerns them. Thus, a company recently entering the Japanese market may want all examples drawn from Japan even though the questions the consultant may be teaching its employees to ask will be relevant in any cross-cultural situation, not just Japan. At times, the consultant may be asked to address two totally unrelated cultures at the same time. For example, I recently presented a training program to a Fortune 100 company doing business in both Korea and Mexico. The culture-general approach allowed me to address these two totally unrelated cultures equally by simply applying the system to both countries and limiting all examples to them.

Diversity Management

The second major area of cross-cultural communication training with increasing demand for the consultant is cultural diversity management. Here the issue is a domestic one. Companies increasingly face a changing work force.

Indeed, estimates of new workers entering the U.S. workforce over the next decade place as high as 85% the number of employees who will be either women, members of minority groups or immigrants. This represents a massive transformation of the workplace from one of relative homogeneously white male domination in the 1950s to a highly diverse workforce, reinforced by the need to compete abroad and to comply with civil rights and Equal Employment Opportunity legislation.

The focus of most cross-cultural diversity management whether as part of a program including women or as an area of concern in isolation -- is pragmatic on the part of client. Generally speaking the consultant will be called upon to address several issues. First, the client is usually interested in creating a multicultural work environment. This includes how to attract the qualified culturally different employee. The consultant here usually provides training in how to interview employees from culturally different backgrounds as well as providing an atmosphere that will be conducive to retaining those employees once they have accepted a job. The consultant may also be called upon to discuss how to manage conflict with cross-cultural roots.

Next, the consultant is likely to be requested to explain how to appeal to customers and clients from diverse cultures. Here the consultant needs to explain how to anticipate and meet the needs of customers and clients from various ethnic groups and often how to create a culturally sensitive service staff that accommodates the needs of immigrant and culturally different groups.

A third area of diversity management deals with discrimination avoidance. Here the consultant is likely to focus on how to reduce culturally linked employee turnover. Even more significant here perhaps is how to reduce the chance of accidental discrimination and the attendant risk of lawsuits.

The consultant can add to this want list one more benefit that the clients often overlook: the actual bottom-line benefits of cross-cultural **synergy.** Here the consultant can show how to maximize the benefit from cross-cultural differences among employees to increase the number of new ideas or to add a new twist to old products or services that might revitalize them resulting in greater market share and profitability.

The Nature of Cross-Cultural Communication Training

Cross-cultural communication training probably takes as many forms as there are cross-cultural communication experts. Here, I can speak only from my own personal experience as the president of one training firm, the Human Resources Advisory Council (HRAC). Whether the training HRAC provides is the best is debatable, but at least in describing the firm's training delivery methods, the communication expert considering the cross-cultural field as an option in training will have some workable approaches to think over.

HRAC provides both international business communication and diversity management training. In both, the trainers use the culture-general approach described above modifying it to the needs of the individual situation as indicated earlier. The format of training takes four forms.

First, HRAC offers a full range of hotel-format programs. The programs are promoted nationally and take place at an advertised date at a hotel in a variety of cities such as New York, Detroit, Nashville, Dallas, Seattle, Boston, Albuquerque, Grand Rapids, Cincinnati, Cleveland, and Columbus, Ohio. By their nature, the hotel-format programs must be fairly general to address the needs of the variety of companies, government agencies and nonprofit organizations which attend.

The second type of training program HRAC offers is in-house training for a specific organization. Here the program is tailored specifically to the needs of the organization, but is again delivered in a lecture format with active audience participation through exercises and discussion. Also, while the focus of this piece has been on training for U.S. companies, it should be noted that a considerable demand exists for foreign companies doing business in the United States and, to a lesser extent, foreign businesses in their home headquarters.

The third service HRAC provides is consultation service. Here HRAC provides a consultant to work with individuals in an organization attempting to shape a cross-cultural communication policy. This policy usually takes the form of a diversification effort or the decision to enter a foreign market. Here, the service is less a training effort than one in which the consultant acts as a facilitator enabling the people involved to crystallize their thoughts on a subject and solve problems they are likely to face in implementing cross-cultural initiatives.

Finally, HRAC designs a prospective policy for an organization when requested. Here, the cross-cultural communication consultant surveys the employees and analyzes the organization's objectives before suggesting a course of action.

In all four cases, HRAC at least has seen an increasing demand for services. Both diversity management and international business needs are growing concerns for U.S. businesses. The area of cross-cultural communication is a promising one for the consultant with the expertise and experience in the field, and promises to be less of a trend than a long-term concern for the foreseeable future.

References

Borisoff, D. & D. A. Victor, D. A. 1989. Conflict management: A communication skills approach. Englewood Cliffs, NJ: Prentice-Hall.
Clifford, J. 1988. The predicament of culture. Cambridge, MA: Harvard University Press.
Condon, J. & Y. Fathi. 1985. An introduction to intercultural communication. New York: Macmillan.
Doob, L. W. 1971. The patterning of time. New Haven, CT: Yale University

Press.

Hall, E. T. 1976. Beyond culture. New York: Anchor Press/Doubleday.

Hall, E. T. 1987. The dance of life: The other dimensions of time. Garden City, NY: Anchor Press/Doubleday.

Hall, E. T. 1966. The hidden dimension. New York: Doubleday.

Hall, E. T. 1959. The silent language. New York: Doubleday.

Hofstede, G. 1984. Culture's consequences: International differences in work-related values. Beverly Hills, CA: Sage.

Hofstede, G. 1991. Cultures and organizations - Software of the mind: Intercultural cooperation and its importance for survival. London: McGraw-Hill.

Kroeber, A. L. & C. Kluckhohn. 1954. Culture: A critical review of concepts and definitions. New York: Random House.

Laurent, A. 1983. The cultural diversity of western conceptions of management. International Studies of Management and Organizations 13: 1-2 and 79-96.

Ricks, D. A. 1983. Big business blunders: Mistakes in multinational marketing. Homewood, IL: Dow Jones-Irwin.

Ricks, D. A. & M. R. Czinkota. 1979. International business: An examination of the corporate viewpoint. Journal of International Business Studies 10: 97-100.

Seelye, H. N. 1984. Teaching culture: Strategies for intercultural communication. Lincolnwood, IL: National Textbook, 1984.

Victor, D. A. 1992. International business communication. New York: Harper Collins.

GENDER AND COMMUNICATION

Sandra L. Herndon

Only in the past two decades has gender become an acknowledged issue in consulting. Initially the impetus was to provide communication skills needed by women in order to be assimilated into organizational cultures which remained predominately masculine in their attitudes, values, and assumptions (see Kanter 1977, Schwartz 1989). Little attention was paid to ways organizations and their members could themselves adapt to a changing workforce; the modus operandi was to "add women and stir."

Gender issues have evolved as part of the larger recognition of demographic changes requiring organizations to adapt to greater diversity in the workforce with an increasing proportion of women. The 1970s saw a rising number of women seeking entry-level jobs. The 1980s revealed problems women faced in moving up and encountering the "glass ceiling" (Hymowitz and Schellhardt 1986, 1[D]). The 1990s are now witnessing the incorporation of these issues into the larger fabric of changing organizational cultures which must adjust to an increasingly diverse workforce at all levels. The resulting changes challenge many of our taken-for-granted assumptions about organizational life.

Consultants attending to gender and communication must be knowledgeable regarding gender expectations and existing information on sex roles as well as the more recent literature on workplace diversity and organizational culture change. However, more than knowledge is required for success. Consultants must possess both a high level of interpersonal skill and sensitivity to the emotional and attitudinal aspects surrounding these issues. Further, the need for recognition of the impact of one's own gender compounds the difficulty of the task. Perhaps more than in any other area of consulting, gender issues (and diversity more generally) are affected by our most fundamental attitudes and beliefs, often in ways outside our awareness.

Why, one may ask, is gender still an issue? Haven't we reached the point where people are recognized and treated fairly based on their merits without regard to their sex?   One need not go far to find evidence to suggest that such is not yet the case.   The fact that we are still faced with wage disparity, occupational segregation, sexual harassment, and the continued existence of the glass ceiling indicates that the "problem" of gender in organizational life has not been "solved" (see Faludi 1991).

The field of communication has played an important role in our understanding of gender. A body of research has addressed sex roles and gender expectations in communication, some studies identifying and interpreting sex differences (see, for example, Arliss 1991; Fine, Johnson,and Foss 1991; Allen, Seibert, and Rush 1990; Lamude and Daniels 1990; Siegerdt 1983), others questioning their significance or even their validity (Putnam 1982, Rakow 1987).

This chapter will first outline some recent research findings and current trends regarding gender and communication training, followed by two cases of gender issues in training. Challenges and ethical considerations relevant to this topic will be explored.   The chapter will conclude with implications for organizational structure and culture.

Research and Trends

It is predicted that women will constitute virtually half of the U.S. workforce by the year 2000, with six out of seven women of working age at work, according to Jamieson and O'Mara (1991). The implications of this change are staggering.   Our habitual expectations regarding female-male work relationships will, of necessity, be revised.   Women will, however slowly, presumably enter executive ranks in substantial numbers; dual-career and single-parent families will increase, requiring additional child-care arrangements; demand will increase for changes in benefits, leave policies, and flexible jobs (Jamieson and O'Mara 1991).

It appears that most organizations are not prepared, or even getting ready, for these changes. Galagan (1991, 43) cites a survey which found that only 27% of 121 Fortune 500 companies provide diversity training, and that mostly to executives.   Only 15% had formal, written diversity policies.   Galagan argues that organizations who are not preparing for diversity now will find themselves facing demographic reality unprepared.

Clearly the major trend involving gender is its inclusion in diversity issues.   Variously described as "valuing diversity," "valuing differences," "managing diversity," "affirming diversity," or "multiculturalism," this movement has the attraction to "follow environmentalism as our next great social movement" (Galagan 1991, 43).   Thomas (1990) defines managing diversity as "enabling every member of your work force to perform to his or her potential," rather than "controlling or containing diversity" (112).   To manage diversity is to manage people--all sorts of people.

What does this mean for communication consultants? According to the heads of many consulting organizations (Galagan 1991), diversity presents the "biggest learning challenges of the next decade" in which success will depend on the "ability of people to work in teams and to communicate with people who are different" (43). Other consultants emphasize the increasing need for "awareness and skills training, especially communication skills training and one-on-one counseling skills" (44). Leadership, according to Butruille (1990, 53), must also change to an empowerment model rather than the more familiar, conventional model of domination.

What needs to be done to prepare for diversity, particularly with regard to gender? Addressing gender within the framework of workplace diversity suggests an inclusive approach, one not focusing on women as the "other" or relying on stereotypes of both genders. Instead this approach suggests appreciation and utilization of individual differences in order to maximize each employee's potential contribution to the organization.

There are many well-established areas for communication skills training, some of which are included in this volume, which are directly relevant to gender. Below I will discuss briefly some of these topics, identifying ways to approach each within the framework of managing diversity as described above.

Leadership and Management Styles. Most models of leadership classify behaviors on the basis of task/achievement and interpersonal/affiliative activities. Traditionally, according to stereotype, task behaviors have been considered in the masculine domain and interpersonal behaviors in the feminine domain with task/achievement concerns considered more essential for organizational success. Consequently, some approaches to this subject have taken the form of workshops for women to provide training in leadership skills which they were presumably lacking, in essence "repair programs for women" to correct their deficiencies (Kanter 1977, 262). Workshops exclusively for men providing training in affiliative leadership skills were not offered since the assumption was that it was women who needed to assimilate into the predominately masculine or task-oriented organizational culture.

However, training in leadership skills may take a different approach in light of diversity. For example, in her study of female and male managers, Mize (1992, 61) conducted workshops designed to help participants of both sexes. She concluded that a plan designed to help women advance (by learning, for example, to reduce their need for approval) should also include men (who may need to learn, for example, to improve encouraging skills).

Conflict Management. Gender issues readily emerge around conflict management. While the traditional stereotyped view of conflict styles depicted men as competitive and women as cooperative, reality presents a more complex picture. According to Putnam (1983), the bigger problem arises when women are expected to behave in contradictory ways: nurturing and cooperative in her role as female, but assertive and independent in her role as manager. In either case, the woman is placed in a potentially no-win situation because of the mutually exclusive roles she is expected to play. This conflict is heightened when an individual is a token or one of a very small number of a subgroup in an organization. Kanter and Stein (1980) illustrate the consequences of a skewed group for both the token and members of the dominant group and argue that both groups need assistance in managing this situation effectively.

Mere instruction in choices of conflict styles does nothing to alleviate this problem, even if provided for both sexes. More fundamental concerns regarding ways we construct our definitions of both genders, categorical expectations we have for groups of people, and the impact of conflict styles must be addressed (see Johnson and Arneson 1991, Borisoff and Victor 1989). Managing diversity offers a framework for restructuring role definitions and expectations for men as well as women, including managing conflict.

Team-Building. Team-building suggests self-management, resulting from a flattened organizational structure. Long an advocate of teamwork, Weisbord (1987) argues that team building is useful for any organizational change. He suggests, "Most team members come away feeling more 'in,' more influential, more competent, more supported, and more committed to their common enterprise" (310). A tool for managing diversity, self-managing teams organize, control, and conduct their own work (Jamieson and O'Mara 1991), thus empowering individuals by enhancing their competence and responsibility.

Listening and Counseling Skills. It seems a safe generalization that most people are inadequately trained in good listening skills, despite a spate of workshops on the subject for the past decade (see Wolvin and Coakley 1991). Listening appears deceptively simple. However, truly listening to another person requires a radical transformation, an opening toward and acceptance of the other (Fish 1987). Such an activity can form a basis for addressing gender concerns as well as other aspects of diversity in organizations.

Counseling, whether under the auspices of career development, employee assistance programs, or other organizational programs, requires skills which elude many people. If done well, such counseling affirms the individual as well as her or his contribution to the organization, thus assisting in the process of managing diversity.

Language. One of the most obvious ways women are excluded, or are relegated to the category of "other," is through our alleged generic language (Miller and Swift 1980). Probably the most fundamental avenue of influence, language both reveals our attitudes and values and shapes our thinking simultaneously. Even in the enlightened 1990s many people, and organizations, trivialize the impact of language, arguing that it is "just words." Organizations, and indeed our culture, will never genuinely accept women as equal to men without representing that value orientation in language (see Maggio 1988). The depth of our socialization is so great that even some communication scholars and practitioners appear unable to comprehend the power of the word.

To fully recognize and draw upon diversity in the workplace demands linguistic parity. Attention to oppressive language, whether sexist, racist, heterosexist, etc., bespeaks a willingness to acknowledge the legitimacy and worth of those who have heretofore been excluded or demeaned. Nonoppressive language is a necessary, albeit not sufficient, component of managing diversity.

Nonverbal Communication. Nonverbal behaviors are a microcosm of power relations between individuals and groups. Considerable research has documented the power differential between females and males as illustrated nonverbally (see Henley 1977, Eakins and Eakins 1978, Bate 1988, Borisoff and Merrill 1992). Men and women stand to benefit by instruction both in nonverbal competence and sensitivity as well as in accurately interpreting others' nonverbal messages (Kirkpatrick 1983). Managing diversity must include not only the appreciation of differences, but also the leveling of power discrepancies between groups in the organization--both of which are revealed, in part, nonverbally.

Sexual Harassment. An issue that has emerged with increasing force in the 1990s, sexual harassment embodies the misuse of power communicated verbally and/or nonverbally. Clearly a gender issue, sexual harassment is directed at men as well as women, and either may be a perpetrator. A major problem in ending such behavior is the conflicting interpretations given to behaviors by the harasser and the target (Jones 1983). One of the goals of successfully managing diversity should be to reduce this discrepancy in interpretations and increase empathy between people as well as to develop organizational education programs in order for sexual harassment to be curtailed (see Bingham 1991; Hickson, Grierson, and Linder 1991).

Legal Issues. Some of the issues concerning gender and communication have legal implications. For example, sexual harassment is considered unlawful, according to a 1980 ruling of the Equal Employment Opportunity Commission (Powell 1988). Employment interviews are circumscribed by bona fide occupational qualifications (BFOQs) which allow only questions pertaining to the applicant's ability to perform the job. Affirmative action guidelines apply to certain organizations doing business with the federal government and are voluntarily subscribed to by others. While compliance with the law is necessary, mere compliance is inadequate to accomplish the goals of managing diversity. Thomas (1990) argues that organizations, while not repudiating affirmative action, for example, must move beyond it to affirm diversity. Indeed training specifically focused on the process of moving, as Thomas suggests, "from affirmative action to affirming diversity" (107) would be in order.

These topic areas illustrate the intersection of gender issues and communication training, all of which can be viewed from the perspective of managing diversity.

Cases of Gender Issues in Training

In this section I will briefly describe two cases, each of which is a blended version of several actual workshops. The first I will refer to as Leadership for Women, the second as Interpersonal Communication for Managerial Effectiveness. In both cases, as will be seen, similar topic areas are discussed and applied. However, since one training group was all women and the other both men and women, the applications were somewhat different.

These workshops raise the question of the wisdom of sex-segregated training. The consultant should be prepared to offer advice or even make a decision regarding separate training. Thomas (1990) poses several test questions: "Does this program . . . give special consideration to one group? . . . Is it designed for them as opposed to us?" (117). If the answer is yes, he argues, then such a program may be a symptom of the very problem being addressed. He goes on to say, however, that if the program addresses a barrier to one group alone, then it may be appropriate.

Originally, as indicated earlier, special programs were designed for the "other," that is, women, members of minority groups, those who needed to be assimilated. Recently, special seminars have been offered for fathers only (The 1990s Father 1989, 3) to address the changing role of fathers around work and family concerns. Such a seminar reflects the shift in focus to include the needs and concerns of all individuals whereas in the past parenting, for example, was considered a woman's issue.

Some guidelines for decision-making might be helpful. For example, consider the following questions regarding special programs for women (Fish 1983): How many women are employed in this organization? In what positions? At what level is the training aimed? What are the exhibited attitudes toward women, their needs and roles in the organization? What is the overall organizational climate as it relates to women? How sophisticated is the management's philosophy? If an organization has few if any women at management level, has no systematic program of development, and exhibits no discernible awareness of the nature of the requisite readjustments stemming from increased numbers of women in the workplace, then women in that organization may need training assistance at the symptomatic level in order for day-to-day communication patterns to be productive and day-to-day working relations to be bearable. Furthermore, in such a situation workshops aimed at men to help them develop skills appropriate to a more diverse workforce might well be in order. Otherwise, singling out one group for special treatment may exacerbate the problems that already exist.

Leadership for Women. This workshop were conducted for federal agencies, sponsored by the Federal Women's Committee which had as its mandate to provide career development for women, particularly in agencies where there were few women and where women were clustered at the bottom in nonprofessional positions. It was also conducted for members of a private industry consortium which offered a variety of training seminars based on member requests.

Leadership for Women was presented as a one- or two-day workshop for women only in order to promote openness, nondefensiveness, and candor among participants. Training consisted of brief presentations on selected topics followed by application to the trainees' work situation and opportunity to practice appropriate skills. Topics included self-concept, leadership styles, conflict management skills, verbal and nonverbal assertiveness, listening skills, and self-assessment.

Probably because the women in this workshop were often isolated and at relatively low levels in organizations with no history of addressing their needs, they were starved for information, for opportunities to talk about their situations, and for contact with other women. They uniformly took the work very seriously and seemed grateful for what they had learned.

Interpersonal Communication for Managerial Effectiveness.   This workshop was also conducted for government agencies as well as members of a private industry consortium. Voluntary participants were both male and female.

The format for this workshop was similar to the one described above. Topics included self-concept, nonverbal communication, assertiveness vs. defensiveness, listening skills, and conflict management skills. Although gender issues were not a prominent feature, they were addressed under nonverbal communication (in an analysis of status unequals), under assertiveness (in terms of socialization), and under conflict management. Responses were generally positive for this workshop, with applications readily made to everyday work situations.

Gender could easily be the framework for this workshop for both sexes. With the same subject matter, participants could learn to see the impact of gender on all aspects of interpersonal communication and to apply new skills to improve their everyday communication.

Challenges and Ethical Considerations

There are a number of challenges unique to training focused on gender issues. One serious consideration is the perceptions of the trainer/consultant by participants. Research as well as experience suggests that women still face some degree of discrimination as consultants (see Selcoe 1988; Gealy, Larwood, and Elliott 1979). However, a female consultant's gender may facilitate greater learning about a number of communication topics such as group dynamics, intergroup relations, and effects of group process on task performance (Correa and others 1988, 228).

One very effective way of defusing the problem of trainer gender is to work in female-male pairs. Co-training has many advantages. First and foremost for our purposes, it highlights the diversity issue. Co-training heightens the learning experience by offering two models of individual styles, especially true "with regard to content areas such as team building, coaching and counseling, conflict resolutions and interpersonal communications" (Miller and Wilson 1982, 95). In addition to different styles, co-training also offers the opportunity to pay closer attention to both task and process.

Co-training is indeed a challenge, requiring the team to exhibit mutual responsibility and to work together themselves as a team in addition to facilitating the learning of participants (Miller and Wilson 1982, 95). This strategy also allows co-trainers to develop areas of expertise which do not conform to stereotyped gender expectations. For example, a male co-trainer could take responsibility for the nurturing/affiliative component in conflict management while the female co-trainer could handle the strategic/confrontational component. Overall, co-training is an excellent strategy for workshops composed of both women and men.

Another challenge, of a totally different sort, is ensuring that diversity training permeates an entire organization. It is unfortunately commonplace for a few people to be trained in new ideas with an ill-defined notion of a trickle-down effect as the only means of dispersion. However, organizations which are making a genuine commitment to managing diversity come to recognize the need for a full-scale effort. Such a process is described by Fish (1991) in which a Fortune 500 company instituted a workshop on men and women at work, mandating it initially for all of the roughly 3000 employees at management level and above. Johnson and O'Mara (1992) have devised an internal-certification process whereby a large organization can provide competent, personalized training for its employees through a train-the-trainer program. Ensuring that effective training reaches all levels of an organization is critical for the success of managing diversity.

Finally, a danger exists for subsuming gender issues under the larger rubric of managing diversity. That danger lies in the possibility that an organization will actually maintain its underlying competitive assumptions which pit one group against another, in which case gender often becomes subordinated to other concerns. Thomas (1991) argues strongly that the very inclusiveness of a managing diversity approach must guarantee that the system works for everyone. Since a move toward managing diversity is by necessity a gradual one, care must taken along the way to ensure that gender needs are not overlooked.

Implications for Organizational Structure and Culture

Addressing gender issues in the context of managing diversity has profound implications for organizational structure and culture. If there is a genuine commitment on the part of principal decision-makers, the consequences will be far-reaching. Even though all individuals in an organization must ultimately be accountable for their part in affirming diversity, the responsibility for creating and supporting such change lies with upper management. It is unrealistic to expect people who have little power or authority, and are vulnerable to those who do, to initiate significant organizational change. Members of an organization which is undergoing significant change can be expected to cooperate and trust if, and only if, the organization creates "the conditions which can allow it to happen" (Pilotta 1983, 5). Further, Schaef and Fassel (1988, 222) warn against substituting skill training in communication for genuine system changes.

What kind of changes can be expected? Essentially what is required is a paradigm shift which reenvisions the nature of organizing and managing.

Jamieson and O'Mara (1991) suggest a flex-management approach which involves shifts in policies, systems, and practices. They argue, for example, that organizations need "fewer, broader policies that aid in individualizing, provide wider latitude and choice, and support desired organizational and employee values" (36). Further, they continue, human resource systems should be redesigned for greater flexibility, and everyday managerial practices must be more versatile. Gordon (1992, 27) identifies performance appraisals, training and development, flextime policies, day care, and job sharing as examples of policies and practices which must be examined as part of organizational systems change in support of managing diversity.

Many organizations have begun this work. For example, some companies are offering benefits covering elder care as well as child care, developing work at home programs, and encouraging networks and support systems (Four by Four 1989). Others are capitalizing on older workers' skills, mainstreaming persons with disabilities, and educating about AIDS in the workplace (Jamieson and O'Mara 1991).

The results of these changes will be a shift in organizational culture. Values, attitudes, and belief systems will inevitably be affected by the mix of people in the workplace and the organizational structures which govern them. These changes promise to be profound, albeit evolutionary. Geber (1990) suggests the importance of "critical mass": "not only do organizations need a critical mass of diverse employees, they need a critical mass of attitude change" (30). And that, she says, happens slowly.

Organizations in the United States are coming face to face with demographic reality, some reluctantly, some with great enthusiasm. Regardless of the various successes or failures of individual programs, organizational life is destined to undergo radical change in the very near future.

References

Arliss, L. P. 1991. Gender communication. Englewood Cliffs, NJ: Prentice Hall.

Allen, M. W., J. H. Seibert, & R. R. Rush. 1990. Gender differences in perceptions of work: Limited access to decision-making power and supervisory support. Women's Studies in Communication 13 (Fall): 1-20.

Bate, B. 1988. Communication and the sexes. New York: Harper & Row.

Bingham, S. G. 1991. Communication strategies for managing sexual harassment in organizations: Understanding message options and their effects. Journal of Applied Communication Research 19 (June): 88-115.

Borisoff, D., and L. Merrill. 1992. The power to communicate. 2nd ed. Prospect Heights, IL: Waveland Press.

Borisoff, D., and D. A. Victor. 1989. Conflict management: A communication skills approach. Englewood Cliffs, NJ: Prentice Hall.

Butruille, S. G. 1990. Corporate caretaking. Training and Development Journal

44 (April): 49-55.

Correa, M. E., E. B. Klein, W. N. Stone, J. H. Astrachan, E. E. Kossek, and M. Komarraju. 1988. Reactions to women in authority: The impact of gender on learning in group relations conferences. The Journal of Applied Behavioral Science 24: 219-233.

Faludi, S. 1991. Backlash. New York: Random House.

Fine, M. G., F. L. Johnson, and K. A. Foss. 1991. Student perceptions of gender in managerial communication. Women's Studies in Communication 14 (Spring): 24-48.

Fish, S. L. 1991. One corporation's attempt to address the issues of gender and race. The Howard Journal of Communications 3: 61-72.

Fish, S. L. 1987. What people can do: Nurturing straight talk in modern organizations. In The bureaucratic experience. 3rd ed., ed. R. P. Hummel, 207-210, 211. New York: St. Martin's Press.

Fish, S. L. 1983. Separate training for women: The communication consultant's dilemma. Organization for Research on Women and Communication Newsletter (Fall).

Four by four: Women in the workplace. 1989. Training & Development Journal 43 (November): 21-24, 27-30.

Geber, B. 1990. Managing diversity. Training 27 (July): 23-30.

Gordon, J. 1992. Rethinking diversity. Training 29 (January): 23-30.

Galagan, P. A. 1991. Tapping the power of a diverse workforce. Training and Development Journal 45 (March): 39-44.

Gealy, J., L. Larwood, and M. P. Elliott. 1979. Where sex counts: Effects of consultant and client gender in management consulting. Group & Organization Studies 4 (June): 201-211.

Henley, N. M. 1977. Body politics: Power, sex, and nonverbal communication. Englewood Cliffs, NJ: Prentice-Hall, Inc.

Hickson, M., R. D. Grierson, and B. C. Linder. 1991. A communication perspective on sexual harassment: Affiliative nonverbal behaviors in asynchronous relationships. Communication Quarterly 39 (Spring): 111-118.

Hymowitz, C., and T. D. Schellhardt. 1986. The glass ceiling. The Wall Street Journal, 24 (March): 1(D) and 4(D)-5(D).

Jamieson, D., and J. O'Mara. 1991. Managing workforce 2000: Gaining the diversity advantage. San Francisco: Jossey-Bass.

Johnson, J., and P. Arneson. 1991. Women expressing anger to women in the workplace: Perceptions of conflict resolution styles. Women's Studies in Communication 14 (Fall): 24-41.

Johnson, R. B., and J. O'Mara. 1992. Shedding new light on diversity training. Training and Development 46 (May): 45-52.

Jones, T. S. 1983. Sexual harassment in the organization. In Women in organizations: Barriers and breakthroughs, ed. J. J. Pilotta, 23-37. Prospect Heights, IL: Waveland Press.

Kanter, R. M. 1977. Men and women of the corporation. New York: Basic Books, Inc.

Kanter, R. M., with B. A. Stein. 1980. A tale of "O": On being different in an organization. New York: Harper & Row.

Kirkpatrick, M. A. 1983. Effective interpersonal communication for women of the corporation. In Women in organizations: Barriers and breakthroughs, ed. J.J. Pilotta, 73-84. Prospect Heights, IL: Waveland Press.

Lamude, K. G., and T. D. Daniels. 1990. Mutual evaluation of communication competence in superior-subordinate relationships: Sex role incongruency and pro-male bias. Women's Studies in Communication 13 (Fall): 39-56.

Maggio, R. 1988. The nonsexist word finder: A dictionary of gender-free usage. Boston: Beacon Press.

Miller, C., and K. Swift. 1980. The handbook of nonsexist writing. New York: Barnes and Noble Books.

Miller, G. V., and P. G. Wilson. 1982. Co-training: A synergistic outcome. Training and Development Journal (September): 94-100.

Mize, S. 1992. Shattering the glass ceiling. Training & Development 46 (January): 60-62.

Pilotta, J. J. 1983. Trust and power in the organization. In Women in organizations: Barriers and breakthroughs, ed. J. J. Pilotta, 1-10. Prospect Heights, IL: Waveland Press.

Powell, G. N. 1988. Women & men in management. Newbury Park, CA: Sage.

Putnam, L. L. 1983. Lady, you're trapped: Breaking out of conflict cycles. In Women in organizations: Barriers and breakthroughs, ed. Joseph J. Pilotta, 39-53. Prospect Heights, IL: Waveland Press.

Putnam, L. L. 1982. In search of gender: A critique of communication and sex-roles research. Women's Studies in Communication 5 (Spring): 1-9.

Rakow, L. 1987. Looking to the future: Five questions for gender research. Women's Studies in Communication 10 (Fall): 79-86.

Schaef, A. W., and D. Fassel. 1988. The addictive organization. San Francisco: Harper & Row.

Schwartz, F. N. 1989. Management women and the new facts of life. Harvard Business Review 67 (January-February): 65-76.

Selcoe, T. L. 1988. The impacts of female consultants. Journal of Management Consulting 4: 43-45.

Siegert, G. A. 1983. Communication profiles for organizational behavior: Are men and women different? Women's Studies in Communication 6 (Fall): 46-57.

The Bureau of National Affairs, Special Report #18. 1989. The 1990s Father: Balancing Work & Family Concerns. Washington, D.C.: The Bureau of National Affairs.

Thomas, R. R., Jr. 1991. Beyond race and gender. New York: AMACOM.

Thomas, R. R., Jr. 1990. From affirmative action to affirming diversity.

Harvard Business Review 68 (March-April): 107-117.

Weisbord, M. R. 1987. Productive workplaces. San Francisco: Jossey-Bass Publishers.

Wolvin, A. D., and C. G. Coakley. 1991. A survey of the status of listening training in some Fortune 500 corporations. Communication Education 40 (April): 152-164.

PUBLIC RELATIONS

Joyce Hauser

As urban living continues to grow in complexity, new challenges are constantly being presented to the public relations consultant. There is a need to restructure present programs, initiate new projects and eliminate old practices to become more relevant to today's needs. Greater emphasis and attention is being placed on communications, to help inform and motivate diverse groups. Today's consultant must be sensitive and attuned to specific needs of ethnic and socio-economic groups of all ages. Consultants must have the expertise to successfully address the public, business, labor or political sectors of a given community, whether on an intimate grass-roots level or through wide-ranging media coverage. They must be fully alert to the many specific considerations involved in public relations outreach, ranging from community center activities to massive national radio and television campaigns.

Isolation has given way to wholesale involvement and confrontation, and the public relations consultants have come to recognize that they live in the complex world of big government, multi-national corporations and powerful pressure groups, and, like it or not, they are engaged in a continual struggle to capture and hold public confidence.

Corporate America needs professionals who are good communicators and have an understanding of the relationship between an organization and its publics. The official statement on public relations formally adopted from the Public Relations Society of America Assembly on November 6, 1982 reads: "Public Relations helps our complex, pluralistic society to reach decisions and function more effectively by contributing to mutual understanding among groups and institutions. It serves to bring private and public policies into harmony."

The trend today is to acquire greater communication skills in public relations. Top management wants the public relations consultant to be more than prescriptive. Besides writing press releases, drafting speeches, etc. the public relations practitioner must know how to research, examine existing data, collect new information, understand communication concepts and theories, perspectives on attitude change and persuasion, systems theory and public relations, choosing communication channels, and a host of communication skills.

If a public relations consultant is to be different from the majority of public relations consultants it is not merely because they can write a press release or teach an inarticulate person to be articulate. Although both are important accomplishments, they are only a small part of the skills a public relations professional must bring to the field.

One distinction that makes a good professional is that they deal with unique ethical and moral matters nearly every moment of a working relationship and they face these challenges with grace under pressure.

The Beginning

Before you can create a public relations program, you must immerse yourself in the workings, goals, problems, strengths, and limitations of the company, service, hospital, etc., you will be working with. The various components of the system, in the vital inter-relationship between a discipline, specialty or service and the internal and external public must be spelled out.

Before the initial program is planned, the consultant goes back to school. Every aspect of the product and the company has to be explored, so to speak. Everything must be seen first hand and every aspect of its operation, its product, and its goals must be absorbed. Without this immersion, public relations turns all too easily into an exercise in glib fatuity.

Once the parameters of any program have been set we move ahead to establish a system of regular two-way communications so that you become one of the client's prime informational resources, a funnel of up-to-date information and a window onto the world of communications. A consultant must have the resources and expertise and, more important, versatility to move on any given day from a meeting with the editorial board of the New York Times to the preparation of a 2,000-word piece explaining what the latest information coming from the company means to the consumer.

Thus, apart from its strong, enduring ties to all the media, print and electronic, the public relations consultant has superb versatility. He must be accomplished writers, capable of preparing speeches, articles and features geared to the needs of the organization to establish its identity. She must be part psychologist, part cheerleader, part swami.

Understanding Public Relations

Public relations is a service, not a product, and unlike marketing and sales which have as their primary objective selling an organization's products, public relations attempts to sell the organization itself. Central to its concern is the public interest.

Unlike advertising, public relation's success in the media depends upon persuasion rather than purchase. Advertising refers to space in a newspaper or magazine, or time on radio or television, that is bought and paid for by the advertiser. The advertiser is guaranteed the space or time and has control over the contents of the ad (Wax,1983 p. 19). The public relations specialist has no direct control over the interests, projects, and activities of the press. To predetermine the concrete results of a public relations media outreach campaign would be the equivalent of asking a lawyer to guarantee winning a case and to stipulate an exact settlement figure in advance.

Certain aspects of public relations, however, do deal with products to a degree. The production of a newsletter, the development of representational literature (e.g.,brochures, and pamphlets), preparations for a media luncheon or press conference, or bulk mailing can all be priced in full, with materials deliverable by certain scheduled deadlines. But definite media response to a public relations outreach campaign can never be assessed in advance, and there is no way to provide tangibles before the fact (in truth, no one else can either). What you can do is structure a work plan with theoretical goals and remain fully accountable for expert follow-through which includes an accurate breakdown of costs for each area of media representation should be known.

Consultants have to be acutely aware of the complexities and ethical considerations involved in achieving the optimum objectives for their client in getting their message out to the different publics. The value of a public relations consultant to an organization is dependent on how well he or she organizes their objectives. Unlike many other professions, public relations programs must be highly personalized and coordinated with and tailored to the individual needs of any organization they serve. Any good public relations program, must include involvement from within; that is, the organization itself.

Marston (1963) suggested that public relations be defined in terms of four specific functions: (1) Research, (2) Action, (3) Communication, and (4) Evaluation, or RACE. Applying the RACE approach involves researching attitudes on a particular issue, identifying action programs of the organization that speak to that issue, communicating those programs to gain understanding and acceptance, and evaluating the effect of the communication efforts on the public.

Public relations practitioners are basically interpreters. On the one hand, they must interpret the philosophies, policies, programs, and practices of their management to the public; on the other hand, they must translate the attitudes of the public to their management.

Objectives

For the public relations consultant, the task is multidimensional. Rather than an effort that defends the past, a deliberate and conscientious effort must be made to guide the continued evolution of the system so that it remains vital and highly responsive to the interests of their publics. This can be accomplished through three major categories of activity:

Category one, strengthening the system as it now exists -- identifying its relative
    weaknesses and acting to correct those weaknesses so that they may not
    become the prey of critics of the system
Category two, advocating for the system -- telling the public at large (but
    particularly telling specific decision makers) in a convincing, credible
    manner about the values and responsiveness of the present system and its
    great potential for the future, and
Category three, maintaining professional control of the evolution of the system--
    forecasting those detrimental forces that would distort its evolution and,
    once they are identified, taking positive steps to meet and cope with those
    external forces.

All of the categories encompass diversified services designed to increase public awareness about your client, including external and internal public relations activities.

External Public Relations Activities

The purpose of public relations is to establish harmony and good will between the organization you represent and its various publics at every single point of contact. It is crucial that the public be given useful information so that decisions that are made are those that will benefit your client.

It is important to sustain solid working relationships with editors of newspapers and periodicals nationwide, specialized publications, business and labor press, network representatives, public service directors, and producers of radio and television programs throughout the country, especially those outlets identified with your client's interests.

1. Securing television and radio coverage in the form of guest appearances, news and feature segments for the client. Securing print media coverage, in daily or weekly newspapers, featuring your client.
2. Coordinating educational and promotional activities and generating electronic and print media coverage of those activities.
3. Serving as liaison between your client and specific educational or political outreach projects. An important sense of community privilege can be instilled by making the public, business and labor communities aware of the sense of the organization's participation.
4. Generating stories in general interest periodicals and magazines, political magazines, lifestyle publications, business press, trade press, and consumer press.
5. Generating news stories about the company for the major press associations

or wire services. The wire services are the backbone of the nation's news system. They provide daily newspapers, weekly newsmagazine, and the electronic media with the bulk of their news and feature content.

6. Assisting the organization in researching and developing new programs and special projects.
7. Counteracting negative publicity. Negative publicity can sometimes be worse than no publicity at all. You must monitor the flow of information appearing in the press, on television and radio and elsewhere, and be prepared to respond immediately and effectively to all issues effecting your client.
8. Improved internal communication among the individuals and groups in the organization can result in more efficient, effective and harmonious outcome for you and the organization.
9. Establish a Speaker's Training Seminar.

Internal Public Relations Activities

The success of any organization and any public relations program begins with the internal publics. A well-motivated and aware population is the key to a successful program. Abraham Maslow identified the "hierarchy of needs" that you must address when you want to build employee enthusiasm and loyalty. He theorized that after human being basic needs (hunger, thirst, air to breathe, shelter and sex), that they are driven to social needs (acceptance, recognition, status and prestige). These social needs include the need to feel secure in their jobs, safe in their homes, and confident about their retirement. Also, people need a sense of "belonging" and so people seek association with others.

As a public relations consultant the challenge is to satisfy the second and third level needs through understanding and group interaction within the organization (Wilcox, Ault, Agee, 1992). Internal publics are those people who are directly involved and identify with the institution. Of course, each institution may have as their internal public a population that is unique to them. Some of the usual target publics would be employees, stockbrokers, dealers, and sales representatives of the company.

As noted by Baskin and Aronoff (1983) Public Relations counselors and consultants communicate with all relevant internal and external publics in the effort to create consistency between organizational goals and societal expectations.

Trends

Most important is being responsive to the many trends and developments that may have an effect on your client. As the media is something akin to a living organism, with all the growth, change and ongoing development that this implies, it is regularly necessary to re-evaluate directions in outreach plans . From month to month throughout the year, the media reflects different needs and interests. The consultant must understand these various media "climates," enabling her to zero in on appropriate outlets for the appropriate event, project, activity or news item. Moreover, you have to analyze and evaluate methods of approach which would best serve your client. According to Robert O. Carlson, dean of Adelphi University's School of Business Administration and former president of the Public Relations Society of America (1988, p.12). "Corporate information programs in the years ahead must be more "issue oriented" and less "public oriented" than they have been in the past."

The consultant must be well-versed and current in the latest issues. Because no organization can stand alone without the help of outsiders, the public relations consultant has become more important as a communicator to tell the organization's story to the public and such self-interest groups as women, environmentalists, and the like. Experience has also shown that media in different statewide areas harbor specific interests at a given time. The consultant must remain aware of these specific areas of interest and stand prepared in the event of regional controversy.

Working with the Media

While it's important to know the media audience, its equally important to know the interviewer or reporter. Reporters, like everyone else, have opinions and attitudes. To a large extent this determines how a subject will be treated in print. It definitely determines the kind of information the reporter will be after. Interviewers on television and radio are governed by the same principles. The types of questions they ask and the tone of the interview that is set are the direct result of the interviewer's opinion.

Broadcasters also have a format to their shows and a style of interviewing. Some are "hard nosed" interviewers out for an expose, others are low key and merely want to explore a subject. For these reasons, it's important to know the interviewers before meetings are scheduled. There are a number of ways this can be done since their work, and often their attitudes, are public knowledge.

To learn the editorial stand of magazine and newspaper reporters, recent issues of their articles should be scanned. For additional background, back copies of publications are usually available in libraries. Newspapers keep their own "morgue" files. This is particularly useful in understanding how reporters have treated past issues, and the trend in their coverage.

Broadcast shows should also be viewed or listened to prior to an appearance. Some of the things to watch for are the interviewer's approach to their guests, their tone, their style of questioning, and attitude toward issues. If the format is a debate situation, the moderator's handling of opponents should be studied. (If possible, before your client appears on the show, study the opponent's position and opinions.)

For personal appearances at clubs or group meetings, the same principle applies. Data on the goals, interests and accomplishment of the audience should be reviewed thoroughly. This should help in structuring the speech, and preparing any questions that might come up.

Encouraging the press to call on your client is only the beginning. What the company's representative says and how she handles herself is the heart of the matter. The reporter is usually seeking a simple, short, and direct answer to a question. You can best establish rapport by providing simple, concise answers. Admittedly most people do not like that kind of an approach. Asking the reporter questions like "How would you phrase what I've just said?" or "Could you play that back to me?" might help to avoid a misquote. However, reporters should not be asked to send a copy of an article before it is printed. Most news organizations have policies prohibiting this practice. That is why it is important to say less than more and edit one's remarks rather than have the reporter edit what they don't want.

Unfortunately, the bulk of today's publicity output never appears in print. Large batches of publicity flood the newsroom of our daily and weekly newspapers only to wind up in the wastebaskets. The reasons for these wholesale rejections are valid and well known. Accordingly, James R. Stephen, who served as city editor of the Bergen New Jersey Record points out very aptly, "Daily newspapers labor continually under two serious shortages, lack of space and lack of time."

News against a company and news from it should be seen as two sides of the same coin. Both are the prerogatives of a free society. The media generally are sufficiently fair to let the bad be answered, as well as the good be told. You should never try to kill an unfavorable story about which you have been forewarned, unless it can be clearly and convincingly proved to the media that the story is inaccurate. Protest without proof does nothing but fan suspicion, and positive articles offered in the future might be viewed with suspicion by media representatives. Credibility, above all else, is essential to media relationships.

There are, however, effective ways for a company to respond to unfavorable stories; this is easier if good media relations have been previously established. After an unfair story appears in a newspaper, an oral or written reply might be prepared, approved, and presented to the media as expeditiously as possible. This reply can take the form of a suggested follow-up story, provided there is a story. A contrasting point of view does not have to be presented on the same program or series of programs. The broadcaster is simply expected to make a provision for the opposing views in the overall programming.

What could be done if, for example, a TV commentator were to broadcast recurrent bias against the company you represent? Beyond informing the commentator of opinions and supportive facts from the appropriate persons, you must still respect the reporters freedom of expression. If the station has a talk show it might be advisable to suggest that a spokesperson from your company be invited as a panelist. However, it is usually best to avoid public confrontation with experienced commentators unless your spokesperson's facts are indisputable and he is able to project them to the audience.

Some newspapers accept guest editorials and articles. A special page opposite the editorial page that uses such contribution (for example, an "Op Ed" page) might be a good place for the submission of an article for publication.

Another way to expose various viewpoints to the public is to organize discussion programs featuring speakers with different affiliation and opinions. The programs could be open to the public, and if media coverage were promoted, they could reach the public at large. Other organizations not directly involved, such as a university, could cosponsor the program.

The only effective way to have favorable news reported to the media is to do newsworthy work that has a positive effect on the community. It may be necessary to notify the media of such activities so that the good news does not slip by unnoticed. Unfortunately, newsworthy activities that have negative side effects are not as likely to slip by. On such occasions the facts must be faced and no attempts should be made to hide from public scrutiny. Honest efforts to correct bad situation are far better than misguided attempts to conceal. It is encouraging to know that the good will usually balance out if, in fact, the good is there.

Evaluation

Every Public Relations campaign deserves a really soul-baring, honest evaluation. What worked and what did not and why? What was accidentally a success? What could have been done better? Far greater attention and emphasis are being placed on public relations programs to meet inflationary trends and the media's awareness.

To make these evaluations successful, it is important to keep all analysis on a professional level; no witch hunts should be permitted. If something did not work, there is usually more than one reason for its failure and more than one person involved in it. The important thing is to use constructive criticism. Egos, especially creative egos, are fragile things, yet no one minds looking in the mirror unless someone in the background is pointing an accusing finger.

The most effective evaluations are continuing programs-- for instance, annual surveys of what happened throughout the year, what was good and what was not. To say after a campaign "it's all over; we can forget it," instead of initiating an ongoing evaluation program means that you will be "constantly reinventing the wheel."

What Do They Want?

A nation-wide survey sponsored by The Public Relations Society of America (1991) sheds light on how corporate clients select and use outside counseling firms. The study was conducted and supervised by Dean Behrend, vice president of Dallas-based Savitz Research Center Inc. The four activities that corporate clients hired counselors to perform most in 1991 were crisis management (51%), media relations (47%), legislative/regulatory affairs (44%), and product/service news (43%).

Overall, 72% of respondents reported using outside counseling firms. About equal proportions (21% to 23%) said they retain counsel on an annual retainer, on an "as needed" basis, or on special assignments created by unforseen circumstances. About 25% said they were not currently using outside counsel.

Freelancers specializing in public relations report that they're very busy these days. Business is "good or better than ever," according to more than half (52%) of the 88 freelance entrepreneurs surveyed by Charet & Associates, a New York City-based executive search firm specializing in communications. Writing remains the top skill sought by employers. Sixty-eight percent said they use writers for either speech writing, press releases or other communications.

According to the study practitioners "market" themselves by measuring the results of their efforts and demonstrating their value to management. Networking in the industry through professional organizations and conferences are important. "The demand on corporations to communicate effectively with their diverse publics is not going to abate nor is the need for the independent counselor," the report summary concluded.

General writing and public relations proficiency count more than specific computer-or technology-related background when hi-tech firms recruit new talent, according to a sampling of top-level executives around the country." (Kador, 1991, p. 14)

Public relations counselors will make invaluable contributions to the success of the company by bringing experience and specialized skills to the varied tasks of communication. Ten major categories summarize the many and diverse work assignments in public relations:

1. Writing. News Releases, newsletters, correspondence, reports, speeches, booklet texts, radio and television copy, film scripts, trade paper and magazines articles, institutional advertisements, product information, and technical materials.
2. Editing. Special publications, employee newsletter, shareholder reports, and other communications directed to internal and external publics.
3. Media Relations and Placement. Contacting news media, magazines, Sunday supplements, free-lance writers, and trade publications with the intent of getting them to publish or broadcast news and features about or originated by the organization. Responding to media requests for information or spokespersons.
4. Special Events. Arranging and managing press conferences , convention exhibits, open houses, anniversary celebrations, fund-raising events, special observances, contests, and award programs.
5. Speaking. Appearing before groups and arranging platforms for others before appropriate audiences by managing a speakers' bureau.
6. Production. Creating communications using multimedia knowledge and skills including art, photography, and layout for brochures, booklets, reports, institutional advertisements, and periodical publication; recording and editing audio and video tapes; and preparation of audio-visual presentations.

7. <u>Research</u>. Gathering intelligence, enabling the organization to plan programs responsive to its publics, both internal and external, and problem situations, monitoring public relations program effectiveness during implementation, and evaluating program impact.

8. <u>Programming and Counseling</u>. Determining needs, priorities, goals, publics, objectives, and strategies. Collaborating with management or clients in a problem-solving process.

9. <u>Training</u>. Working with executives and other organizational representatives to prepare them for dealing with the media, and for making presentations and other public appearances. In-service staff development.

10. <u>Community relations</u>. Counsel on public relations programs at the community level; liaison with local news media; assistance in executing special events, such as arranging for showings of audio visual aids and participation in exhibitions; and in establishing liaison with community organizations (Fraser, 1984).

Inherent in public relations objectives is the essential need of the company, profession, or service to increase public recognition and identification of itself and its services. Objectives include:

1. To provide a goal-oriented public relations program specifically directed to the public.

2. To provide a plan of public information actions aimed directly at this goal and designed to familiarize the public with the company.

3. To provide a plan of public service actions which will demonstrate social and professional concerns for the public.

4. To provide a measurable public relations program which can be implemented at regular intervals.

5. To enhance public recognition and prestige of the company at the community, state, regional, and national level.

Timing plays a key role in obtaining the greatest possible public relations impact for any specific public relations activity. Because of this fact, timing must become an integral part of planning for all activities which are involved--either directly or indirectly.

It should be added, however, that planning must always begin with a definite consideration of time. Generally speaking, most projects should be carefully planned and meticulously mapped out at least three months in advance, hereby allowing adequate time for internal consultation, definition of responsibilities, clear assignments to individuals or committees, preparation and dissemination of news about the activity, communication with external organizations involved, transportation or expense arrangements to be completed, unexpected considerations to be analyzed, and last minute preparations to be worked out.

Public Opinion

People, groups, organizations, and the relationships between them are the basic components of public relations. As a public relations consultant, one of your primary concerns will always be the subjective world of the consumer. In this private consciousness, what motivates him or her to choose a certain product or service? What motivates that same person to reject another product or service, especially when objective data show it to be equal or superior in quality to the one actually purchased? How does he or she feel about certain products or services after having bought and/or used them?

These decisions are made in a highly complex mental and physical environment. Therefore, the study of consumer behavior becomes the study of many sciences: economics (including the basic concept of supply and demand), psychology (e.g.,cues and symbols), social psychology (e.g., the social rewards, perceptions and sanctions that accompany certain purchases and ownerships), sociology (particularly role theory, and the role expectations of those around us) and even anthropology (the cultural myths, folklore and past behavior patterns that may influence behavior today), and communications (speech-communication models of source-message-channel-receiver-feedback) (Pavlik, 1987).

Public relations efforts to create attitudes where none exist is illustrated in many national campaigns to get people with ingrained resistance because of the human habit to resist change. A steady barrage of persuasive communication, using films, posters, public service spots, news stories, television documentaries, etc can be instrumental in persuading people to change. This is evident by the reduction of in the number of smokers, exercise and dietary changes for better health, buckling up for safety, etc.

Public opinion gets its power through individuals, who must be persuaded and organized. To deal effectively with this potent force, one must understand there is no single public, that the public consists of many publics, groups of individuals joined by a sense of common characteristics or attitudes.

When asked why he never took a client unless the client agreed to research, usually a survey by Gallup or Harris or Roper, Edward Bernays (1991) stated "You have to find out what attitudes about the client are and who hold them. Then choose a method of affecting these attitudes."

Strategies and Case Studies

Formerly in comparative isolation, the corporate America of today is more than ever dependent upon the solidarity and support of their individual constituencies, governmental movements and decisions, and the need to capture public confidence. "Image" has become the watchword, and out of necessity greater attention and importance is being placed on public relations programs.

Without outside assistance, most corporations are rarely in a position to thoroughly and effectively grapple with public relations exigencies by themselves.

An effective program demands round-the-clock surveillance, active staff response, and on-call representation well beyond the ken of the busy practitioner or company official. Working closely with an expert public relations specialist, however, considerable gains and achievements can be made.

In order to successfully create and implement an effective public relations program, as mentioned, a consultant must have knowledge of the workings, goals, problems, strengths and limitations of the various components of the corporation. In addition, it is most important to understand the vital inter-relationship between a discipline and the public served.

The Tylenol Incident

In 1983 the Public Relations Society of America's Honors and Awards Committee gave a Silver Anvil Award to Johnson & Johnson Company and its public relations firm, New York-based Burson-Marsteller, for the way in which the company responded to the fatal poisoning crisis, the result of tampering once the product was on the retail shelf.

Johnson & Johnson management faced a devastating public relations problem. Caught totally by surprise and without very little information, Johnson & Johnson learned from the media what had happened. They were inundated with calls for information. The company decided not to remain silent and hope that the problem would go away. Instead, Johnson & Johnson knew that it needed the media to get out as much information to the public as quickly as possible, and in so doing, attempt to prevent a panic. Johnson & Johnson, together with its public relations consultants, immediately made the decision to be completely open with the news media.

The second day of the crisis, Johnson & Johnson discovered that an earlier statement that no cyanide was used on its premises was wrong. Its public relations consultants immediately announced that the earlier information it had sent out was not true. While it might have been embarrassing to admit your mistakes, the company's openness was rewarded with the public's feeling of trust toward the company.

Through advertisements, Johnson & Johnson offered to exchange Tylenol tablets for caplettes. Two months later, a press conference was held to introduce a new Extra-Strength Tylenol package. They also commissioned a nationwide opinion survey to assess the damage done to the company because of the Tylenol poisonings. The survey showed that 87 percent of Tylenol users said that they realized the maker of Tylenol was not responsible for the deaths. It was not long until Tylenol had regained its full market share.

Jerry Knight of the Washington Post (1982) said about the Tylenol Crisis, "Serving the public interest has simultaneously saved the company's reputation. That lesson in public responsibilities, and public relations, will survive at Johnson & Johnson regardless of what happens to Tylenol."

The Exxon Valdez Fiasco

While Johnson & Johnson has become a textbook episode of what to do in a crisis, Exxon is an example of what not to do when an unexpected crisis thrusts a company into the limelight. The Exxon's Corporation's reputation was bound to suffer after the Exxon Valdez ran aground off Alaska and dumped 250,000 barrels of oil into Prince William Sound. This was one of history's worst environmental accidents, and a public relations case so mismanaged that the public perceived the Exxon Corporation as a company that just didn't care, a company more concerned with profits than the damage they had caused.

Beyond the accusations that the tanker's captain might have been drinking before the Valdez accident, how Exxon responded afterward heightened the criticism of the company. The biggest mistake was that Exxon's chairman, Lawrence G. Rawl, sent a succession of lower-ranking executives to Alaska to deal with the spill instead of going there himself and taking control of the situation in a highly visible way.

Exxon made another mistake by concentrating its news briefing in Valdez, a small Alaskan town with limited communications operations, thereby making the dissemination of information nearly impossible.

Top Exxon executives declined to comment for almost a week after the spill, increasing the impression of a company that was not responding adequately. Public statements by the Exxon contradicted information from other sources. Exxon said their concern was an operational one, getting the remaining million barrels of oil off the tanker. But the emphasis on operations at the expense of public opinion was a very costly lesson for Exxon. Companies have learned that they should have a plan that will provide information quickly and give the impression that they are on top of the crisis.

Public Relations consultants and the companies they represent have learned. A few months after the Exxon disaster, the American Trader, a tanker leased by British Petroleum, spilled oil two miles off the Southern California coast. Approximately 400,000 gallons of oil poured into the Pacific and threatened to flow onto popular beaches.

British Petroleum, aware of Exxon's mistakes, reacted quickly. Private public relations specialists were brought in to augment the companies' staff. The Chairman, James Ross, flew to the scene immediately. An organized cleanup operation went immediately into effect. British Petroleum officials appeared on local and national television programs. The company even went so far as to provide underwater photos of holes in the tanker's hull. British Petroleum's response gave the impression they cared. They emerged with positive news coverage and virtually no complaints from media or public.

Over the last decade, business has developed some clear rules on "crisis management." A company must not only deal with the emergency but also do so with the entire nation, if not the entire world, looking on.

Resources

Professional associations are the best places to network, to find people who work in the field, take the pulse of the field, and to keep you involved in the world of communication and public relations. Some of the organizations of interest are:

1. The Public Relations Society of America.
2. The Public Relations Student Society of America. (PRSSA) is the collegiate counterpart of PRSA, and its membership is limited to undergraduate and graduate students.
3. The International Association of Business Communicators.
4. The Association for Business Communication.
5. Women in Communications, Inc.
6. The Institute of Public Relations.

References

Baskin, O. & C. Aronoff. 1983. Public relations. Dubuque, IA: Wm.C. Brown.

Carlson, R. 1988. Precision public relations. White Plains, NY: Longman.

Center, A. & F. Walsh. 1985. Public relations practices. Englewood Cliffs, NJ: Prentice-Hall.

Frey, S. 1991. A conversation with Edward L. Bernays, Fellow, PRSA. Public Relations Journal (Nov): 31-33.

Kador, J. 1991. Hi-tech firms seek computer friendly recruits. Public Relations Journal (July): 14-15.

Knight, J. 1982. Tylenol's maker shows how to respond to crisis. Washington Post, 11 October, Washington Business: 1.

Marston, J. 1963. The nature of public relations. New York: McGraw-Hill.

Maslow, A. 1970. Motivation and Personality. New York: Harper & Row. Quoted in J. Pearson & P. E. Nelson, Understanding and Sharing. 4th ed., Dubuque, IA: Wm.C. Brown.

Newson, D. & S. Alan. 1985. This is PR. Belmont, CA: Wadsworth Publishing Co.

Pavlik, J. 1987. Public relations: What research tells us. Newbury Park, CA: Sage Comtext.

Seitel, F. 1989. The practice of public relations. Columbus, OH: Merrill Publishing.

Shell, A. 1991. How and why corporate clients select and use outside counseling firms. Public Relations Journal (August): 12-13.

Wilcox, D., P. Ault, & W. Agee. 1992. Public relations strategies and tactics. New York: HarperCollins.

COMMUNICATION STYLES AND PREDISPOSITIONS

Andrew S. Rancer

This chapter details the design, development, and delivery of communication training and development efforts which focus on communication styles and communication predispositions. Although a myriad of communication predispositions have been identified (see Infante, Rancer, and Womack 1990, chapter 5), this chapter will describe training efforts designed to enhance an individual's ability to argue constructively by focusing on two communication predispositions: argumentativeness and verbal aggressiveness. The chapter will describe the need for this type of training, summarize research on those traits, review the development of training programs focusing on these predispositions, and offer suggestions regarding the delivery of these programs.

This chapter will also explore why training and consultation in communication predispositions (in particular, argumentativeness and verbal aggressiveness) continues to emerge as an important and necessary area of communication training and development. Finally, the appendix of this book contains the instruments which are critical for the successful delivery of these training programs.

Communication Traits and Predispositions

Communication traits and predispositions have occupied a central place in the communication discipline for almost thirty years. A perusal of the journals in communication underscores this observation. A large percentage of the research and theory building activity in the discipline has been directed at understanding how communication traits and predispositions emerge, and how they influence not only our actual communication behavior, as well as our communication-based perceptions.

When we mention such traits as openness, friendliness, aggressiveness, and argumentativeness, we readily conjure up images of individuals we know whose communication behavior is defined by those terms. Understanding the communication behavior of others can be enhanced by knowledge of the traits individuals possess, as well as by understanding factors associated with the situation they communicate in. "Communication traits provide a basis for what to expect from others in various situations" (Infante, Rancer, and Womack 1990, 135).

When we interact with others, especially individuals we do not know very well, uncertainty is quite high. Research suggests that people are uncomfortable communicating under conditions of high uncertainty (Berger and Calabrese 1975). When high uncertainty exists, people attempt to reduce that uncertainty. Knowledge of communication traits and predispositions may be effective ways of reducing uncertainty when we communicate with others. Understanding our own predispositions, as well as those of others, enhances our ability to predict and interpret outcomes of communication interactions. Knowledge of communication traits alerts us as to what to expect when we interact with others.

Communication traits and predispositions can be viewed as a subset of personality traits. That is, communication traits are concerned directly with human symbolic (i.e., communication) behavior. A communication predisposition as "an abstraction which is constructed to account for enduring consistencies and differences in individuals' message sending and message receiving behaviors" (Infante, Rancer, and Womack 1990, 143).

Over the last fifteen years, several communication traits and predispositions have been the focus of scholarly research and theory building activity. Communication predispositions have been classified into four categories: Apprehension traits (e.g., communication apprehension, receiver apprehension, unwillingness to communicate), Presentation traits (e.g., communicator style, disclosiveness), Adaptation traits (e.g., rhetorical sensitivity, communication competence, interaction involvement), and Aggression traits (assertiveness, hostility, argumentativeness, verbal aggressiveness).

Many of these traits have stimulated intense pedagogical activity inside traditional secondary and college classrooms. A few of these predispositions have been profitably applied in andragogical contexts, outside the traditional classroom. The following sections of this chapter will detail the utilization of research on two aggression traits (argumentativeness and verbal aggressiveness) in developing training programs for applied contexts. "The ideal strategy for conceptualizing training and development from an interpersonal perspective may well be to draw upon both the established, 'pure' theoretical literature and to look for applications within the parameters of concern and interest for training and development specialists" (Kaye 1985, 46). Over a decade of research on aggressive communication predispositions has been conducted. The findings from this body of knowledge have been profitably applied in developing training programs designed to enhance an individual's ability to argue constructively.

Specific Skills/Training Necessary for Consultants in this Area

Trainers or consultants wishing to engage in training and development activities on communication styles and communication predispositions in general, and/or on these traits in particular, should possess the following:
1. basic knowledge of communication theory
2. content knowledge of the traits of argumentativeness and verbal aggressiveness
3. basic knowledge of interpersonal conflict models and interpersonal conflict research
4. basic knowledge of the principles of argumentation

If an individual is going to engage in training on communication styles and predispositions, it is imperative to have a basic knowledge of communication theory. This knowledge is critical for several reasons. First, trainers must be conversant with the terminology of the discipline. Trainers must be able to understand the terminology and translate it for non-academic audiences. Communication theory provides this terminology. Second, trainers must be able to recognize how the study of communication traits and predispositions fits into the larger context of "message sending and message receiving behaviors." That is, trainers must be able to show trainees how communication traits influence the larger goal of communication competence in message sending and message receiving. A general knowledge of communication theory, with a focus on source, message, channel, and receiver variables allows for this discussion of developing overall communication competence.

Concomitant with a general knowledge of communication theory, the trainer/consultant must possess content knowledge specifically regarding the predispositions of argumentativeness and verbal aggressiveness. Fortunately, these constructs have stimulated a considerable amount of research which is available and easily accessible in communication journals and textbooks. For example, Infante (1988) and Infante, Rancer, and Womack (1990) synthesize a great deal of this research and theory building on aggressive communication predispositions. [1]

Basic knowledge of the models, causes and manifestations of interpersonal conflict is also a prerequisite for the development and presentation of training and development programs on argumentativeness and verbal aggressiveness. As interpersonal conflict is often the catalyst for the display of these predispositions, a basic understanding of interpersonal conflict is fundamental to this type of training. Again, a plethora of articles and several texts on interpersonal communication conflict from a communication perspective exist to help the trainer. Borisoff and Victor (1989), and Hocker and Wilmot's (1991) contributions are among the most widely cites sources of information on conflict from a communication perspective.

Finally, some basic content knowledge of effective argumentation skills and strategies would also enhance a trainer's ability to conduct these programs.

Infante's (1988) text, <u>Arguing Constructively</u>, can bring the trainer "up to speed" in this area, and is used as the manual/handbook for the workshops on argumentativeness and verbal aggressiveness described here.

The Infante text is unique because of its dual focus. It is a hybrid text in that it brings together the areas of interpersonal communication and argumentation. Most interpersonal communication texts have little to say about arguing, despite knowledge that arguing is a ubiquitous form of interpersonal communication behavior. Instead, many interpersonal communication texts (and most interpersonal communication courses and training programs) tend to emphasize how to achieve satisfying relationships. These texts and training programs often stress the concepts of "warm, open, and supportive" communication with others. Empathy, supportiveness, self-disclosure, and listening are concepts which are emphasized. This focus ignores the presumption that a frequent form of interpersonal communication involves individuals advocating different positions on controversial issues, and refuting other's positions while attempting to defend their own. What was just described, of course, can be defined as informal or interpersonal argumentation. Recently, interest in argument in informal and relational contexts has received a great deal of attention (see especially Infante 1988; and Trapp 1990). The literature on marital and family communication suggests that informal argument is a pervasive form of communication in those contexts (see especially, Pearson 1989; and Yerby, Buerkel-Rothfuss, and Bochner 1990 for a review of family communication research; and Cahn 1990 for a synthesis of marital conflict research).

Traditional texts on argumentation usually say little about <u>informal</u> argumentation. Most texts which focus on argumentation present theory, research, and application directed at the formal "debate" context. This approach is often less than satisfactory for interpersonal communication training programs because of the emphasis on the use of argumentation in the formal legislative and judicial contexts.

The Infante (1988) text is used as part of the training materials provided to the participants of the program. It's content follows closely that of the actual training program. The text can also be used as a self-study guide for the trainees after they have completed the program. Participants are able to work through the exercises at the end of each brief chapter, then use the techniques and skills in their daily interactions with others.

Research and Trends

One approach to managing conflict productively is to enhance individuals motivation and skill in argumentative communication (for a comprehensive examination of other conflict management techniques and programs, see Deborah Borisoff, <u>Conflict Resolution</u>, in this volume). Several conceptual frameworks have been proposed which utilize the identification of <u>personal</u> variables in the management of interpersonal conflict. Louis (1977) suggests that the individual differences perspective is a useful training approach to understanding interpersonal conflict. Warehime (1980) also suggests the profitability of employing the individual difference perspective in developing training programs on conflict management.

The predispositions of argumentativeness and verbal aggressiveness have received considerable attention from communication scholars over the last decade Argumentativeness and verbal aggressiveness can be placed along a "constructive - destructive" continuum. Symbolic aggressive behavior is considered constructive if it facilitates interpersonal communication satisfaction, while symbolic aggressive behavior is considered destructive if it produces dissatisfaction, and/or if relational quality is reduced (Infante 1987).

Assertiveness and argumentativeness are placed on the constructive side of the continuum, while hostility and verbal aggressiveness are placed on the destructive side of the continuum. Assertiveness has been the subject of numerous training programs during the last twenty years. Assertiveness has been defined as a "person's general tendency to be interpersonally dominant, ascendant, and forceful" (Infante 1987, 165). Numerous conceptualizations of hostility have been offered including hostility as a "generalized conceptualization of the affect of anger" (Costa and McCrae 1980, 93).

The focus of this chapter is on the communication predispositions of argumentativeness and verbal aggressiveness. Argumentativeness is defined as a generally stable trait which predisposes individuals in communication situations to advocate positions on controversial issues, and to verbally challenge the positions others take on those issues (Infante and Rancer 1982). Verbal aggressiveness is the predisposition to engage in attacking an adversary's self-concept, instead of, or in addition to their position on controversial issues (Infante and Wigley 1986).

Verbal aggression can include character attacks, competence attacks, profanity, teasing, ridicule, threats, maledictions, and nonverbal emblems. Several explanations have been posited for the development of verbal aggressiveness: a psychopathological basis involving transference (verbally aggressing against those who symbolize some unresolved conflict existing, perhaps at a subconscious level); disdain; social learning; and an argumentative skill deficiency.

Clinical intervention is perhaps the best way to treat those who verbally aggress due to psychopathology (Infante 1988). While disdain (severe dislike) for another accounts for some verbally aggressive behavior, it is thought that most people avoid communicating with those whom they dislike greatly. It may be those times when we are required to interact with people we dislike greatly that verbal aggression becomes manifest. The social learning explanation suggests that verbally aggressive behavior is shaped by sources in society. These sources (family, reference/peer groups, environment, the media) exert strong influences on our developing communication behavior. From these influences, we "learn" to approach conflict by employing verbal aggression.

The fourth cause of verbal aggression, the argumentative skill deficiency explanation, may be the most positively influenced by training, and has been examined through empirical research. Several studies have been conducted (e.g., Infante, Chandler, and Rudd 1989; Infante, Chandler Sabourin, Rudd and Shannon 1990) testing this explanation for verbal aggression, and a great deal of support has been found for it. The argumentative skill deficiency explanation suggests that individuals low in motivation to argue have great difficulty generating arguments when they are placed in social conflict situations. That is, individuals low in motivation and skill in argumentative communication quickly "run out of things to say" (arguments) when they are engaged in an argument with someone. This explanation suggests that these low argumentative individuals have weak inventional systems (systems which help us invent arguments).

In social conflict episodes, we are placed in an "attack-and-defend" mode. Our attention is focused on attacking the position our adversary holds on the controversial issue, and on defending our own position on the issue. People with weak inventional systems have great difficulty in generating arguments to support their position, and quickly "use up" their supply of arguments. If the conflict continues, the attack-and defend mode is still operational. Thus, individuals still feel the need to say something to defend themselves and attack their opponent. If they cannot attack their adversary's position on the controversial issue with arguments (argumentativeness), they redirect their attack to the person's self-concept (verbal aggressiveness).

The argumentative skill deficiency explanation for verbal aggressiveness presents a raison d'etre for the development of training programs on constructive argument in interpersonal and small group contexts.   "Deficiencies can be corrected. People can be taught to argue skillfully and constructively" (Infante 1988, 27).

Argumentativeness and verbal aggressiveness are theoretically and empirically distinct predispositions.   That is, individuals who enjoy attacking positions on controversial issues (argumentativeness) might also enjoy attacking an adversary's self-concept (verbal aggressiveness).   This type of individual would be high in both argumentativeness and verbal aggressiveness. While their tendency to attack an adversary's position on controversial issues is quite high (and thus, constructive), their predisposition to attack an adversary's self-concept is also quite high (hence, destructive). Training efforts therefore would attempt to reduce this individual's level of verbal aggression while maintaining their level of argumentativeness. Conversely, individuals can be low in both aggressive predispositions.   That is, while their motivational tendency to attack an adversary's self-concept is low, their tendency to challenge an adversary's position on issues through the use of arguments is also quite low. This type of person would benefit from training efforts which would raise their motivation and skill in argument and argumentativeness, while keeping their predisposition to verbally aggress against others low.

Of course, several other combinations of these two aggressive traits exist. Perhaps the most dangerous and destructive combination would be the individual low in argumentativeness and high in verbal aggressiveness. This type of individual may have extreme difficulty in generating arguments during social conflict episodes, and often resorts to verbally aggressive behavior when in these situations.

Aggressive Communication in Three Contexts

Studies have examined the influence of these two aggressive communication predispositions in a variety of communication contexts including: organizational, marital/family, and intercultural. The research suggests that organizational outcomes are more favorable for superiors who are higher in argumentativeness (Infante and Gorden 1985). Subordinates appear to be more satisfied when their superiors are high in argumentativeness and low in verbal aggressiveness (Infante and Gorden 1991). Superiors were also more satisfied with a subordinate's job performance when the subordinate was higher in argumentativeness, lower in verbal aggressiveness, and exhibited an affirming communicator style (Infante and Gorden 1989).

An "Independent-Mindedness Model of Organizational Productivity" has emerged from this body of research (Infante and Gorden 1987). The model contends that American corporate productivity can be enhanced by nurturing employees who exhibit this trait of "independent-mindedness." Independent-mindedness is composed of high argumentativeness, low verbal aggressiveness, and an affirming communicator style (highly attentive, highly relaxed, highly friendly). The model runs counter to conventional wisdom which suggests that, in organizational contexts, subordinates should not "argue with the boss." The research conducted in this area generally supports the independent-mindedness model. The model offers an alternative to the Japanese management models which stress collectivism and deference to authority, values and behaviors which run counter to the American value of freedom of speech.

The application of the research on argumentativeness and verbal aggressiveness into the marital/family context has generated much interest in the academic community, as well as in the applied sector. Numerous scholarly and popular articles have appeared describing the consequences of engaging in destructive forms of conflict, many of which involve verbal aggression. Research has demonstrated that communication styles in general, and methods of arguing in particular, greatly influence marital satisfaction (Gottman 1979).

Much of the research exploring aggressive communication traits and marital/family interaction has focused on distressed families and interspousal violence. An interactionist model of intrafamily violence has been proposed (Infante 1987, 1988) which suggests that the interaction of personal, situational, and societal conditions may lead to physically aggressive behavior among family members and between spouses. The model also utilizes the argumentative skill deficiency explanation for verbal aggressiveness. In the context of marital and family interaction, this argumentative skill deficiency may lead to greater verbal aggression, and hence, greater physical aggression between spouses and among family members. According to this model, spousal abuse is culminated by physical aggression which is often preceded by verbal aggression. Infante and his colleagues (e.g., Chandler Sabourin, Infante, Rudd, and Payne 1989; Infante, Chandler, and Rudd 1989) discovered that husbands and wives in violent relationships were lower in argumentativeness and higher in verbal aggressiveness than husbands and wives in nonviolent marriages.

The last few years have witnessed an increased emphasis on the subject of conflict management and violence prevention in general. One example of this interest is the Boston Violence Prevention Project (Prothrow-Stith 1987). This project includes a training program designed to teach individuals, particularly inner city adolescents in high violence-prone areas, alternative methods of managing conflict productively. Constructive argumentation is one facet of that multi-dimensional program that attempts to teach young adults alternative methods of conflict-solving.

Aggressive predispositions have also been applied to the study of intercultural communication and conflict. Examining the two constructs across cultures, races, and ethnic background may help illuminate and clarify differences in conflict styles across cultures. This pursuit appears worthy as differences in these predispositions may contribute to perceived or actual intercultural conflict.

Nicotera, Rancer, and Sullivan (1991) examined race as a factor in argumentativeness, verbal aggressiveness, and beliefs about arguing. While participants showed a relative commonality in argumentativeness and in beliefs about arguing, the results also revealed that African-Americans as a group reported significantly more self-reported verbal aggressiveness than did whites as a group.

Sanders, Gass, Wiseman, and Bruschke (1992) also found significant ethnic differences for verbal aggressiveness. Interestingly, Asian Americans reported higher verbal aggressiveness than did Hispanic Americans and European Americans. The researchers speculate that since Asian culture generally opposes argumentation, Asian American students may not have received adequate encouragement to argue and argumentative skill training in the home. Hence, Asian American students "may exhibit a greater preference for verbal aggression" (Sanders et al. 1992, 55). This speculation is entirely consistent with the argumentative skill deficiency explanation for verbal aggressiveness.

Differences in communication predispositions and conflict management styles may be factors which contribute to racial tensions and racial violence. Thus, the research, training programs, and workshops (such as the one outlined in this chapter) appear needed to help stem the tide of racial and ethnic conflict which emerges with an increasing frequency across the country and throughout the world.

Case Studies of Past Clients

The next section of this chapter will describe an application of the theory and research presented in the development of a training program called "Arguing Is Good For You." This program has been delivered to a number of diverse groups and organizations, ranging from insurance companies to student government organizations on several college and university campuses. This section will describe in some detail, the design and delivery of this program to a large group of College and University Support Staff members from the New England Region. This group of admission counselors, university clerical support staff, and college recruiters meets several times each year to provide training and workshop activities as well as to share concerns and accomplishments. Although this section will detail the delivery of the training to this particular organization, the content of the program is rather generic, and can be applied to almost any group or organization.

Program Design: "Arguing Is Good For You"

Arguing is a common form of human communication. We argue at home, on the job, and in many other social situations. We argue with our spouses and other intimates, with colleagues, superiors and subordinates on the job, and even with strangers. Indeed, our democratic society puts a premium on constructive arguing. Effective arguing is considered a valuable social skill in conflict situations. It is an important tool to use when you want one thing, and another person wants something else. Despite this emphasis on the benefits of arguing, many individuals hold unfavorable feelings about arguing and argumentative communication. This training program will illustrate the positive aspects of "arguing constructively." Some of the objectives of this program are outlined below. Upon completion of this program you should be able to:

1. Understand two important communication predispositions which   influence the way you approach conflict and argumentative communication.
2. Discover your predispositions toward aggressive communication. That is, you will (objectively and systematically) discover how you score on these two aggressive communication predispositions.
3. Distinguish constructive aggressive communication from destructive aggressive communication.
4. Enhance your motivation and skill in arguing by learning and using a system designed to help you generate arguments for any conflict situation. This system can be used during any argument, regardless of who you are arguing with, or the topic of the argument.

Program Sequence and Content

In this section, the sequence of the program "Arguing Is Good For You" will be described. While we try to adhere to the time frames outlined, the size of the group and the ego-involvement of the trainees mandate that this framework be somewhat flexible.

First Day Session

10:00 - 10:30 Introduction of Trainer and Program.
This introduction is necessary for the establishment of the trainer's credibility. The program description and the objectives of the program are covered. Program participants have the opportunity to ask questions of the trainer regarding their experiences in conflict situations in general, and about their argumentative ability in general. A brief discussion of the nature and scope of interpersonal conflict is presented. At this point, the trainer asks the participants to outline a recent conflict episode they have had which was not managed constructively. That is, they describe a recent "argument" they have had. It is beneficial to ask them to think about their argumentative behavior in general, but to tailor their example to the organizational context. These examples are then presented to the entire group by the program participants who volunteer to share their experiences. The trainer must remain nonjudgmental during these presentations.

10:30 - 11:00 The Administration of Argumentativeness and Verbal Aggressiveness Scales.
At this point in the program, both the Argumentativeness and Verbal Aggressiveness Scales are administered to the program participants (copies of these instruments can be found in the Appendix of this Volume). It is important to note that the instruments should not be labeled or identified, e.g., "Argumentativeness Scale." This is done to prevent any potential social desirability effects or demand characteristics from influencing the participants self-report of the two predispositions. It is helpful to reproduce both scales on different color paper. Trainers should stress that participants must respond honestly and accurately to the items contained in both instruments. Trainers should circulate among the seminar participants to address any questions they may have regarding any of the items on both scales. The Argumentativeness Scale (Infante and Rancer 1982) and the Verbal Aggressiveness Scale (Infante and Wigley 1986) are employed as the diagnostic tools which provide trainees with a conscious awareness of their underlying trait predispositions.

11:00 - 12:00 - Instruct Participants On Scoring Both Instruments.
Scoring instructions for both instruments are distributed to the participants. The scoring instructions should also be placed on an overhead transparency and projected to the group. This section of the program is quite critical. After completing and scoring the scales, participants discover where they are placed on the continuum of high to low in both predispositions. Thus, a careful and systematic illustration of the scoring of both instruments should be conducted. A separate set of scoring instructions for both instruments, color-keyed to the instruments (e.g., yellow paper for the Argumentativeness Scale, yellow paper

for the scoring instructions for the Argumentativeness Scale) is distributed to trainees. As the Argumentativeness Scale scores range from positive to negative numbers, it is important for the trainer to circulate among the trainees to address any questions regarding scoring the instruments, and to help ensure that a proper and accurate ARGgt (general tendency to be argumentative score) and VA (verbal aggressiveness score) be obtained by each participant.

At this point in the program, the trainer should encourage the participants reveal, in general, how they scored on the instruments. That is, participants are asked if they scored high, moderate, or low in argumentativeness and verbal aggressiveness. Trainers should not place any value judgments on participants scores at this time. This particular activity is helpful because it demonstrates to the trainees that they are not alone in their orientations toward aggressive communication. It is especially comforting for those individuals low in argumentativeness to see that there are (usually) a number of other individuals who scored similar to them. The trainer should suggest that regardless of how they scored, the remainder of the program will help them better understand these predispositions toward aggressive communication, and help them enhance their ability to argue constructively.

It is helpful during this part of the program to discuss the psychometric adequacy of both instruments. That is, it is important for trainers to stress that both instruments have been subject to extensive testing prior to their publication, and have met the demands of reliability (internal consistency) and validity (does the instrument measure what it purports to measure?). Both instruments have been used for many years, in several geographical regions, and with diverse cultural, ethnic and age groups.

The trainer should be prepared to address any individual questions trainees may have about their scores on the scales. Trainers should stress that both predispositions are not static constructs, but are fluid and can change with time and training. Indeed, trainers should indicate research has revealed that training can modify an individual's score in a relatively short period of time (see especially, Anderson, Schultz, and Courtney-Staley 1987; Infante 1985; Schultz and Anderson 1982). This information leads participants into the second half of the seminar.

12:00 - 1:00 Lunch

1:00 - 2:00 Discussion of Argumentativeness and Verbal Aggressiveness as Communication Predispositions.

At this point in the seminar, an explanation of the constructs of argumentativeness and verbal aggressiveness is presented. This part of the program is dedicated to a discussion of distinguishing arguing and argumentativeness from verbal aggressiveness. Trainees are taught that an argument is often thought of as any disagreement, from the most polite discussion to the loudest verbal battle. Arguments range in intensity from being very emotional and loud (both verbally and nonverbally), to being very sedate and unemotional. The key element, however, in distinguishing constructive from destructive arguments is to be able to identify the locus of attack. To do that, two communication predispositions have been identified which separate constructive from destructive forms of argument.

The definitions of argumentativeness and verbal aggressiveness are presented. Examples of verbal aggressiveness are highlighted, e.g., "You're so stupid," "You never do anything right," and nonverbal examples of verbal aggression are also presented (e.g., rolling the eyes, looks of disgust, smirks, nonverbal emblems such as raising the middle finger, etc.). The four probable causes of verbal aggression are discussed, and the argumentative skill deficiency explanation is highlighted. Participants are informed that if they become more motivated to argue and more skilled at generating arguments, then verbally aggressive behavior becomes less likely. Thus, developing skill in argument significantly reduces the chances that individuals will resort to verbal aggression in social conflict and argumentative situations.

At this point in the training session, a videotape is played for the participants. The videotape illustrates different types of communication behavior exhibited during social conflict episodes. The first example demonstrates pure verbal aggressiveness. A couple is arguing about who is responsible for cooking dinner after work. The "argument" quickly deteriorates into a shouting match with both spouses using profanity and engaging in other forms of verbal aggression. The second example, employing the same scenario, demonstrates an argument which contains both argumentativeness and verbal aggressiveness. This is done to reinforce the concept that both traits are separate and distinct, and individuals can be high, low, or moderate on each trait. The last example, again using the same scenario, demonstrates "pure" argumentativeness. The couple is shown attacking each other's positions on controversial issues, while being careful not to attack each other's self-concepts. This underscores the type of behavior which accompanies argumentativeness.

2:00 - 2:30 - Participants "Argue" With Each Other.

During this part of the training program, participants have an opportunity to "argue" with each, and to test out their own ability to generate and deliver arguments. It is important to note here that argumentative skill training has not been covered. This part of the program allows both the trainer and the participants to get a benchmark of their argumentative ability (as well as their use of verbal aggressiveness).

Participants are randomly paired together to form dyads. A "roommate scenario" case is presented to them. The case involves a dispute between two roommates over the financial obligations of a long-term guest. Each dyad partner receives the same case information but from a different perspective. [2] Participants are randomly assigned to one side of the argument. Each member of the dyad is given ten minutes to try to develop some arguments to present to their "adversary." After this time period, participants engage in the "argument" with their adversary. These arguments usually last about ten minutes.

2:30 - 3:45 - Debriefing Occurs.

After the mock argumentative discussion, a debriefing is then conducted. Participants are asked: (1) if the conflict has been resolved; (2) how easy or difficult it was to generate arguments used for the argumentative discussion; and (3) how much verbal aggression they and their partner exhibited during the discussion.

It is not atypical for participants to reveal that it was quite difficult for them to generate many arguments, that a great deal of verbally aggressive behavior was exhibited during the discussion (e.g., character attacks, competence attacks, maledictions, profanity), and the conflict actually escalated rather than diminished. The remainder of the session is dedicated to a review of the day's content and activities.

Second Day Session

9:00 - 9:30 - Brief Review.

The content of the previous day is reviewed. The differences between argumentative and verbally aggressive behavior are reiterated. The benefits of arguing constructively are discussed with the participants. Trainees are then prepared for the remainder of the program.

9:30 - 11:00 Training In The Use of The Inventional System.

At this point in the program, trainees receive actual instruction in the use of the Inventional System, the method for generating arguments. The content for this part of the training follows the presentation of the material in the participant manual, Arguing Constructively (Infante 1988).

The first part of this training instructs the participants on how to state the nature of a controversy in propositional form. Participants are instructed that the first argumentative skill is concerned with gaining a clear understanding of the argumentative situation. That is, the first skill involved in arguing constructively involves having the parties decide exactly what they are arguing about. There is little chance of resolving the controversial issue if both parties are arguing different issues or proposals (propositions). Following the format of the manual used in the training, arguments are conceptualized as "controversies over proposals" (Infante 1988, 35). When individuals argue in favor of a proposition, they are making a proposal to those who oppose the proposition. Thus, arguments are viewed as controversies over proposals.

The three types of propositions (fact, value, and policy) are defined and distinguished from each other. A key concept presented in this part of the training is that, according to this model of argumentative competence, people must recognize propositions as they emerge during daily, informal, argumentative communication. Trainees must learn to recognize propositions by what their adversary claims: "Did the individual claim something happened, is happening, will happen? (propositions of fact), Did the person imply that something should be evaluated favorably or unfavorably? (propositions of value), Did the person propose that an action should be taken? (propositions of policy)" (Infante 1988, 36).

The next section of the training involves training participants in the use of the inventional system. We review how difficult it was for many participants to stay on topic, and to generate actual arguments during the previous day's argumentative role-play. Participants are informed that just like any other skill, an argumentative skill can be taught. Inventing arguments comes as a result of analyzing the proposition being argued (Infante 1988). Once an individual can state the nature of the controversy in propositional form, they can analyze it, and determine what arguments to use.

The Infante (1988) Inventional System for the generation of arguments is presented.   Participants are supplied with a handout which contains this inventional system. Trainees are informed that they can use this handout as a review (cue) sheet during the session, but that the best way to utilize the inventional system is to memorize it for occasions where they are not able to make use of the cue sheet.

The Inventional System employed is the following:

Table 1: The Inventional System

Major Issues and Sub-Issues

1. Problem
    a. What are the signs of a problem?
    b. What is the specific harm?
    c. How widespread is the harm?
2. Blame
    a. What causes the problem?
    b. Is the present system at fault?
    c. Should the present system be changed?
3. Solution
    a. What are the possible solutions?
    b. Which solution best solves the problem?
4. Consequences
    a. What good outcomes will result from the solution?
    b. What bad outcomes will result from the solution?

(from Infante, Dominic, A. 1988. Arguing Constructively.
      Prospect Heights, IL: Waveland Press, Inc. 47).

Trainees spend some time examining the inventional system, and any questions about it are addressed at this time. Examples of using the system in informal argument are presented and discussed. One example uses the system to invent arguments to address whether a person should start looking for a new job. Each part of the system (problem, blame, solution, consequences) is covered using the examples.

After we have illustrated how to use the inventional system when trainees want to present a proposal to another person, we examine how to use the system to generate arguments when someone presents a proposal to them. Participants are suggested to explore: 1. Which of the four major issues (and sub-issues) were ignored by the adversary?, 2. Whether the adversary said enough about each issue discussed; 3. Whether they agree with what was said about each issues presented (Infante 1988).

The content information for this portion of the training also presents several additional points to consider during an argument. Participants are instructed as to how to proceed with the presentation of information during an arguments, and how to proceed when they are defending their own position on the controversial issue. A brief section on how to attack an adversary's evidence is also covered.

It is important to note that the material presented in this part of the training program is also contained in the participant's manual (the Infante text) distributed during this part of the program. Thus, trainees can follow along in the manual, or use the text as a refresher after they have completed the program.

11:00 - 11:30 - Getting Ready to Argue Constructively.

Participants review their materials, and prepare to use the inventional system for an argumentative situation. Questions about any aspects of the content are addressed.

11:30 - 1:00 Lunch

1:00 - 2:30 Participants Use The Inventional System To Argue.

At this point in the training, the participants are able to test out their newly acquired skill in developing arguments and arguing constructively. Trainees are randomly assigned into dyads to argue another case. An "Office Conflict" scenario is presented. Again, two versions of this case is presented, and participants are assigned to be either the support staff member, or the office manager. The case involves a dispute between a superior and subordinate regarding assigned work tasks, and general superior-subordinate interpersonal conflict issues. [3]

Participants are instructed to use the inventional system presented earlier to help them generate arguments. They are told to use the cue sheets distributed during the seminar if they have not had enough time to commit the system to memory. Participants are given twenty minutes to prepare the list of arguments they plan to present during the argumentative discussion.

After using the inventional system to generate the arguments, participants are given twenty minutes to engage in an argument with the adversary assigned to them. Dyads are also told that in addition to presenting their arguments they should also try to develop a solution to the controversy.

After the dyads have completed their "arguments," the trainer requests that one or two dyads engage in the argumentative discussion in front of the rest of the trainees. After each presentation, the trainer reviews the skills learned: stating the nature of the controversy in propositional form, and the use of the problem-blame-solution-consequences topical system of generating arguments.

2:30 - 3:30 Debriefing, Questions and Answers, Wrap-Up.

The remainder of the training program is dedicated to addressing any issues the trainees may have regarding the use of the inventional system, attacking an adversary's evidence, or how to behave during argumentative communication. At this point in the session, a evaluation of the program and the trainer(s) is requested.

Outcome of the Training

Although a day and a half program is not enough time to dramatically alter an individual's lifetime of established communication behavior during argumentative interactions, a number of positive outcomes are usually evident as a result of the training. Upon completion of this program, trainees possess some knowledge of what constitutes constructive and destructive behavior during an argument. In addition, they have used a system that can help them generate more, and better quality, arguments. Participants also have knowledge of the importance of arguing in our American society, as well as how motivation and skill in arguing can enhance their personal and professional lives.

Challenges of this type of training

It is gratifying to observe the changes in attitudes toward conflict in general, and arguing in particular, as participants progress through the training program. Of particular note is their recognition that verbal aggression is a destructive form of communication behavior, and that argumentation is not the same as "fighting." This new orientation to arguing, however, is still difficult for many participants to internalize. Even after the training, a few trainees will offer comments like, "My spouse and I never argue. We discuss controversial issues by presenting and defending our sides calmly and objectively." What this individual has just described is, of course, argumentation. Prior to the training, most participants have been led to believe that arguing is bad, that arguing escalates conflict, and that anger, hurt feelings and hostility are unavoidable outcomes of argumentative encounters. The media and reference groups reinforce this negative and distorted view of arguing. The communication discipline has long advocated the necessity of argumentation, and the benefits of constructive arguing. Many trainees are startled to learn that ancient communication theorists such as Aristotle taught people how to argue constructively 2500 year ago!

Still, motivating people to engage in argumentative behavior is a challenge. This is especially true of those participants who score on the lower end of the trait argumentativeness distribution. However, by pointing out the advantages to be gained by high motivation and skill in arguing, it is hoped that individuals who go through this type of training will slowly and systematically gain more confidence during argumentative encounters. Rancer, Kosberg, and Baukus (in press) suggest that the enhancement of skill in conflict management should develop from two directions: (1) enhancing the self-concept so that the individual chooses to confront the other in an effort to resolve the conflict (increase motivation to argue); and (2) provide skill development techniques to enhance actual behavior during arguments. The content of this training program is designed to accomplish both objectives.

References

Anderson, J., B. Schultz, and C. Courtney-Staley. 1987.   Training in argumentativeness: New hope for nonassertive women. Women's Studies in Communication 10:58-66.

Berger, C. R., and R. J. Calabrese. 1975.   Some explorations in initial interaction and beyond: Toward a developmental theory of interpersonal communication. Human Communication Research 1:99-112.

Borisoff, D., and D. A. Victor. 1989. Conflict management: A communication skills approach. Englewood Cliffs, NJ: Prentice-Hall.

Cahn, D. D. 1990.   Intimates in conflict: A communication perspective. Hillsdale, NJ: Lawrence Erlbaum Associates.

Chandler S., T. A. Sabourin, D. A. Infante, J. E. Rudd, & M. Payne. 1989. Verbal aggression, argumentativeness, and marital satisfaction: Using couple data to test the argumentative skill deficiency model of interspousal violence.   Paper presented at the annual meeting of the Speech Communication Association, San Francisco, CA, November.

Costa, P. T. and R. R. McCrae. 1980.   Still stable after all these years: Personality as a key to some issues in adulthood and old age. In Life-span development and behavior, Vol. 3, ed. P. B. Baltes and O. G. Brim, 65-102. New York: Academic Press.

Gottman, J., M. 1979.   Marital interaction: Experimental investigations. New York: Academic Press.

Hocker, J. L., and W. W. Wilmot. 1991.   Interpersonal conflict. 3d ed. Dubuque, IA: Wm. C. Brown Publishers.

Infante, D. A. 1985.   Influencing women to be more argumentative: Source credibility effects. Journal of Applied Communication Research 13:33-44.

Infante, D. A. 1987. Aggressiveness. In Personality and interpersonal communication, ed. J. C. McCroskey & J. A. Daly, 157-192. Newbury Park, CA: Sage Publications.

Infante, D. A. 1988. Arguing constructively. Prospect Heights, IL: Waveland Press.

Infante, D. A., T. A. Chandler, and J. E. Rudd. 1989. Test of an argumentative skill deficiency model of interspousal violence. Communication Monographs 56: 163-177.

Infante, D. A., T. C. Sabourin, J. E. Rudd, & E. A. Shannon. 1990. Verbal aggression in violent and nonviolent marital disputes. Communication Quarterly 38:361-371.

Infante, D. A., and W. I. Gorden. 1985. Superiors'argumentativeness and verbal aggressiveness as predictors of subordinates' satisfaction. Human Communication Research 12:117-125.

Infante, D. A., and W. I. Gorden. 1987. Superior and subordinate communication profiles: Implications for independent mindedness and upward effectiveness. Central States Speech Journal 38:73-80.

Infante, D. A., and W. I. Gorden. 1989. Argumentativeness and affirming communicator style as predictors of satisfaction/dissatisfaction with subordinates. Communication Quarterly 37:81-90.

Infante, D. A., and W. I. Gorden. 1991. How employees see the boss: Test of an argumentative and affirming model of superiors' communicative behavior. Western Journal of Speech Communication 55:294-304.

Infante, D. A., and A. S. Rancer. 1982. A conceptualization and measure of argumentativeness. Journal of Personality Assessment 46:72-80.

Infante, D. A., A. S. Rancer, and D. F. Womack. 1990. Building communication theory. Prospect Heights, IL: Waveland Press.

Infante, D. A., and C. J. Wigley. 1986. Verbal aggressiveness: An interpersonal model and measure. Communication Monographs 53:61-69.

Kaye, M.. 1985. Applications of interpersonal communication theory to the field of training and development. Australian Journal of Communication 8:41-47.

Louis, M. R. 1977. How individuals conceptualize conflict: Identification of steps in the process and the role of personal/developmental factors. Human Relations 30:451-467.

Nicotera, A. M., A. S. Rancer, and R. G. Sullivan. 1991. Race as a factor in argumentativeness, verbal aggressiveness, and beliefs about arguing. Paper presented at the annual meeting of the Speech Communication Association, Atlanta, GA, November.

Pearson, J. C. 1989. Communication in the family. New York: Harper & Row.

Prothrow-Stith, D. 1987. Violence prevention curriculum for adolescents. Newton, MA: Education Development Center.

Rancer, A. S., R. L. Kosberg, and R. A. Baukus. In press. Beliefs about arguing as predictors of trait argumentativeness: Implications for training in argument and conflict management. Communication Education.

Sanders, J., R. Gass, R. Wiseman, and J. Bruschke. 1992. Ethnic comparison and measurement of argumentativeness, verbal aggressiveness, and need for cognition. Communication Reports 5:50-56.

Schultz, B., and J. Anderson. 1982. Learning to negotiate: The role of argument. Paper presented at the annual meeting of the Eastern Communication Association, Hartford, CT, May.

Trapp, R. 1990. Arguments in interpersonal relationships. In Perspectives on argumentation, eds. R. Trapp and J. Schuetz, 43-54. Prospect Heights, IL: Waveland Press.

Warehime, R. G. 1980. Conflict-management training: A cognitive/behavioral approach. Group and Organization Studies 5:467-477.

Yerby, J., N. Buerkel-Rothfuss, & A. P. Bochner. 1990. Understanding family communication. Scottsdale, AZ: Gorsuch Scarisbrick, Publishers.

APPENDIX A

The Argumentativeness Scale[1]

Instructions: This questionnaire contains statements about arguing controversial issues. Indicate how often each statement is true for you personally by placing the appropriate number in the blank to the left of the statement. If the statement is almost never true for you, place a "1" in the blank. If the statement is rarely true for you, place a "2" in the blank. If the statement is occasionally true for you, place a "3" in the blank. If the statement is often true for you, place a "4" in the blank. If the statement is almost always true for you, place a "5" in the blank.

_____1. While in an argument, I worry that the person I am arguing with will form a negative impression of me.

_____2. Arguing over controversial issues improves my intelligence.

_____3. I enjoy avoiding arguments.

_____4. I am energetic and enthusiastic when I argue.

_____5. Once I finish an argument I promise myself that I will not get into another.

_____6. Arguing with a person creates more problems for me than it solves.

_____7. I have a pleasant feeling when I win a point in an argument.

_____8. When I finish arguing with someone I feel nervous and upset.

_____9. I enjoy a good argument over a controversial issue.

_____10. I get an unpleasant feeling when I realize I am about to get into an argument.

_____11. I enjoy defending my point of view on an issue.

_____12. I am happy when I keep an argument from happening.

_____13. I do not like to miss the opportunity to argue a controversial issue.

_____14. I prefer being with people who rarely disagree with me.

_____15. I consider an argument an exciting intellectual challenge.

_____16. I find myself unable to think of effective points during an argument.

_____17. I feel refreshed and satisfied after an argument on a controversial issue.

_____18. I have the ability to do well in an argument.

_____19. I try to avoid getting into arguments.

_____20. I feel excitement when I expect that a conversation I am in is leading to an argument.

SCORING INSTRUCTIONS FOR ARGUMENTATIVENESS SCALE

1. Add your scores on items: 2, 4, 7, 9, 11, 13, 15, 17, 18, 20

(A) Total =

2. Add your scores on items: 1, 3, 5, 6, 8, 10, 12, 14, 16, 19

(B) Total =

3. Subtract your (B) total from your (A) total

INTERPRETATION OF ARGUMENTATIVENESS SCORES

If the result is any number between 14 and 40, you have high motivation to argue.

If the result is any number between -4 and 13, you have a moderate motivation to argue.

If the result is any number between -5 and -25, you have a low motivation to argue.

---

[1]Infante, D. A., and A. S. Rancer. 1982. A conceptualization and measurement of argumentativeness. Journal of Personality Assessment 46:72-80.

Used by permission of authors.

APPENDIX B

THE VERBAL AGGRESSIVENESS SCALE[2]

This survey is concerned with how we try to get people to comply with our wishes. Indicate how often each statement is true for you personally when you try to influence other persons. Use the following scale:

1=almost never true
2=rarely true
3=occasionally true
4=often true
5=almost always true

_____1. I am extremely careful to avoid attacking individuals' intelligence when I attack their ideas.

_____2. When individuals are very stubborn, I use insults to soften their stubbornness.

_____3. I try very hard to avoid having other people feel bad about themselves when I try to influence them.

_____4. When people refuse to do a task I know is important, without good reason, I tell them they are unreasonable.

_____5. When others do things I regard as stupid, I try to be extremely gentle with them.

_____6. If individuals I am trying to influence really deserve it, I attack their character.

_____7. When people behave in ways that are in very poor taste, I insult them in order to shock them into proper behavior.

_____8. I try to make people feel good about themselves even when their ideas are stupid.

_____9. When people simply will not budge on a matter of importance I lose my temper and say rather strong things to them.

_____10. When people criticize my shortcomings, I take it in good humor and do not try to get back at them.

_____11. When individuals insult me, I get a lot of pleasure out of really telling them off.

_____12. When I dislike individuals greatly, I try not to show it in what I say or how I say it.

_____13. I like poking fun at people who do things which are very stupid in order to stimulate their intelligence.

_____14. When I attack a person's ideas, I try not to damage their self-concepts.

_____15. When I try to influence people, I make a great effort not to offend them.

_____16. When people do things which are mean or cruel, I attack
their character in order to help correct their behavior.

_____17. I refuse to participate in arguments when they involve
personal attacks.

_____18. When nothing seems to work in trying to influence
others, I yell and scream in order to get some movement
from them.

_____19. When I am not able to refute others' positions, I try
to make them feel defensive in order to weaken their
positions.

_____20. When an argument shifts to personal attacks, I try very
hard to change the subject.

SCORING INSTRUCTIONS FOR VERBAL AGGRESSIVENESS SCALE

1. Add your scores on items: 2, 4, 6, 7, 9, 11, 13, 16, 18, 19

2. Add your scores on items: 1, 3, 5, 8, 10, 12, 14, 15, 17, 20

3. Subtract the sum obtained in step 2 from 60

4. Add the total obtained in step 1 to the result obtained in
step 3 to compute your verbal aggressiveness score.

INTERPRETATION OF VERBAL AGGRESSIVENESS SCORES

If you scored between 59-100, you are considered high in verbal
aggressiveness.

If you scored between 39-58, you are considered moderate in
verbal aggressiveness.

If you scored between 20-38, you are considered low in verbal
aggressiveness.

----

[2]Infante, D. A., & C. J. Wigley. 1986. Verbal aggressiveness: An
interpersonal model and measure. Communication Monographs 53: 61-
69.

Used by permission of authors.

Note: For a comprehensive list of works on argumentativeness and verbal
aggressiveness, or for copies of either scenario, please write the author of this
chapter.

INTERVIEWING STRATEGIES

Rebecca L. Ray

Though attacked as a poorly devised means of identifying successful employees (Goodall & Goodall, 1992; Latham & Saari, 1984), the often unstructured job interview remains the primary means of candidate selection in corporate America (McComb & Jablin, 1984). Interviewers are surprisingly poorly trained for the interview process given the relative importance of the task (Goodale, 1977; Lahiff, 1977; Posner, 1981). Without a structured interview and with no or minimal training, interviewers reveal biases and rely on instinct as an "accurate" means of predicting success (Downs, 1969). A review of the literature indicates that if a moderately structured interview with a series of targeted questions can be coupled with a trained interviewer, the possibility of selecting a successful candidate increases dramatically (Downs, Smeyak, & Martin, 1980; Goodall & Goodall, 1992; Stewart & Cash, 1991).

Convincing corporate America that training in the area of interviewing can be a critical success factor is not difficult. They are all too aware of the cost of hiring and training new employees, the real cost of employee turnover, and the cost of litigation when candidates claim, and in many cases prove, discrimination in the interview process. Estimated cost of finding, hiring, and training a new employee is roughly 50% of the annual salary (Squadrilli, 1989). For executive searches, add the recruiting costs of 20-35% of the annual salary. If all does not go well in the interviewing process and the candidate files a claim with the Equal Employment Opportunities Commission and presses his or her case in court, the settlement costs could be staggering. Even if there is no litigation, image the frustration of the staff which continues to limp along without the key people it so desperately needs - losing sales, reducing productivity, lowering morale. Small wonder, then, that interviewing training is a large part of the communication training menu.

Communication consultants who wish to offer this type of training would be well served to be well-versed in a number of areas. An understanding of interviewing principles and concepts as well as the current research in the area is, of course, a baseline competency. Many of us teach a class in interviewing strategies, probably relying on the classic Stewart & Cash (1991) text, where students, after studying the basics, engage in interview simulations which are, in many cases, videotaped for their analysis. Consultants need to add to the mastery of interviewing principles an understanding of the structure of interviewing (or lack thereof) as it is all too often conducted in the corporate setting.

Understanding the pressured atmosphere in which managers conduct interviews and the structured series of interviews which normally transpire in the hiring process are important factors in relating the interviewing material to the workshop. It is critical to know the guidelines for interviewing and the hiring process in such legislation as the Americans with Disabilities Act and the guidelines set forth by the Equal Employment Opportunity Commission in order to help workshop participants phrase questions and present information. Publications from the field of human resource management will provide a wealth of information about the practical application of interviewing principles in light of those guidelines. The suggestions are a natural extension of the research done in the field of communication with regard to gender, diversity, conflict, listening, response strategies, nonverbal communication, impression management, and interpersonal communication.

Given the need to present information about the structure of the interview and the role of the interviewer, a workshop should devise a way of disseminating that information without running the risk of alienating a group of successful executives who probably feel as though they do well enough at the task of interviewing as it is. This initial revelation about the lack of interviewing training that is the case in most of America must be handled in a way that does not offend while at the same time creating the kind of atmosphere where trainees can take risks and try new skills. Finally, participants need to acknowledge that the interview process, from the interviewer's chair, must be a continual process of self-observation and evaluation in order for real change to occur. Training is intended only as a launching point.

Given what the research indicates about the relative importance of the face-to-face employment interview and the lack of training for provided to the interviewer, a two-day workshop for managers could address the major concerns of the organization (careful employee selection, adherence to EEOA and ADA guidelines, and avoidance of litigation) as well as the concerns of the interviewers (avoiding costly mistakes, highlighting the organization's best points, and controlling aspects of nonverbal behavior and interpersonal communication in order to increase the supportive nature of the interview process). Critical to this training is the use of the videocamera to allow participants to monitor their own nonverbal behavior.

Interviewing Basics

In an attempt to produce real change in the interviewing setting, the communication consultant will need to cover not only the communication aspects of the interchange but the legal parameters as well.   While interviewing incorporates by necessity a variety of communication skills in order to be effective, it is possible to convey to trainees information which will make an impact on the quality of the interviewing process.   All of this must be done with a great deal of sensitivity to the fact that managers most often believe that they are successful interviewers.

Nonverbal communication plays a key role in the interview setting. Because there is an imbalance of power inherent in the interview setting, trainees need to know that their body language will communicate attitudes to the applicant which may influence the applicant's response which may, in turn, influence the interviewer's response to the candidate (Goleman, 1986; Goodall & Goodall, 1992; Knapp, 1980; Leathers, 1992; Duncan, 1974). Burgoon, Buller and Woodall (1989) discuss the impact of an applicant's paralanguage, gender, and mode of presentation on impression management. These factors, as well as the nonverbal communication of the interviewer, are important areas to discuss with trainees so that they can monitor their own behavior as well as that of the applicant.

Trainees need to be aware of their management style.   Extensive work has been done with personality testing.   Using the Myers-Briggs Type Indicator (MBTI), trainees can not only understand the kind of person they are but also the kind of manager their employees must deal with.   Benfari (1991) takes the principles of the MBTI and applies it to a variety of settings; as part of the total picture of the manager, he explores the "dark side" of management. Because so many executives have already become familiar with the MBTI, it is a natural extension to talk about its implications in the interview setting.

Critical to the success of the interview is the ability of the interviewer to structure the interview so that it determines key areas of interest necessary for the decision-making process.   Trainees need to have a structure within which to obtain information.   To that end, the trainees should have a variety of formats from which to choose and know the value of each.   Questioning strategies should also be discussed so that the maximum amount of information can be obtained from the candidates.   The 80/20 split is a guideline for the minimal portion of the interview the interviewer should spend talking.

Questioning strategies, the design of questions, the order of questions, and the areas of probing are discussed as they relate to the success of the interview setting.   No training session is complete without an overview of the legal landmines inherent in the interview.   Trainees need to have current information about EEOC guidelines and be able to justify any question asked in the interview as a bona fide occupational question (BFOQ).

The Interviewing Workshop

What follows is a non-industry specific workshop designed for twelve middle managers who are responsible for the initial screening interview and upon whom companies depend for accurate and detailed information with which to decide whether or not to continue the interview process with particular candidates.

"Effective Employment Interviewing Skills for Managers"

Day One
(8:30 am - 5:00 pm)

30 minutes   *Introductions*

Participants introduce themselves (name, office, how long with the company, and favorite interviewing question and answer). I tell them that after a short exercise, I will provide more detail about the next two days.

60 minutes   *Icebreaker: Interview Jeopardy*
                         Categories include: BFOQs, EEOA, ADA, Bits and
                         Pieces, and Famous Lawsuits

Participants divide into three teams of four, select one member of the team to start and then play the game which is modeled after the original. At intervals, the team representative is replaced by another and the game continues. The purpose of the game is to test their prior knowledge about federal guidelines. As each question is answered, the response is corrected, if necessary, by illuminating the question. At the end of the game, we have done several things: we have gotten to know each other as all have actively participated and are much more likely to continue to do so, the trainees have learned that there are many things that they do not know and, thus, have perhaps decided that this workshop may have value afterall, and we have set the tone for the remainder of the workshop.

45 minutes   *Discussion: The Interview Setting*

After giving them an overview of the workshop, I ask participants to tell me what they hope to gain from this workshop. I write the responses on a flipchart and attach the list to the wall. I tell them that we will cross-check the list at the end of tomorrow. I ask for their input as we discuss the nature of the interview setting and determining what to look for in a candidate. I ask them to tell me what qualities they look for in a candidate and I list the responses on the flipchart. Almost without exception, the responses can be broken down into these categories: Ego, Achievement, Courage, Focus, and Discipline. I then present a chart for recording the applicant responses that indicate those qualities during an interview. We discuss the role of the interviewer as information-seeker as well as information-provider, using the 80% interviewee and 20% interviewer time split.

15 minutes   *Break*

90 minutes   *Discussion: Your Interviewer/Personality Style*

I discuss the Myers-Briggs Type Indicator as a means of understanding their personality style and how it interacts with that of others. Based on the work of Carl Jung, the four major personality types are sensors, who relate to experience through sensory perceptions and are present-oriented do-ers; feelers who relate to experience through emotional reactions and thrive on human contact; thinkers who are logical, systematic, orderly, structured, and data-oriented; and intuitors who conceive ideas, look to the future, and are concerned with planning and setting goals. I ask participants to make an educated guess as to which type they might be. Then, I reveal the results of the MBTI, which they completed and returned for scoring prior to the workshop.

This leads to a discussion of common pitfalls: making an immediate judgement and seeing through that filter, imposing one's own attitudes and values on the situation and/or the candidate; falling for the concept of "mutual fit," that is, being very much like the interviewer or like the company profile. We discuss the "halo" effect and the "smart" applicant who uses verbal and nonverbal techniques to model and pace the interviewer.

The goal of this section is have participants know their personality type, understand its positive and negative aspects, and adjust for a more open and flexible style which will help put candidates at ease and build rapport. Before breaking for lunch, I ask participants to outline the interview structure they use most often and prepare a list of questions they commonly ask applicants in each setting and bring it back to the training room after lunch.

90 minutes   *Lunch and Preparation*

90 minutes   *Interview Structure*

After returning, I ask one of the participants to outline the interview structure. Invariably, the structure looks like: introduction, body, and conclusion. After discussion, I reframe the interview into these goals: establish rapport, explain purpose, gather predictive information, describe the position and the organization, answer questions and allow for candidate input, and terminate. I ask for a breakdown of exactly what is covered in each of those sections. I offer the 4Cs of resume scrutiny: "completion, care, congratulations, concerns." I then discuss with the participants the structure, the relative length of each section, methods of organizing the body of the interview (funnel, inverted funnel, tunnel, covertly sequenced, and freeform), the areas to ask about (experience, accomplishments, education, personality, and applicant concerns), and the types of questions (open-ended, closed, follow-up, probing, leading, and mirror). Before the break, I give participants a list of poorly phrased questions to rephrase.

30 minutes   *Break and Preparation*

30 minutes   *Question Revision*

Participants are asked to take one sheet of the flipchart paper and write the awkward question and the revised one below it. We discuss them briefly. I offer suggestions about the practice of notetaking and their legal implications.

60 minutes   *Strategies for the Interviewer*

I facilitate discussion regarding the difficult or the evasive applicant and offer response strategies. For example, when applicants are evasive, the interviewer can adopt a number of strategies in order to refocus the question or pinpoint the response. When applicants are verbose, interviewers can make the most of the 80/20 split by having the applicant provide more concrete information and more direct answers. Before describing the interview simulations for the next day, I ask if there are any questions that they have regarding any of the area covered. After those questions have been answered, I tell participants that they will be involved in two twenty-minute interview simulations and will role-play both interviewee and interviewer during the day. To that end they will be given a brief overview of the simulation, the personality type to portray they will be involved in, and a mock resume to review for their stint as an applicant. Trainees will be given copies of the book <u>LifeType</u> which will allow them to read the section which matches their test result and that of the types they are to portray. In addition, they will be given a human resources overview of hiring guidelines for reference.

Sample simulation "personality types," similar to those below, detailed job descriptions, company profiles, and applicant "resumes" are given to the participants in preparation for the next day.

<u>SIMULATION A</u>

<u>Manager</u>. You are the manager whose personality style is "feeler." You have never met this applicant who comes right out of college, your alma mater. You know that you can spot successful material by the way in which people interact. Make every effort to use nonverbal communication to make the applicant feel at ease.

<u>Applicant</u>. Your personality style is "sensor." You are a graduating senior and want to follow in your father's footsteps: same school, same fraternity, successful broker, etc. You may have a difficult time describing it, but you know that a broker is what you want to be. You are greatly impressed with the hallowed halls of company X and very nervous about this important interview. You have worked very hard on the "right" answers to the questions you feel sure will be asked. You feel that your weak points are lack of experience and youth. You feel that your strong points are dedication and drive and have been all of your life as evidenced by...

SIMULATION B

<u>Manager</u>. Your personality style is "intuitor." You are able to run a successful office because you run "a tight ship." You expect a great deal from employees and no less from yourself. You have very definite ideas about how even your office can improve itself and you have projected what the office can do within the next few months and years to achieve those goals. You have an appointment in 30 minutes and will need to cut the interview shorter than you would like and may not have time to look at all of the materials the applicant has brought.

<u>Applicant</u>. Your personality style is "thinker." You are a recently retired military officer whose combat duty and leadership experience have been recognized many times. You hope to take that experience and parlay it into a successful career. You have a resume that lists every honor, achievement, and activity you have had. You have brought letters from commanding officers and samples of projects on which you have worked. You are still adjusting to civilian life but look forward to its challenges.

Day Two
(8:30 am - 5:45 pm)

30 minutes   *Overview of Simulation Schedule and Questions*

After allowing for any questions participants may have from the previous day's work, I walk through the simulation schedule. During each block of time during which the simulations occur, other participants remain in the room and offer feedback. After each simulation ends, those two participants will take their videotape to a breakout room, view it, and return to the main room when finished to provide feedback for the others.

90 minutes   *Interview Simulations*

Pairs A, B, and C complete simulations. Others provide feedback.

15 minutes   *Break*

90 minutes   *Interview Simulations*

Pairs D, E, and F complete simulations. Others provide feedback.

30 minutes   *Group Feedback and Questions Session*

With the entire group, the simulations are analyzed in terms of adherence to the interviewing practices discussed in the previous day's session as well as the participant's reactions to the videotape of their performance in terms of nonverbal communication, language choices, transitions, control of the interview, etc.

60 minutes   *Lunch and Preparation*

90 minutes   *Interview Simulations*

Pairs D, E, and F complete simulations. Others provide feedback.

15 minutes   *Break*

90 minutes   *Interview Simulations*

Pairs A, B, and C complete simulations. Others provide feedback.

60 minutes   *Group Feedback and Questions Session*

Final analysis of the simulations with the group. All participants are encouraged to discuss the value of the videotaped simulations. I review the list of goals the participants had for the workshop and check to see that any remaining questions are addressed.

It should be noted that this is a relatively expensive workshop for the client because of the relatively small number of trainees per session, the need to purchase and have scored the MBTI, copies of LifeType, videocamera rental, handbooks, participant reference materials, and prizes.

This workshop generally has good reviews. What managers indicate at the end of the two-day session is that they were now much more aware of the role of nonverbal communication in the presentation of themselves and the company to the prospective employee. Many had not seen themselves in this type of interaction on videotape and appreciated the opportunity to do so. Managers realized how much they needed to know about federal guidelines in order to limit the exposure to litigation. Most managers cited the ability to interact with other managers about the interview process and the number one benefit of the workshop.

Swink (1993) offers these guidelines for conducting simulations: establish rapport with participants long before asking them to become involved with the simulations, set up as much realism in the format and in the surroundings as possible, find ways to bring in observers and make them accountable for the quality of the entire process, and bring the simulation to closure by relating it back to the concepts introduced before the simulation.

Critical to the success of this workshop is the facilitation skill of the instructor. Slick (1993) cites the critical ability of the facilitator to draw information out from the trainees and ask the right questions rather than simply impart knowledge.

References

Benfari, R. 1991. Understanding your management style. New York: Lexington Books.

Burgoon, J., D. Buller, & W. G. Woodall. 1989. Nonverbal communication: The unspoken language. New York: Harper & Row.

Downs, C. W. 1969. Perceptions of the selection interview. Personnel administration, (May/June): 8-23.

Downs, C. W., G. P. Smeyak, & E. Martin. 1980. Professional Interviewing. New York: Harper & Row.

Duncan, S. (1974) Some signals and rules for taking speaking turns in conversations. In Nonverbal communication, ed. S. Weitz, 298-311. New York: Oxford University Press.

Goleman, Daniel. 1986. Studies point to power of nonverbal signals. New York Times, 8 April, C1.

Goodall, D. B. & H. L. Goodall. 1992. The employment interview: A selective review of the literature with implications for communication research. In Readings in organizational communication, ed. K. L. Hutchinson, 372-382. Dubuque, IA: Wm. C. Brown.

Goodale, J. G. 1977. Tailoring the selection interview to the job. In Readings in interpersonal and organizational communication, 3d ed., eds. R. C. Huseman, C. M. Logue, & D. L. Freshley, 433-441. Boston: Holbrook.

Hequet, M. 1993. The intricacies of interviewing. Training (April): 31-36.

Hirsh, S. & Kummerow, J. 1989. LifeTypes. New York: Warner.

Hutchinson, K. L. 1992. Personnel administrators' preferences for resume content: A survey and review of empirically based conclusion. In Readings in organizational communication, ed. K. L. Hutchinson, 364-371. Dubuque, IA: Wm. C. Brown.

Knapp, M. 1980. Essentials of nonverbal communication. New York: Holt, Rinehart, and Winston.

Lahiff, J. M. 1977. Interviewing for result. In Readings in interpersonal and organizational communication, 3d ed., eds. R. C. Huseman, C. M. Logue, & D. L. Freshley, D. L., 395-414. Boston: Holbrook.

Latham, G. P. & L. M. Saari. 1984. Do people do what they say? Further studies on the situational interview. Journal of Applied Psychology 69: 569-573.

Leathers, D. G. 1992. Successful nonverbal communication. 2nd ed. New York: Macmillan.

Mandel, J. E. 1977. A strategy for selecting and phrasing questions in an interview. In Readings in interpersonal and organizational communication, 3d ed., eds. R. C. Huseman, C. M. Logue, & D. L . Freshley, 427-441. Boston: Holbrook.

McComb, K. B., & F. M. Jablin. 1984. Verbal correlates of interviewer empathetic listening and employment interview outcomes. Communication Monographs 51: 353-371.

Posner, B. Z. 1981. Comparing recruiter, student, and faculty perceptions of important applicant and job characteristics. Personnel psychology 34: 329-339.

Ralston, S. M. 1993. Applicant communication satisfaction, intent to accept second interview offers, and recruiter communication style. Journal of Applied Communication Research, 21: 53-65.

Ray, R. L. & A. Squadrilli. 1989. What's your interviewing IQ? Executive Female, May/June, 31.

Schmidt, P. 1988. Ask the right questions before taking that new job. Financial Manager, November/December, 70.

Slack, K. 1993. Training for the real thing. Training & Development (May): 79-85.

Squadrilli, A. 1989. How to hire the right person. Financial Manager July/August, 72.

Stewart, C. & C. J. Cash. 1991. Interviewing principles and practices. 6th ed. Dubuque, IA: Wm.C. Brown.

Suters, E. T. 1993. The unnatural act of management. New York: HarperBusiness.

Swink, D. F. 1993. Role-play your way to learning. Training & Development (May):91-97.

CONTRIBUTOR PROFILES

Deborah Borisoff (Ph.D., New York University) is Associate Professor and Director of Speech and Interpersonal Communication, and Deputy Chair of the Department of Culture and Communication at New York University. Deborah is the co-editor of *Women and Men Communicating* (Harcourt Brace Jovanovich, 1993) and *The Power to Communicate* (Waveland Press, 1985), *Conflict Management* (Prentice-Hall, 1989), and *Listening in Everyday Life* (University Press of America, 1991) and is the co-author or co-editor of three additional books on communication. She has published twenty book chapters and articles, and has presented nearly 100 convention papers and keynote addresses at state, regional, national, and international conferences. In addition, she has served as a communication consultant to Fortune 500 companies, government agencies, and individual executives. The former president of the New York State Speech Communication Association, she currently serves as the editor of The Speech Communication Annual.

Judi Brownell (Ph.D., Syracuse University) is Associate Professor of Managerial Communication at the School of Hotel Administration, Cornell University. She teaches graduate and undergraduate courses in organizational and managerial communication and participates regularly in the School's executive education programs. She has served as a consultant and has designed and conducted training programs for a wide range of service, educational, and other organizations. She is the author of *Building Active Listening Skills* (Prentice-Hall, 1986) and co-author of *Organizational Communication and Behavior: Communicating for Improved Performance 2+2=5* (Holt, Rinehart, and Winston, 1989). The author of more than forty scholarly articles, Judi is currently president of the International Listening Association and past president of the Southern Tier Chapter of the American Society for Training and Development.

Joyce Hauser (Ph.D., Union Institute) is Assistant Professor in the department of Communication and Culture at New York University. Some twenty years ago, she became the Chief Operating Officer of Marketing Concepts and Communications, Inc., whose client roster included retail chains, health care consortiums, and political entities. For thirteen years, Joyce was regularly featured on NBC Radio. In 1985, she served as a mediator and arbitrator for the Victim Services Agency and the Institute for Mediation and Conflict Resolution. Joyce is the author of numerous articles on public relations, mediation, and communication in the nontraditional family. She was elected to Marquis' "Who's Who in the World," "...the East," "...in Industry and Finance," and "...in Advertising," as well as "American Women." She was recently honored by the National Cancer Society as one the "Top Fifteen Women in America."

Sandra L. (Fish) Herndon (Ph.D., Southern Illinois University) is Professor and former Chair of the Corporate Communication Department, Ithaca College, Ithaca, NY. Author of numerous articles including "Preparation for the Year 2000: One Corporation's Attempt to Address the Issues of Gender and Race," in The Howard Journal of Communications (1991), she is co-editor of *Qualitative Research: Applications in Organizational Communication* (Hampton Press/Speech Communication Association, under contract for 1993) and *Talking to Strangers: Mediated Therapeutic Communication* (Ablex, 1990). Past President of the Eastern Communication Association, she coordinated the 1989 annual convention on the theme of "Communication in a Multicultural World." She was a Commissioner on the Tompkins County Human Rights Commission (1988-89) as well as President of the Board of Directors of Suicide Prevention and Crisis Service of Tompkins County, Inc. (1985-86). She has been associated with Training for Change, Inc., Ithaca, NY, and has designed and conducted communication training programs for both the public and private sectors since 1977.

John J. Makay (Ph.D., Purdue University) is Professor and Chair, Department of Interpersonal Communication at Bowling Green State University. He is the author of *Public Speaking: Theory Into Practice* (Harcourt Brace Jovanovich, 1992) and six additional textbooks. **Leigh Makay** (Ph.D., The Ohio State University) is Assistant Professor of Communication at Wright State University.

Michael W. Purdy (Ph. D., Ohio University) is University Professor and Chair of the Division of Communication at Governors State University. He has published articles and presented papers on listening, interpersonal communication, communication philosophy, qualitative research, and communication technology. He also conducts training and workshops for business, government, religious, and service organizations on listening, management communication, conflict management, and customer service. He co-edited *Listening in Everyday Life: A Personal and Professional Approach* (University Press of America, 1991) with Deborah Borisoff. Currently, he is working on a book on the historical conceptualization of listening and a trade book on listening and empowerment.

Rebecca L. Ray (Ph.D., New York University) An active corporate consultant, she provides a variety of consulting and training services for such clients as Merrill Lynch, The First Boston Corporation, the public relations firm of Howard J. Rubenstein, Deloitte & Touche, Ernst & Young, Ziff-Davis Publishing, and Pearson, the financial holding company for Penguin Books, Royal Doulton China, and London's Financial Times. Rebecca has made over fifty presentations to professional organizations and community and professional groups on various communication topics with a focus on presentation skills, media training, interviewing strategies, and diversity. She has been elected to serve as the Applied Communication Interest Group Chair of the Eastern Communication Association in 1994. Rebecca teaches at New York University.

Andrew S. Rancer (Ph.D., Queens College) is Associate Professor of Communication in the School of Communication at the University of Akron. The main area of his research is interpersonal communication with a focus on the influence of predispositions of argumentativeness and verbal aggressiveness on human communication behavior. His research has been published in leading communication journals as have book chapters. He is co-author of two texts, *Building Communication Theory* (Waveland Press, 1990) and *Exploring Careers in Communication and Telecommunications* (Rosen Publishing, 1985). An active corporate consultant, Andrew serves as the Applied Communication Interest Group Chair of the Eastern Communication Association.

David A. Victor (Ph.D., University of Michigan) is Associate Professor of Management in the Eastern Michigan University College of Business University in Ypsilanti. He is the co-author of *Conflict Management* (Prentice-Hall, 1989) and the author of *International Business Communication* (Harper Collins, 1992). David is the president of the Human Resources Advisory Council, a training firm which specializes in international business communication and diversity management training for corporations in the United States and abroad.